For John Ishee,
Dear friend. With
gratitude for your decency —
Tom
May 28, 1995

DEFICITS, DEBT AND THE ECONOMY

Getting Out of the Financial Maze

Thomas F. Dernburg, Ph. D.

ISBN 0-9644810-0-6

Published by:
TD Economics
1103 Shiloh Drive
Nashville, Tennessee 37205

Produced by:
JM Productions, Brentwood, Tennessee 37024-1911

Cover Design:
Ron Watson

Preface

The manuscript of this book was sent to the publisher shortly before the political upheaval occasioned by the November 1994 elections. Rather than rendering the message conveyed by the book obsolete such things as the Republican "Contract with America" have, in fact, made it all the more timely and important. The contract's principal obsession is with the budget deficit of the federal government and that's what this book is about. There's little doubt that this is an important problem. The danger is that draconian and poorly thought out remedies may do severe harm to the overall economy, to State government programs, as well as to specific groups in the economy that benefit and rely on Federal Government financial assistance for education, health care, and many other important social problems. Let's take steps to reduce the deficit and the growth of the national debt. But let's study how to do it intelligently so as to minimize the dangers.

Although little in this book has been changed at the last minute, recent events have occasioned a minimal amount of updating. The most significant of these is an elaboration of the discussion of a Constitutional Balanced Budget Amendment in Chapter 2.

I wish to thank the Reverend Dr. John Ishee, my good friend, pastoral counselor, and publisher, as well as his son Mark for undertaking the publication of the work. Thanks are also due to my many fine colleagues in the College of Business at Austin Peay State University, where I had the pleasure of holding a chair the past two years, for their support and valuable suggestions. And finally, I wish to thank Mrs. Dorothy Rudolph whose research assistance was especially valuable with respect to the discussion of taxes and tax expenditures of Chapter 8. I alone am responsible for errors and omissions.

Thomas F. Dernburg

Clarksville, Tennessee

Contents

1

Getting Started

The Search for a One-Armed Economist

President Harry S. Truman was said to have been in perpetual search for a one-armed economist. One who couldn't always say "on the one hand; but then on the other." The search proved fruitless. The simple truth is that the answers to most of the economic questions that concern us differ depending on economic conditions that are in a state of perpetual flux.

To illustrate the point consider the following three questions. Your job is to circle the correct answers.

Question 1: An increase in the Federal budget deficit is inflationary. (true, false, sometimes)

Question 2: An increase in federal borrowing depresses government and other bond prices and it therefore raises interest rates. The higher interest rates act as a deterrent to private investment in new machinery, equipment, and structures thereby "crowding out" investment and reducing the rate of economic growth. (true, false, sometimes)

Question 3: Inasmuch as an increase in government borrowing raises interest rates, this causes foreign investors to sell their own domestic securities in search of the higher yielding U.S. securities. This raises the international value of the dollar, makes imports cheaper, makes exports more difficult to sell, and is therefore responsible for our trade deficit. (true, false, sometimes)

Now let's see how well you did. If you answered all three questions true you would pass the test. If you answered them all false you would also pass. But if you gave the economist's typical answer of "sometimes" your instructor would give you an A.

The person who answered true to all the questions probably has in mind the presence of a well functioning economy characterized by low unemployment and a level of total production roughly equal to the economy's potential production. Have a look at ***Table 1-1*** so that you can get a closer fix on what is meant by these concepts.

The value of the economy's total new production of goods and services during the year is called its *gross domestic product* or GDP for short. During periods of recession such as 1982-83 the economy's GDP falls substantially short of what it could have produced if unemployment had been low and if the economy's other productive resources had been fully utilized. We call this concept of what the economy is capable of producing *potential output* or *potential GDP*. Of course, if we were overly ambitious and tried to attain a potential output level that was too high, we would find that we had labor shortages and capacity bottlenecks that would cause inflation. Therefore, we need to be reasonable about our estimate of potential output and stipulate that it is the most output the economy is capable of producing without causing inflation to accelerate.

Column 1 of the table shows estimates of potential output, while column 2 shows the actual record of real GDP as reported by the Department of Commerce. Column 3 shows actual output deducted from potential output. This gives an indication of the *GDP Gap* which is a measure of the difference between what was actually produced and what could have been produced had the economy been functioning well. The next column then expresses the magnitude of the gap as a percentage of actual GDP. All figures in the table are expressed in constant 1987 prices. That way we won't be misled by changes caused by inflation. When prices are arbitrarily held constant the GDP figures are called *real GDP*. When output is valued in current prices the GDP is figure is called *nominal* GDP. Annual data are shown for the years 1978-1988. Thereafter quarterly data are provided so that recent developments may be studied more carefully.

The final column shows the civilian unemployment rate. This is, perhaps, the most newsworthy of all the economic indicators. It is the ratio of total unemployment to the civilian labor force. Notice that when the unemployment rate rises the GDP gap also tends to

Table 1-1
Estimates of Potential Real GDP

Year	1 Potential GDP	2 Actual GDP	3 GDP Gap	4 Gap, % of Actual	5 Unemployment Rate
1978	3,664.3	3,703.5	-39.2	-1.06	6.0
1979	3,758.1	3,796.8	-38.7	-1.02	5.8
1980	3,854.4	3,776.3	78.1	2.07	7.0
1981	3,953.1	3,843.1	110.0	2.82	7.5
1982	4.054.4	3,760.3	294.1	7.82	9.5
1983	4,158.2	3,906.3	251.9	6.45	9.5
1984	4,264.7	4,248.5	16.2	0.38	7.4
1985	4,374.0	4,279.8	94.2	2.20	7.1
1986	4,486.0	4,404.5	81.5	1.85	6.9
1987	4,600.9	4,540.0	60.9	1.34	6.1
1988	4,718.7	4,718.6	0.1	0	5.4
Quarter					
1989-1	4,793.8	4,809.4	-16.0	-0.33	5.2
2	4,842.2	4,832.4	-8.2	-0.17	5.3
3	4,854.8	4,845.6	9.2	0.19	5.3
4	4,885.6	4,856.7	28.9	0.59	5.3
1990-1	4,916.6	4,898.3	26.0	0.53	5.2
2	4,947.8	4,917.2	30.7	0.62	5.2
3	4,979.2	4,906.5	72.7	1.48	5.5
4	5,010.8	4,867.2	143.6	2.95	5.9
1991-1	5,042.6	4,837.8	204.8	4.23	6.5
2	5,074.6	4,855.6	219.0	4.51	6.7
3	5,106.8	4,872.6	234.2	4.81	6.8
4	5,139.2	4,879.6	259.6	5.32	7.0
1992-1	5,171.8	4,922.0	249.8	5.08	7.2
2	5,204.6	4,965.5	239.1	4.82	7.4
3	5,237.6	4,988.2	249.9	5.00	7.5
4	5,270.8	5,068.3	202.5	4.00	7.2
1993-1	5,304.2	5,078.2	226.0	4.45	7.0
2	5,337.9	5,102.1	235.8	4.62	6.9
3	5,371.8	5,138.3	233.5	4.54	6.7
4	5,405.9	5,212.1	193.8	3.72	6.5

rise. Indeed, both pieces of data tell roughly the same story except for the fact that the unemployment rate tends to be a lagging indicator which means that frequently the economy can be in the process of deteriorating while unemployment, at least for a time, remains low. The year 1989 provides a good illustration of this problem. The GDP gap shows that the economy began to deteriorate in the third quarter of 1989; but the unemployment rate held steady for another whole year before beginning to rise.

Full employment should coincide with the absence of a GDP gap. But how low can the unemployment rate be pushed? It would not be accurate to say that there is a consensus unemployment rate that represents full employment. What can be said is that full employment implies the lowest unemployment rate consistent with the absence of non accelerating inflation. If one had to pick a consensus number it would probably be between 5.0 and 6.0 percent of the labor force. Therefore, in the spirit of compromise let's pick 5.5 as our NAIRU. NAIRU is an ugly acronym that stands for non accelerating inflation rate of unemployment. The thing to bear in mind is that the difference between the actual unemployment rate and the NAIRU carries roughly the same message as the GDP gap. Therefore when the unemployment rate is 5.5 percent, the GDP gap should be roughly zero.[1]

On the surface economics seems extremely confusing. People can give completely opposite answers and they can all be both correct and incorrect. Economic conditions change and that's why the answers change. Its not that if all the world's economists were laid end to end that they still wouldn't reach a conclusion, it's that their answers could very quickly change just by giving them news of an unanticipated development such as a sharp increase in the cost of oil imports. Although people are in constant search of eternal verities, in economics there aren't very many such verities that can be relied upon on a consistent basis. But that does not justify the all

1.Why is it not possible to push unemployment much below 5.5 percent without causing inflation? Such types of unemployment are not caused by inadequate spending. Structural unemployment is the kind of unemployment that occurs because technological developments render the skills of certain workers obsolete. Even if demand for the product of the industry were to increase, such workers would not get their jobs back. Similarly, a major component of unemployment is frictional. Such unemployment occurs when people are in transition between jobs or when they are engaged in job search. Frictional unemployment is actually a very good thing because it is an indication that our labor force is highly mobile and adaptable too common conclusion that economists don't know what they are talking about.

As noted, the person who answered yes to all three questions had in mind a well functioning economy in which unemployment was low and the GDP gap was insignificant. Table 1.1 shows that 1988 was such a year. Unemployment was 5.4 percent and the GDP gap was zero. Since GDP is a measure of total spending in the economy, the absence of a gap means that total spending was just about right – high enough to achieve potential output but not too high to cause inflation. In such a situation a rise in the federal budget deficit would surely be expected to be inflationary. A tax reduction, for example, would raise the after tax incomes of individuals. This would cause them to increase their consumption spending. Since this means that spending becomes excessive, the increase in the budget deficit is clearly inflationary. At the same time the rise in the deficit forces the government to engage in additional borrowing. Thus the government must print and market additional government securities. This increase in the supply of government securities tends to depress government bond prices and this raises interest rates.[2] This in turn increases the cost of raising money by business and is therefore apt

2. It's very important to have a clear understanding of why bond prices and interest rates move in opposite directions. So if this is not clear to you, read this footnote, which tries to clarify the issue. In the case of a bond with a lengthy maturity the relationship between the market value, V, of the bond and the yield, or interest rate, i, may be approximated by the simple formula $V = R/i$, where R is the coupon value of the bond. This is the annual amount of interest that the bondholder is guaranteed to receive on his loan. The important thing to keep in mind is that this coupon value is a fixed sum. Now if R is fixed, a rise in i would obviously lower V, the market value of the bond, whereas a fall in i would raise V. Does this make sense?

Suppose that you are in possession of a bond and suppose that the annual coupon value is \$100 and that the current rate at which money can be borrowed is 10 percent. Suppose also that you are considering the sale of the bond. Speaking to a friend you ask him if he would be

be willing to pay you \$2000 for the bond. He replies: "With friends like you I don't need any enemies. If I take my \$2000 and lend it at the current interest rate of 10 percent I will earn \$200 during the year. If I buy your bond I'll only earn \$100. What kind of deal is that?" He then returns the insult by telling you that he'll give you \$500 for the bond. Its now you turn to complain: "I may be crazy but I'm not stupid. My bond pays me \$100 in interest, but if I take your \$500 and lend that out at 10 percent I'll only earn \$50.

Its obvious that there is only one possible market value for the bond and that is \$1000—the coupon value of the bond divided by the current market rate of interest. Now suppose that interest rates fall from 10 to 5 percent. The formula tells us that this should double the value of the bond to \$2000. Why? Because that is how much you would now have to lend in order to earn the \$100 that the bond guarantees to pay you.

to cause some investment projects to be postponed. Since there will be less investment spending by business, the increase in the budget deficit *crowds out* private investment. Because this means that the economy will have less capital stock (productive facilities) with which to work, the rate of economic growth is slowed because of the increase in the budget deficit.

Finally, when interest rates rise in the United States this causes foreign investors to see a profitable opportunity to rearrange their financial portfolios to take advantage of the higher yields available in the U.S. A British investor would therefore sell some of his domestic assets in return for British pounds. However, to buy the U.S. bonds he needs dollars. He therefore goes to the *foreign exchange market* where national currencies are traded to convert his pounds into dollars. Finally, he uses the dollars to purchase the higher yielding U.S. securities. A flow of funds of this kind is called a capital inflow. When capital inflows increase this raises the demand for the dollar and this causes the value of the dollar to increase relative to the value of foreign currencies. The dollar, in other words, appreciates. When this happens Americans find that they need to spend fewer dollars to obtain the foreign currencies needed to purchase imports. Thus, as seen by Americans, foreign goods become cheaper in terms of dollars. This provides a clear incentive to purchase foreign produced goods rather than domestically produced goods. Imports, therefore, rise. At the same time foreign citizens see that they must now put up more of their own currencies to acquire the dollars needed to buy American exports. Since this means that American goods become more expensive to foreigners, there will be a decline in exports. In combination the rise in imports and decline in exports imply an increase in the trade deficit. Its for this reason that the term *twin deficits* has arisen. The concept captures the idea that an increase in the government budget deficit is an important causal factor in producing a widening trade deficit. Between 1981 and 1985 the federal budget deficit increased $122.3 billion. During that same period of time the value of the dollar rose 31 percent relative to a market basket of foreign currencies, while the trade deficit swung into the red by $177 billion.

What about the person who answered no to all three questions? If his analysis is valid it is because he is thinking of how a rise in the budget deficit affects an economy that is performing poorly. It has a high unemployment rate and a high GDP gap. Suppose he has 1992 in mind. The GDP gap averaged about $300 billion (in 1987 prices) and the unemployment rate averaged 7.3 percent.

Its obvious that changes in the budget deficit have significant effects on the economy. Perhaps less well known, but equally important, is the fact that the condition of the economy has major effects on the budget. Indeed, intelligent discussion of the budget and the economy is impossible unless this is kept firmly in mind at all times. That is why nearly all of the next chapter is devoted to that all important subject.

In 1991 the budget deficit of the federal government was $210.4 billion. In 1992 the deficit jumped to $297.8 billion, an increase of $87.4 billion. How could this possibly happen with a conservative President in the White House who neither proposed nor agreed to any major spending initiatives or tax reductions? It happened because the economy continued to deteriorate. The unemployment rate continued to rise and this meant that laid off workers went to the unemployment office to draw unemployment compensation. If the unemployment office gives a jobless person $1,000, this automatically increases the budget deficit by $1,000. Because actual output was so far below potential output in 1992 virtually all sources of income were depressed. Therefore, the yield from the individual income tax and the corporate income tax were all far below what they would have been at potential output. Payrolls, too, were depressed thereby automatically reducing the yield from the various payroll taxes that finance the nation's social insurance programs.

Such automatic increases in the budget deficit are called increases in the *cyclical deficit*. How do such increases affect the answers to the three questions? Suppose that I earn $4,000 per month in take-home pay. However, the economy deteriorates, my company's sales decline sharply, and I am laid off. My monthly purchasing power declines by $4,000 for as long as the lay off lasts. However, I am able to go to the unemployment office where I am given a check for $1,000 as partial replacement for my lost wages. Therefore, instead of a $4,000 loss in purchasing power my net purchasing power loss is $3,000. In the meantime the federal budget deficit automatically increases by $1,000.

Does this increase in the deficit cause inflation? My wife and I talk the situation over and decide that we have no choice but to economize. She had been hoping to purchase a new fur coat and I had been hoping to buy a new car. But we agree that the purchase of these items will have to be postponed until I get my job back. How will the resulting loss of business affect the furrier and the auto dealer? Elementary economics tells us that when successful firms lose business they tend to cut prices rather than raise them. The auto dealer is likely to increase his discounts and the furrier is likely to put his coats on sale. Obviously, then, the increase in the deficit of $1,000 cannot possibly be inflationary. Prices are likely to drop; not increase. My ability to get $1,000 at the unemployment office does not raise my purchasing power; rather it prevents my purchasing power from falling *as much as would otherwise have been the case.* Had I not lost my job but had to take a pay cut instead, I again lose purchasing power. Fortunately, however, my income and payroll tax liabilities decline automatically so that my purchasing power falls by *less than would otherwise have been the case.* Declining purchasing power means declining business sales and creates a deflationary environment. Clearly then, an *increase in the cyclical deficit can never be inflationary.*

What about interest rates and investment crowdout? When the amount of business the economy does declines, the amount of money and credit needed to finance business activity also declines. Fewer potential borrowers walk into banks to request loans. How do the banks respond? Do they raise lending rates or do they lower them? If they are intelligently run and try to complete with other banks for customers, they will surely lower their lending rates. Since interest rates fall instead of rise as the economy deteriorates, and since the deficit automatically increases, we can conclude that an increase in the cyclical deficit *can never crowd out business borrowing and investment spending.* Investment might decline because business is pessimistic over future sales prospects and other adverse factors; but it cannot decline because of higher interest rates.

By the same token since a rise in the cyclical deficit caused by a weakening economy cannot raise interest rates, it cannot induce the capital inflow that raises the value of the dollar and therefore adds to the trade deficit. Indeed, when the economy weakens total spending declines and part of that spending decline is reflected in a decline in imports. The trade deficit therefore nearly always declines when the cyclical deficit increases.

It's been a somewhat lengthy story but certainly an important one.

When a public official or a pundit makes a pronouncement about what will happen if the budget deficit is widened, our first question must be: Does he have a strong or a weak economy in mind? Often he himself will not bother to tell us. That is why we have to be exceptionally alert when bombarded by public pronouncements.

Can I Benefit from this Book?

Did you understand what was explained in the previous section? Did you learn anything useful from it? If the answer to both questions is yes, then this book is definitely for you. It's about the budget deficit of the Federal Government of the United States, about the national debt, and how they interact with the functioning of the economy. It is designed to be accessible to the general reader. A modest background in economics, though helpful, is not essential. Rather than telling you what we ought to do about the deficit the book largely just asks questions and tries to provide the tools and information that permit you to answer the questions intelligently and constructively.

President Clinton's budget proposals barely squeaked through the Congress in the summer of 1993. And in 1994 there was another cliff hanger. Nearly all major issues are budget issues. The great health care debate came to nothing, but you can be sure that it will persist well into the future. You can bet that well over half the time the debate will either be about how to pay for a program or how to cut its cost. Budget issues will arise as soon as the President sends the very next program to Congress be it health care, jobs, poverty or anything else that costs money. Indeed, the principal obsession of Speaker Newt Gingrich's "contract with America" is the drive to amend the Constitution to require a balanced federal budget.

People say they are alarmed about the deficit. But do they know the countless ways the deficit and the debt affect their own well being? Are simple answers to a complex problem possible? When cutting the budget do we dare ignore the side effects? Federal budget policy can create jobs or take them away. It can cause inflation or be used to slow inflation. It can reduce economic growth or be used to stimulate it. It can improve the distribution of income or worsen it. Do we dare ignore these things?

A number of books intended to communicate with the average

citizen on the subjects of debt and deficit already exist. Some are of the gloom and doom variety while others carry the message that the deficit and the debt are not going to kill us and that our worst fears are unwarranted. Neither carries a balanced nor particularly useful message. This book takes a different tack. Instead of trying to alarm you or attempting to calm your fears, it tries to provide some simple tools, and considerations you may not have thought of, to enable you to make informed judgements about government expenditure and revenue programs. It takes the view that the most useful service an economist can perform is to separate out which claims are warranted and which are not, to spell out the reasons, and to suggest constructive, rather than draconian, ways of dealing with important problems.

Questions, Questions, Questions

The following are some of the additional budgetary questions that this book attempts to answer. You have no doubt heard that deficits are inflationary because governments that cannot make ends meet are resorting to the printing press. Is this true? Is it sometimes true? When is it likely to be true? What difference does it make? You have also heard that deficit financing places a burden on future generations. Is this true, and in what sense is it true? Is it true that the trade deficit is similar to the budget deficit because it means the country is living beyond its means and that future generations will have to pay the price for the extravagances of the 1980s?

What harm is caused by all that interest that the Federal government must pay on its debt? Could the interest costs of the debt become so huge that there would be no room for anything else in the budget? Are interest costs a burden? If so to whom? What are the appropriate signals to indicate that the burden is increasing or possibly even decreasing?

Is it possible to eliminate the deficit without harming the economy? What would happen to production and employment if government expenditures were reduced and taxes were raised by an amount equal to the current deficit? Will such action in fact eliminate the deficit? Will the national debt have to be repaid? Should it be repaid? Can it be repaid?

Reducing the budget deficit has become such an over-riding goal of economic policy that other important goals are being compromised and endangered. It is easy enough to say nowadays that the large deficit shows that we cannot afford to spend additional money on education, health, and poverty programs. Equally important, the large budget deficit is making it all but impossible to use the government's taxing and spending powers to regulate total spending in the economy. Policies designed to accomplish this are called fiscal policies. Aware that the economy was in need of stimulation, President Clinton proposed a modest fiscal stimulus program in early 1993. The proposal failed to make it through Congress largely because it would have widened the deficit. Subsequently, President Clinton proposed a substantial package of tax increases designed to reduce the deficit. But many questioned such a program because it was very likely to weaken an already weak economy that had, for an extended period of time, shown very little ability to create an adequate number of jobs. Reduce the deficit and weaken the economy. Or strengthen the economy and increase the deficit. That appeared to be the unpleasant choice. Are there other options? That is the $64,000 question that is addressed in Chapter 5.

Polls disclose that people have been greatly concerned about the economy. But it's not at all clear whether this means concern over jobs or concern over the deficit. Clarity about such things is essential since intelligent policy decisions can't be made otherwise.

The conflict between deficit reduction and the desire to achieve full employment is a clear example of why it is very important to organize thinking about economic policy systematically. Good policy must focus on the achievement of not one but several objectives or targets simultaneously. Its easy enough to reduce the deficit. But can this be done without increasing unemployment or destroying the anti-poverty safety net? Conversely, can employment be raised without increasing the deficit? Can more resources be put into investment to raise economic growth without reducing the current standard of living?

The good new is that just about *any single* major economic objective can be achieved within a reasonable period of time. Employment can be raised, economic growth can be accelerated, inflation can be slowed, the deficit can be reduced, and so can the trade deficit. The bad news is that policies that move the economy in the direction of one target often have the effect of making other targets even more remote. Attempting to design policy so that several objectives can be reached simultaneously is what makes so-called macroeconomics really interesting and useful.

Sources of Confusion: The Information Gap

A historian, a rabbi, and an economist were debating the issue of which of their disciplines was the oldest. The historian claimed that the history of the world went back to the creation. The rabbi then said that since God created the world out of the prevailing chaos, religion surely had precedence over history. Winning the contest hands down, the economist asked, "Who do you think created the chaos?"

Why are we confused by what economists say? We've already discussed the first, and by far the most important and difficult to grasp. And that is that the effects of an increase in the Federal Budget deficit, to take but one example, will differ sharply depending upon prevailing economic conditions. But there are other culprits that add to the confusion. And sadly much confusion is deliberately spread because it is designed to promote hidden agendas.

Confusion by Priority

A major source of the kinds of confusion and conflict that make economists and policy makers look inept arises from different sets of normative priorities. Such confusion is most likely to occur in so-called *dilemma* situations. One such situation occurred in 1975 when both unemployment and inflation were excessive, and it exists again today because of the seemingly incompatible goals of reducing the budget deficit while simultaneously attempting to use the budget to restore full employment.

Let your imagination drift back to 1975 and suppose that you are privy to a discussion in President Gerald Ford's Oval Office. It is a horrible year. In the preceding year the OPEC oil cartel had quadrupled the price of imported oil. Not only had this caused inflation to accelerate sharply, it had also brought about the worst recession since the Great Depression of the 1930s because people had far less income left to buy other things after paying their higher energy bills. Suppose now that the President has just called in his team of economic advisers to discuss the terrible economic condition of the country. The President is greatly upset that his WIN button, intended to convey the message "whip inflation now," has been turned upside down (NIM) and has become an object of ridicule by changing the message to, "No Immediate Miracles." The President is especially incensed to learn that many people have further modified the message to "Nothing In Mind."

"Is it true?" asks the President, "Are we as bereft of constructive policy ideas as the critics are saying?"

One adviser points out that inflation is accelerating sharply. He therefore suggests that a tax increase to reduce consumer spending would be appropriate. The second adviser then tells the President that unemployment is edging up to 9 percent. He therefore suggests tax reduction to raise consumer spending so as to simulate the economy. What is the President to do? Should he ask Congress for a tax increase; should he ask for a tax cut; or should he just fire his advisers and halt distribution of the embarrassing WIN button?

The source of the conflict is quite independent of economic analysis. The two advisers may have received their degrees at the same graduate school. They may have taken the same courses, had the same professors, and read the same books and journals. They may also agree with respect to every detail of economic analysis. What separates them is not economic analysis, it is, rather, different normative priorities. The first adviser is more concerned about inflation than he is about unemployment, whereas the second adviser is more worried about high unemployment than about inflation.

The budget debate of 1993 provides another excellent example of a dilemma situation. A tax increase was indicated to achieve the objective of reducing the budget deficit. But tax increases would destroy purchasing power and weaken an economy that was already alarmingly weak. Under the circumstances it didn't matter whether you were a Republican or a Democrat. You could justify your vote in either direction and easily justify changing your position without the need for elaborate explanations. A Republican might say, "Sure I want to reduce the deficit but if I vote for a tax increase those tax and spend Democrats are just going to raise spending and we won't get any deficit reduction out of it." Other Republicans, suddenly sounding like liberal economists, could say that, although deficit reduction is important, a tax increase would further weaken the economy and we can't tolerate that. Similarly, a Democrat might say, "I favor a tax increase because otherwise it will be impossible to maintain the spending on health care and poverty that we so desperately need." Or, he too could oppose the tax increase on the grounds that it would weaken the economy.

Under the circumstances it isn't hard to see why the budget debate was such an unpredictable cliff hanger. Vice President Gore had to break two ties in the Senate, and the entire package would have gone down to defeat had only one yes vote been changed to a no in the House of Representatives.

Congress and the Media: Information by Osmosis

Although Congress makes the laws it is ill equipped to do so when it comes to economic issues. Indeed, most congressmen and senators are confused by economic problems and wish that economists and economic problems would just go away.

Much of the information given to Congress comes from committee hearings. However, if you ever attend an open hearing of the House and Senate Banking Committees, the Joint Economic Committee, the Budget Committees of the two Houses, or the House Ways and Means and Senate Finance Committees you will quickly find yourself engulfed in chaos. Congressmen drift in and out of the hearings snatching only bits of testimony. At the same time there will be rafts of staff people buzzing around them like flies whispering continuously into their ears. Witnesses are apt to represent extreme points of view from opposite poles of the political spectrum. Their ideological differences cause them to give sharply conflicting testimony and sometimes they fall to brawling over technical minutia. It is too much to expect legislators to sort out the reasons for the differences in the testimony. And, since the expert witnesses can't agree, there is a tendency for the members simply to ignore the testimony and vote their predispositions. Thus the congressional hearing, ostensibly designed to provide expert information to Congress, often as not simply provides a convenient cover for ignoring such information. It is the mainstream that needs to be heard in Congress, but the mainstream gets little attention. In its superficial insistence on even-handed representation of the issues, Congress often gets the opposite.

You don't have to have witnessed the sorry spectacle of a congressional hearing to understand the communications problem. Just consider a public affairs TV program allegedly devoted to an economic issue. If there are two guest panelists they are very likely to represent radically different points of view. If there is a third guest present to represent the middle ground, he will be interrupted and shouted down by the others whose rudeness and boorishness generally escalate in direct proportion to the extremity of their positions. The noise makers are the ones with axes to grind, and that means the middle ground isn't heard. Consequently, much of what passes for public information is not that at all. It is, rather, high-decibel tub-thumping designed to promote hidden ideological agendas rather than to promote practical solutions to practical problems.

The popular press isn't much help either. The economists most often quoted in the press do not generally represent the thoughtful mainstream. Shooting from the lip raises more public interest and sells more newspapers than the sexless mainstream.

Yes, Virginia there is a mainstream and that is where thoughtful, well reasoned, and carefully researched approaches to problems of economic policy originate. But the public hearing the mainstream gets is far less than the attention given to the extremes. This fact has always been at the heart of the information gap between the layman and the economist. Efforts to reduce this gap are what give rise to books such as this.

It must be added that economists themselves are not entirely free from responsibility for the information gap. It is truly remarkable how quickly an economist who ascends to a policy making or advisory position can become an amateur politician. The words "politically feasible" immediately come to dominate his thinking process. Because of this the advice given often is not good advice. It is, rather, advice heavily biassed by the economic adviser's judgement as to what is acceptable to his superior. Then, when he is interviewed on television, he feels obliged to support whatever it is that his superior proposes even when this runs completely counter to his best *economic* judgement. Economists could do everyone a favor by sticking to economics, giving the best advice that their training and research provide, while leaving politics to politicians.

Self-Appointed Expertise

Conversely, there is the problem of non economists posturing as economic experts. This is a chronic disease to which many business leaders are particularly susceptible because they believe that meeting a payroll is all they need to know about economics. Ross Perot is a perfect example. During the election campaign of 1992 he proposed a 50 cent per gallon increase in the federal gasoline tax. He estimated that $265 billion could be raised over a four year period with this tax alone. The idea was intriguing – boost federal revenue, balance the budget, reduce energy consumption, reduce air pollution, and provide incentives to utilize car pools and public transportation. Regrettably, however, Perot showed himself either to be ignorant of economic history or of how to interpret it. It is necessary only to go back to the year 1974 to see why.

In that year the OPEC cartel quadrupled the price of oil from a pre embargo price of $2.40 per barrel to over $10.00 per barrel. The effect on oil importing countries was devastating. Not only were energy-using businesses forced to absorb huge increases in costs, but many of them found their productive facilities suddenly uncompetitive and obsolete. To absorb the cost increases prices had to rise so that consumer prices, in the United States, rose 9.1 percent in 1975. Meanwhile consumers, having little choice but to pay the higher gasoline and heating oil prices, were forced to increase their expenditures on energy. Having to spend more on energy, they were left with far less to spend on other things, so that non-energy consumption fell sharply. The outcome was the worst recession since the Great Depression of the 1930s.

This was no ordinary recession. Not only did unemployment rise to 8.5 percent of the labor force in 1975 but, unlike the Great Depression when prices fell, consumer prices rose 9.1 percent. Add these two rates together and you get what the late Arthur Okun, Chairman of the Council of Economic Advisers under President Lyndon Johnson, called a "discomfort index" of 17.6 percent.

Economists were quick to point out that the rise in oil prices was the practical equivalent of a huge excise tax on energy. With oil imports running at an average rate of 7 million barrels a day, the pre OPEC annual cost of oil imports of $5 billion jumped to $20 billion. In today's economy, that would be roughly $60 billion, not much different than what Perot's gasoline tax would raise in a year.

While reductions in energy consumption may be desirable, the experience of the 1970s should serve as a reminder that heavy tax increases slow the economy. Therefore, if a heavy gasoline tax is put in place, this would have to be accompanied by equivalent reductions in other taxes so as to offset the purchasing power impact of the gasoline tax. But if that were done, no progress would be made against the budget deficit. With experts like Perot serving as a daily model it would be far better to turn economic policy over to a class of college economics majors. Thanks to his enormous wealth, Perot is able to play the loose cannon, a role that he seems greatly to enjoy. However, by continuously making a public ass of himself, he provides a daily reminder that success in business does not necessarily qualify a person as an expert economist. Perot likes to ask: "If you're so smart, why aren't you rich?" The inverse would be more appropriate: "If you're so rich, why aren't you smart?"

What Do We Want From Government?

Do you know how to cut government spending? What specifically do you propose? Chapters 6, 7, and 8 provide some grist for your decision-making mill. You're the tax payer. Are you getting an adequate bang for your tax buck?

What do we want from the federal budget and from government economic activity? Here's a list of some major objectives:

1. We want the budget to act as a stabilizing balance wheel to cushion the effects of swings in the economic cycle. The next chapter looks very closely at this all-important function.

2. We need budget outlays to provide infra-structure investments of a kind the private sector either would not or could not provide, and that have the beneficial effect of raising rates of return on private investment.

3. We want the distribution of income in our society to be equitable and we have therefore created an enormous income redistribution machine in the form of the federal budget. This

machine takes income from taxpayers and distributes it to the beneficiaries of public programs – retirees, sick persons, the poor, and others.

4. We use the budget as a way to increase the share of resources used for specific social priorities such as when preferential tax treatment is extended to corporate outlays on research and development, or when we subsidize home ownership by permitting homeowners to deduct mortgage interest and property taxes from taxable income.

5. Painful experience tells us that a large fraction of our population cannot, or will not, save towards a nest egg adequate to provide for education, emergencies, and retirement. We therefore ask the government to do this saving for us by levying taxes to finance public schools, health care, and social security.

6. Finally, we want government to provide *public goods* that the private sector either could not provide efficiently, or perhaps not at all.

To explain the meaning of the term public goods consider that, even if you don't like the cops that ticket you for rolling ever so slowly through a stop sign and if you think there's entirely too much over-stuffed military brass, you will have to admit that we all benefit from police protection and national defense. You would enjoy these benefits even if you, personally, didn't have to pay for them. If you were in this position you would be a *free rider*.

In the old days the absence of adequate protection by the law caused private groups of ranchers to form their own vigilante forces to protect themselves against cattle rustlers. However, it never took long for an individual in the group to realize that if he dropped out and became a free rider, thereby saving time and avoiding the risk of getting shot, he would still receive the benefits since cattle rustlers would likely be driven out of the territory. Private vigilante forces are not apt to be effective for very long because it pays for each member of the group to drop out and become a free rider. The solution, therefore, is to beef up public law enforcement and have each taxpayer contribute his fair share.

Education has a public good content. When my neighbor's children become educated and sufficiently civilized to stop vandalizing my property, this is of considerable benefit to me. This benefit would accrue to me even if I didn't have to pay for it. It costs me nothing to reap the enjoyment of driving through a beautiful national or state park, but if society weren't willing to pay for it the park wouldn't be there. It also costs me nothing to pollute the air when I drive my car down the street. Yet it costs society a great deal. Although I realize that energy conservation is in the national interest, why should I go to the inconvenience of doing it when nobody else does it? The government has to have a hand in these things. They wouldn't get done otherwise.

Where Do We Go From Here?

The book is divided into three distinct parts. They all have in common the fact that the issues raised are all very closely related to government deficits and debt.

Part I, consisting of Chapters 2 through 5, looks at the relationship between the budget deficit and the economy.

- Chapter 2 provides facts about the federal budget deficit and suggests appropriate ways to interpret them. Attention focusses on that part of the deficit that *affects* the economy as distinct from that part that is *caused* by the economy. Can the deficit be inflationary and crowd out investment, is this true only for a part of the deficit, and when is it true? Can federal fiscal policy be used constructively so as to moderate fluctuations in national income and employment? What are the likely economic consequences of attempting to eliminate the deficit?
- Chapter 3 focuses on deficits, money, and inflation. Does a deficit mean that the government is printing and spending money? Are there times when this is appropriate? When is it most likely to happen, and what are its economic consequence? Why does deficit financing in war time and in developing countries usually cause inflation? Why is this not necessarily true during peace time in the United States?
- Chapter 4 looks at the cumulative national debt. Who owns it, who owes it, and in what sense is it a burden to the present and to the future? In what sense is the interest paid on the debt a burden and when is this burden growing excessively?

Are there constructive uses of federal debt? What would happen if we tried to repay the national debt?

- Chapter 5 takes up the $64,000 question: Can deficit reduction be reconciled with economic recovery? The chapter therefore considers how apparently conflicting economic objectives can be achieved simultaneously. Can monetary policy be ignored when the deficit is cut? Is an overall strategy necessary to achieve multiple goals?

Part II looks at specific government programs to see where budget savings could be effected by spending tax dollars more efficiently. This part of the book therefore takes a look at specific programs to see where savings can be found and to see how programs can be made more efficient.

- Chapter 6 considers social security and the financing of social insurance in general.
- Chapter 7 provides an analysis of health care financing designed to enable the reader to see the nature of essential reforms.
- Chapter 8 takes up agriculture, defense, and so-called tax expenditures – providing subsidies via tax breaks rather than direct payments.

Part III focusses attention on international issues.

- Chapter 9 looks at the international implications of government deficits and debt. How are the budget deficit and the trade deficit related? Is there a fundamental difference between government debt held domestically and government debt held by foreigners? Is the latter more burdensome? Can the trade deficit be eliminated by eliminating the budget deficit?
- Chapter 10 discusses the global debt problem. Is it related to the federal budget deficit? Why do some countries appear to have to run continuing trade deficits in order to prosper? Why is the opposite the case for other countries?
- Chapter 11, finally, discusses economic integration. What are the benefits of forming regional free trade areas such as the European Economic Community and NAFTA? What is the

importance of monetary integration? Would such integration, currently being introduced in Europe, be appropriate for the western hemisphere?

PART I

THE ECONOMY AND THE DEFICIT

2

The Federal Budget Deficit

The Record

The annual budget deficit of the Federal Government is the difference between the government's outlays and its tax receipts. The Federal debt is the cumulative total of all past budget deficits. Therefore, today's deficit represents the year's increase in the national debt. This chapter focusses attention on the annual deficit. The debt, or cumulative deficit, is a subject for a later chapter.

The government finances its deficits by the sale of government bonds of varying maturities. Private investors and financial institutions find that government bonds are highly desirable earning assets and there is, therefore, a brisk market for government securities. The taxing power of the Federal government stands behind these debt instruments and they are therefore viewed by investors as the most gilt of all gilt edged securities. This is not meant to imply that government debt is good or that government debt certificates are better than private debt paper.

The Federal government has three budgets--the Cash Budget, the Administrative Budget, and the National Income and Product accounts (NIA) budget. Economists find the NIA budget to be the most useful because it is the most helpful in assessing the economic impact of the budget. NIA differs from the cash budget primarily with respect to timing. Receipts and expenditures are recorded on an accrual basis rather than on a cash basis. The Administrative budget's usefulness is limited because it is affected by sometimes arbitrary and unanticipated policy changes that have little or no economic impact. For example, in the summer of 1992 the Director of the Office of Management and Budget (OMB) announced that the fiscal year deficit had suddenly fallen by some $25 billion. Was he happy about this seeming windfall? Not at all. He went on to rail against Congress because the deficit was reduced by congressional failure to approve $25 billion in savings and loan bail out funds.

Its time now to look at the NIA budget. ***Table 2-1*** presents a *time-series* of Federal receipts and expenditures for the calendar years 1975 through 1993. Beginning from the left the table shows the several sources of tax receipts. It then moves down where the various categories of expenditure are entered. The next to the last

Table 2.1
Federal Receipts and Expenditures
(NIA Basis, Billions of Dollars)

Receipts

Calendar Year	Total	Personal Income Tax	Corporate Tax	Indirect Business Taxes	Contributions for Social Insurance
1975	294.8	125.4	43.6	24.2	101.7
1976	339.9	146.4	54.6	23.8	115.0
1977	384.0	169.1	61.6	25.6	127.7
1978	441.2	193.8	71.4	28.9	147.1
1979	504.7	229.7	74.4	30.1	170.4
1980	553.0	256.2	70.3	39.6	196.8
1981	639.0	297.2	65.7	57.3	218.8
1982	635.4	302.9	49.0	49.7	233.8
1983	660.0	292.6	61.3	52.5	252.6
1984	725.8	308.0	75.2	57.8	284.8
1985	788.6	342.8	76.3	58.6	310.9
1986	827.2	357.4	83.8	53.5	332.5
1987	913.8	400.6	103.2	58.4	351.5
1988	972.3	410.1	111.0	60.9	390.4
1989	1,059.3	461.9	117.1	61.9	418.5
1990	1,111.4	484.3	116.4	65.8	444.8
1991	1,127.8	474.9	107.1	79.1	466.7
1992	1,183.0	490.8	120.2	81.3	490.7
1993	1,267.6	521.2	141.0	87.4	517.9

Table 2.1 (continued)

Expenditures

Year	Total	Purchase	Transfer	Grants	Interest	Subsidy	Deficit Actual	Deficit %GDP
1975	364.2	129.4	150.3	54.6	23.0	10.4	69.4	4.38
1976	392.7	135.8	163.0	61.1	26.8	9.7	52.9	2.99
1977	426.4	147.9	173.5	67.5	29.1	11.8	42.4	2.18
1978	469.3	162.2	186.2	77.3	34.6	12.8	28.1	1.26
1979	520.3	179.3	209.8	80.5	42.1	12.7	15.7	0.63
1980	613.1	209.1	252.0	88.7	52.7	15.6	60.1	2.22
1981	697.8	240.8	287.1	87.9	71.7	15.3	58.8	1.94
1982	770.9	266.6	332.8	83.9	84.4	19.6	135.5	4.30
1983	840.0	292.0	347.5	87.0	93.7	27.1	180.1	5.29
1984	892.7	310.9	353.7	94.4	113.1	30.0	166.9	4.42
1985	969.9	344.3	378.2	100.3	127.0	31.5	181.4	4.49
1986	1,028.8	367.8	395.5	107.6	131.0	36.2	201.0	4.69
1987	1,065.6	384.9	412.2	102.8	136.6	39.5	151.8	3.34
1988	1,109.0	387.0	436.3	111.3	146.0	28.4	136.6	2.79
1989	1,181.6	401.6	471.5	118.2	164.8	25.5	122.3	2.33
1990	1,274.9	426.5	514.1	132.3	176.5	25.6	163.5	2.95
1991	1,331.2	445.9	522.1	153.0	157.6	22.6	203.4	3.55
1992	1,459.3	448.4	624.5	171.4	187.1	27.5	276.3	4.58
1993	1,493.4	443.4	650.0	185.9	180.6	33.6	225.8	3.53

Source: Department of Commerce, Office of Business Economics

column in the lower part of the table is the deficit obtained by subtracting tax receipts from expenditures. During this period the smallest deficit was President Jimmy Carter's 1979 deficit of $15.7 billion and the largest was the 1992 deficit of $276.3 billion. The last column is an addendum designed to relate the magnitude of the deficit to the size of the economy. Viewed from this perspective it can be seen that although the deficit has grown rapidly, this growth really has not, until very recently, drastically outstripped the growth of the economy. Also, it can be seen that the magnitude of the deficit has equaled or exceeded 5 percent of GDP only in 1983 when the economy experienced its worst slump since the depression of the

1930s. These years have in common the fact that these were both years during which the economy operated at well below its potential output.

Receipts are divided into four categories. There are, first, receipts from the personal income tax. The second category of receipts is the corporate profits tax. The third category, Indirect Business Taxes, consists of so-called consumption taxes. These include Federal excise taxes such as taxes on airline tickets, alcohol, tobacco and gasoline, as well as import duties. The final category, Contributions for Social Insurance, consist of payroll taxes specifically earmarked to finance retirement under social security, health care under Medicare, and unemployment compensation. Notice that at the beginning of the period the individual income tax raised considerably more revenue than the social insurance taxes. The latter have, however, risen so sharply during the period that payroll tax receipts now roughly equal receipts from the individual income tax. This is a very important development that has major economic implications to be discussed in chapter 6.

Federal expenditures are divided into five categories. Federal purchases are expenditures made to provide goods and services for the Federal government. Major purchases are defense purchases, federal construction projects, purchases of equipment and supplies, and government wages and salaries. Purchases constitute direct injections into the economy's expenditure stream and are therefore a component of GDP. They represent the government's claim over currently produced output. Government purchases increased 244 percent during the period covered by the data, substantially less than the increase in overall spending of 310 percent.

The other components of Federal spending, which amounted to 70.3 percent of total outlays in 1993, do not represent direct claims over resources and are, therefore, not a part of GDP. Government transfer payments are unilateral income transfers to individuals. The most important of these are social security benefits, medical benefits under Medicare and Medicaid, and unemployment compensation. Since these are unilateral income transfers and do not represent the purchase of a good or service, they do not add to GDP. They do, however, have indirect effects on GDP because such things as social security benefits and unemployment compensation raise the after tax (disposable) incomes of the recipients and therefore are reflected in higher levels of consumer spending. Also, when the government pays your medical bills, this leaves you with more income to spend on other things. Inasmuch as income taxes represent unilateral transfers from individuals to government, whereas transfer outlays are the opposite, economists often think of government transfer payments as negative taxes. Equal increases in taxes and reductions in transfer payments have identical effects on total after tax income.

Grants in Aid are Federal government transfers to State and Local Governments. Over the data period grants have risen by 240 percent, substantially less than the increase in total Federal outlays.

The next category of expenditure is interest on the public debt. Because of the sharp increase in the national debt, as well as interest rates that, during the 1980s, were high by historical standards, this component of government spending has risen far faster than any other component. Over the period covered by the table interest payments have risen 685 percent. This increase has been a cause of considerable alarm that merits major attention in chapter 4.

The Structural and the Cyclical Deficits

Actual deficit figures such as those presented in Table 2-1 are not always easy to interpret. For example, why did the deficit rise by over $87 billion in 1992 when, in fact, defense spending slowed significantly while the Bush Administration took no major fiscal action such as a new expenditure program or a significant tax reduction? Or, why was the deficit so much larger in 1975 than it was in 1979? Did this represent fiscal excess by President Ford's administration, or fiscal conservatism by the Carter administration? Is there another explanation?

To answer these questions as well as other questions such as the impact of the deficit on the economy, including the effect of deficits on inflation, economists have developed the concepts of *structural* and *cyclical* deficits. Indeed, intelligent discussion of the Federal budget and Federal fiscal policy is virtually impossible without this distinction.

The idea is to divide the actual deficit into two parts. The structural part is the deficit that would be observed if the economy operated at potential output. Very frequently the structural deficit differs sharply from the actual deficit because failure to attain potential output increases the actual deficit automatically. For example, unemployment increases when the economy enters a slump. Because of this government outlays on unemployment compensation and welfare increase automatically, and government transfer payments therefore increase sharply when the GDP gap widens. Similarly, when GDP is below its potential, personal income, corporate profits, and payrolls are all less than they would have been at potential output. Therefore receipts from personal income, corporate profits, and payroll taxes are all lower than they would have been. Such increases in the deficit, caused by the failure to achieve potential output, are called increases in the *cyclical deficit* and the various sources of increases in the cyclical deficit are called *automatic fiscal stabilizers.*

As shown in ***Table 2-3***, roughly 26 percent of the total 1993 deficit of $225.8 billion was cyclical. Remember the three questions asked in the first chapter? First, it is often said that increases in the deficit are inflationary. However, increases in the cyclical deficit can *never* be inflationary. Second, it is often claimed that increases in the deficit raise interest rates and crowd out investment. Increases in the cyclical deficit can *never* do this. Third, it is said that increases in the budget deficit cause increases in the trade deficit. Increases in the cyclical deficit can *never* do this. The reasons for these blanket statements were explained in Chapter 1. Be sure to remember the reasons at all times: that alone is half the battle of gaining a clearer understanding of federal government finance.

Cyclical deficits are automatic reflections of the effect of the economy on the budget. Changes in the structural deficit, on the other hand, reflect fiscal decisions by the President and the Congress. Such increases occur when a new government program is introduced or when existing programs are deliberately increased or when Congress legislates a tax reduction. These increases reflect the budget's influence on the economy.

Table 2-3 provides rough estimates of the structural and the cyclical deficits over the period covered by the last three recessions. The estimates are based on the assumption that the years 1974, 1979 and 1989 were years during which potential output was achieved. There is, therefore, no cyclical deficit during these years. With these estimates in hand, it becomes far easier to interpret the movement of the deficit.

Table 2-3
Structural and Cyclical Deficit Estimates
(Billions of Dollars)

YEAR	ACTUAL	STRUCTURAL*	CYCLICAL*	%CYCLICAL
1974	6.8	6.8	0	0
1975	69.4	35.0	34.4	50
1976	52.9	23.8	29.1	55
1977	42.4	19.6	22.8	54
1978	28.1	23.1	5.0	18
1979	15.7	23.7	0	0
1980	60.1	22.4	37.7	63
1981	58.8	44.9	13.9	24
1982	135.5	56.6	78.9	58
1983	180.1	74.8	105.3	58
1984	166.9	96.2	70.7	42
1985	181.4	123.8	57.6	32
1986	201.0	136.2	64.8	32
1987	151.8	130.3	21.5	14
1988	136.6	112.0	24.6	18
1989	122.3	122.3	0	0
1990	163.5	145.0	17.7	11
1991	203.4	143.8	59.6	29
1992	276.3	215.1	61.2	22
1993	225.8	168.0	57.8	26
Cumulative	2,478.8	1,732.5	762.6	31

----

*Author's Estimates

The economy attained full employment (potential output) in 1973 and 1974. However, 1974 was the year in which the OPEC cartel raised the price of imported crude oil from $2.40 per barrel to well over $10 per barrel. Because of the higher energy costs business costs, and therefore prices, increased sharply. At the same time there were huge increases in the cost of gasoline and other fuels to the consumer. Since consumers had to continue to buy gasoline and heat their homes, they had little choice other than to pay the higher energy prices. Because of this they had less income remaining to spend on other goods, and this was a major cause of the sharp recession of 1975, a recession that was far more severe than any recession since World War II.

The effects on the cyclical and the overall budget deficits were dramatic with the actual deficit rising to a level not seen since World War II. But this was only marginally due to government fiscal action. It was, rather, primarily the consequence of the severe recession which raised the cyclical deficit by over $30 billion.

Recovery began in 1976 and continued until 1979 so that both the cyclical and the actual deficits declined steadily during that time. After a lull in 1976, the rate of inflation continued to rise powered, in 1979, by the second OPEC oil shock. With inflation appearing out of control, the Federal Reserve System and its new Chairman, Paul Volker, felt that there was little choice other than to engage in a harshly restrictive monetary policy.

Careful looks at how the Federal Reserve (Fed) conducts monetary policy are taken in chapters 3 and 5. However, its not difficult to understand the bare essentials of monetary policy, so that just a few words of explanation at this time are sufficient to comprehend what happened. The basic money supply of the economy consists of currency and checkable bank deposits. When the Fed wishes to slow inflation it sells government bonds to individuals who pay for the bonds by writing checks. The money supply of the private sector of the economy therefore declines when the Fed conducts an *open-market sale.* Because there is an increase in the supply of government bonds, government bond prices decline, and interest rates rise. At the same time, because people have reduced their holdings of bank deposits, banks find themselves with less money to lend and this, too, raises interest rates. The effect of the high interest rates is to reduce borrowing and spending in the economy.

The high interest rates also attracted large amounts of foreign short term capital. To buy the higher yielding U.S. financial assets foreign nationals converted their domestic securities into their own currencies. They then went to the foreign exchange market where currencies are traded, and sold their own currencies in exchange for dollars. The dollars, finally, were used to purchase U.S. financial assets. This represented an enormous increase in the demand for dollars, and the dollar therefore began to rise in value relative to other currencies. This had the effect of cheapening the cost of foreign goods as seen by Americans which, in turn, led to a sharp increase in imports. At the same time American goods became more expensive as seen by foreigners and this caused exports to stagnate. Rising imports replace domestically produced goods while stagnating exports slow the growth of production in export industries. As a result, the restrictive monetary policies produced a harshly deflationary effect on the economy. The economy weakened in 1980, recovered somewhat in 1981, and then crashed into the worst recession since the Great Depression of the 1930s. It must be added, however, that the attempt to slow inflation was highly successful. After rising at a rate of 11.5 percent in 1979, consumer price inflation slowed to 3.2 percent in 1983.

Changes in the cyclical deficit reflected these events. The cyclical deficit rose sharply in 1980. It then declined substantially in 1981. But then jumped again in 1982 and 1983. It is important to note that, although the structural deficit began to rise significantly after 1980, these increases were eclipsed by increases in the cyclical deficit. It can therefore be seen that the era of $100 plus billion deficits, which began in 1982, was initially caused by the severe recession of 1982-83, and only secondarily by any real or imagined government spending spree.

The recession touched bottom during the winter of 1982-83. Thereafter the economy embarked on an extended period of recovery that continued until 1989. Much of the impetus for the recovery was provided by the major tax reductions and defense spending increases enacted at the request of President Ronald Reagan. These fiscal policies produced substantial increases in the structural deficit that continued through 1986. Therefore, even though the cyclical deficit declined steadily between 1983 and 1989, growth of the structural deficit caused the overall deficit to reach the $200 billion mark in 1986.

The period of fiscal excess was not 1981-84 when the economy was in the grips of recession and early recovery, rather it was the subsequent years of late recovery when virtually nothing was done to reduce the structural deficit. Remarkably enough the highly expansionary increases in the structural deficit failed to raise the rate of inflation which actually declined to 1.9 percent in 1986. The continuing rise in the international value of the dollar played an important role in this favorable inflation outcome. As the overall budget deficit widened the U.S. Treasury was obliged to increase its sale of government bonds. This increase in the supply of government bonds caused bond prices to fall, and when bond prices fall, interest rates rise. Inasmuch as the higher yields make U.S. government bonds relatively more attractive, foreign investors react by doing exactly what they did in 1980. They sold their domestic securities in return for foreign currency. They then exchanged the foreign currency for dollars. And they then used the dollars to buy the higher yielding U.S. assets. Once again, therefore, the demand for the dollar increased so that its international price continued to rise. Indeed the dollar appreciated by some 59.1 percent between 1979 and 1985. The effect, once again, was to make imports cheaper, and since imports enter the cost of living, the effect of the dollar appreciation was to reduce the rate of increase of consumer prices. At the same time cheaper imported raw materials, semi finished goods, and machinery and equipment reduced business costs thereby also helping to lower inflation.

The economy attained potential output in 1988 as the civilian unemployment rate fell to 5.4 percent and the cyclical deficit was eliminated. The economy remained strong in the first half of 1989, but then began to weaken. Thereafter the gap between actual and potential output widened and unemployment increased. The cyclical deficit has therefore increased sharply in recent years reaching about $132 billion in 1992. This combined with a structural deficit of $166 billion produced an overall budget deficit of $298 billion in that year.

Over the entire period 1975 to 1992 the cumulative deficit came to $2,227 billion. Out of this $1508, or about two-thirds, was structural while one third was cyclical. Notice that the cyclical deficit actually outstrips the structural deficit during years of severe recession.

The presence of a cyclical deficit implies that the economy is in a period of recession or, as at present, in a period of stagnation. Purchasing power is inadequate and unemployment is far too high. If taxes are increased to reduce the deficit this further destroys purchasing power and widens the GDP gap. If unemployment compensation is reduced, this will have the same effect. Clearly, then, it would be a huge mistake to attempt to eliminate a cyclical deficit by a program of budget cutting. Because of this it seems obvious that budget cutting *should only take place when there is no significant cyclical deficit or when the cyclical deficit is declining sharply.*

Unfortunately it's not easy to implement this principle. Why? Because politicians understand the concept of cyclical deficit only when it is convenient to do so. Budget cutting causes the least harm when the economy is growing briskly. But because of rapid economic growth the cyclical deficit and probably also the actual deficit will be declining. Policy makers may then be led to believe that because the deficit is declining there is no need for budget cuts. Therefore, failure to be clear about the difference between the cyclical and the structural deficit could easily cause the best opportunity to cut the budget to be lost. The time was ripe for budget cuts from 1986 to 1988. But because the deficit declined automatically due to a falling cyclical deficit, the budget appeared to be heading in the right direction and the opportunity to gain greater control of the budget was frittered away.

Can the structural deficit be eliminated? Of course it can, but the price the economy would have to pay is likely to be unbearably high. Consider a situation such as existed in 1989. The economy had attained full employment and there was no cyclical deficit. The structural deficit and the actual deficit totalled approximately $120 billion. Now suppose that the President and the Congress collaborate on a program that reduces Federal purchases by $120 billion. Although it is hard to imagine how this can be accomplished--slashing defense in half and firing one third of the Federal bureaucracy perhaps--assume, for the sake of the argument, that it can be done.

What are the repercussions? Inasmuch as defense purchases and government wages and salaries are a part of GDP, GDP immediately falls by $120 billion. Since this involves a $120 billion income loss, consumption spending declines. As a result production in consumer goods industries declines so that there is a further income loss. This, in turn, further reduces consumer spending. Clearly then there will be a chain of contracting *feedback* effects that will reduce GDP by more than the initial $120 billion impact. This chain is called the *multiplier.* It has been estimated that the value of the multiplier in the U.S. economy is somewhere between 2.0 and 2.5. Taking the smaller number this implies that overall GDP will fall by at least $240 billion.

When *nominal* GDP – that is, GDP valued in current prices – falls this has both a price and a quantity effect. Roughly 10 percent of the immediate effect is a slowing of inflation while 90 percent is in the form of output loss. Consequently *real* GDP – GDP measured in constant prices – falls by 0.9 times $240 billion, or roughly $216 billion in 1987 prices. The value of real GDP in 1989 was $4,719 billion. Dividing 216 by 4,719 shows that the decline in real output (GDP) comes to 4.6 percent.

What is the effect on employment? We estimate that a two percentage point drop in real GDP will cause the unemployment rate to rise by one percentage point. Therefore, the unemployment rate will rise by 2.3 percentage points. Since the civilian labor force in 1989 was 111.3 million persons, this rise in the unemployment rate implies that at least 2.5 million persons will lose their jobs.[1]

Next, consider the feedback budgetary impact. A one dollar decline in nominal GDP costs the Treasury roughly 20 cents in lost tax revenue and 6 cents in higher transfer outlays. Therefore with a $240 billion reduction in nominal GDP the cyclical deficit can be expected to rise by about $60 billion. Inasmuch as the initial reduction in Federal purchases was $120 billion, and the feedback increase in the cyclical deficit is $60 billion, it follows that only one half of the initial deficit will in fact have been eliminated.

Carrying this exercise to its painful conclusion, it appears that a one dollar budget cut actually ends up reducing the deficit by only 50 cents. Therefore, to rid the economy of the remaining deficit of $60 billion, the budget would have to be cut another $120 billion. Real GDP would, therefore, fall by another 4.6 percent, the unemployment rate would rise by another 2.3 percent, and the total job loss would then be at least 5 million.

These are the harsh realities of draconian budget slashing. Although these estimates are based on ball park figures and back of the envelope calculations, they illustrate the problems that major

1. In Chapter 5 we explain why the job loss is actually likely to be quite a bit larger than the loss estimated here.

budget slashing is likely to cause. If the deficit is to be reduced, this will have to be done very slowly and very carefully so as to give the economy time to absorb the shock without major disruption.

Fiscal Policy

There is a very important and fundamental difference between the expenditures and revenues of the federal government and the expenditures and revenues of individual businesses. Individual businesses cannot take it upon themselves to solve the nation's unemployment and inflation problems. No well run business would increase production and hire more workers than its sales justify in order to raise employment. It is, however, widely recognized that raising employment is a major responsibility of the Federal government, a responsibility that is acknowledged in such legislation as the Employment Act of 1946, which created the Council of Economic Advisers, and the Humphrey-Hawkins bill of the 1970s.

Anti cyclical deficit spending serves a very useful purpose. Without it swings in economic activity would be far greater in magnitude than otherwise. There would have been a higher average level of unemployment, a lower level of production, and possibly more inflation without these swings in the budget. The *automatic fiscal stabilizers* such as unemployment compensation and automatic revenue losses caused by recession are a considerable boon to the economy. The cyclical deficits caused by them can hardly be cited as evidence of Federal waste and overspending and, as explained earlier, they cannot be inflationary or crowd out private investment. As seen in Table 2-3, roughly 44 percent of the 1992 deficit of $297.8 billion was cyclical, and over the entire period covered in the table 33 percent of the cumulative deficits were cyclical.

The term fiscal policy is used to describe budgetary policies that are designed to affect the level of total spending in the economy. The idea of using the federal budget in this manner was not seriously considered until the depression of the 1930s. Prior to that time it was not believed that fiscal action could be effective as a countercyclical device. Issues concerned with government expenditure and revenue were described by the term public finance. Although there are still numerous people, including economists, who oppose the use of certain forms of fiscal policy or regard them as ineffective, hardly any knowledgeable person favors the elimination of automatic stabilizers.

Fiscal policies are generally classified as *discretionary* fiscal policy and *automatic* fiscal policy. Usually, but not always, discretionary fiscal policies affect the structural deficit. Examples of discretionary fiscal policies are legislated tax changes designed to raise purchasing power during recession or to lower it during inflation, public works projects such as TVA and other projects such as introduced during the depressed 1930s, and recession-inspired increases in such transfer outlays as social security benefits. At the request of President John F. Kennedy an investment tax credit was introduced to stimulate investment in the early 1960s. Kennedy also asked for an income tax reduction to boost the economy. Although the tax bill was eventually passed, the President did not live to have the satisfaction of signing it. Taxes were raised in 1968 in an effort to offset the inflationary effects of accelerated defense spending. They were again lowered in early 1975 to combat unemployment. At that time Congress also granted extensions of unemployment compensation in excess of the normal twenty six weeks. Recovery from the severe recession of 1980-83 was greatly facilitated by sharp tax cuts during the first term of President Reagan's administration.

Another, sometimes overlooked, category of fiscal policy consists of discretionary changes that make the automatic stabilizers more effective without changing the structural deficit. Examples of such policies are the Comprehensive Employment and Training (CETA) and Anti-Cyclical Revenue Sharing programs introduced during the deep recession which began in 1974. The amount of money spent on these programs was designed to change as the unemployment rate changed. A rise in the unemployment rate would trigger a rise in outlays; a drop in the unemployment rate would automatically reduce them. Since the outlays were designed to be phased out automatically when the economy reached full employment, they increased the cyclical deficit when unemployment was high but had no effect on the structural deficit.

Triggered programs are popular because they by-pass a number of the problems associated with discretionary policy. If taxes are lowered during recession, shouldn't they be raised again once the economy recovers? But will they? If they aren't, the tax cuts could then be inflationary. But if they are, people could come to expect recession tax cuts to be temporary, and the cuts might therefore be ineffective because people would just increase their savings instead of their consumption. Evidence suggests that this is likely to be the case in response to windfall income? If a public works project is started during a recession, will the bulk of the spending occur quickly, when it is most need to create jobs, or will the bulk of the outlays come on stream after the economy has recovered and the spending becomes inflationary? If a new program is started and a bureaucracy is hired to administer it, can the program be discontinued when it is no longer need it, or will the bureaucracy have such a vested interest and be so firmly entrenched that it can't be dismantled?

Because of these, and other, problems its a good thing the economy has its automatic stabilizers. Undoubtedly the most important of these are unemployment compensation and the individual income tax. The individual income tax is stabilizing not only because taxes decline automatically when personal income declines, but also because taxes decline proportionately more because of the *progressive* rate structure. Under 1992 tax law heads of households were taxed at a rate of 15 percent on the first $28,750 of taxable income and at a rate of 28 percent on any additional income up to $74,150. Thereafter any additional income was taxed at a rate of 31 percent. Suppose that your taxable income comes to $50,000. You pay 15 percent on the first $28,750, or $4,312.50, and 28 percent on your remaining income of $21,250 ($50,000 - $28,750). This amount is $5,950.00 so your total tax bill comes to $10,262.50. Your average tax rate is your tax divided by taxable income. This rate is 20.5 percent.

Now suppose that the economy enters a recession and that you suffer a reduction in your taxable income of $10,000 to $40,000. Since you remain in the 28 percent bracket, this reduces your tax liability by $2,800 thereby causing $2,800 of the income loss to be absorbed by the government. Your disposable (after tax) income declines by $7,200 rather than the $10,000 loss in your pre-tax income, and you and the economy therefore benefit from the fact that you are forced to reduce your consumption spending by less than if you had to absorb the entire loss. Since your total tax bill is now $7,462 while your taxable income is $40,000 your average tax rate declines from 20.5 percent to 18.7 percent. The example shows that your tax bill falls both because you have less income available to tax and because the remaining income is taxed at a lower average rate. It is important to recognize, as well, that your average tax rate declines even though you remain in the 28 percent bracket. That is the key ingredient of a *progressive* tax; higher income taxpayers pay a larger fraction of their income in taxes than lower income tax payers and this is true even if both their incomes fall in the same tax bracket.

Congress could increase the stabilizing effect of the individual income tax by increasing the number of brackets and imposing successively higher bracket (marginal) rates on these brackets, and this could be done without changing the taxes you have to pay if your income remains at $50,000. However, if your income then falls again by $10,000 the decline in your tax liability would be greater than before, and this would be true for your average tax rate as well. Such legislation would be another way to widen the cyclical deficit during a recession, thereby cushioning the loss of purchasing power, without affecting the structural deficit.

The phrase "fiscal fine tuning" has earned an unenviable reputation, one that is probably deserved when applied to efforts to make incremental tax and expenditure adjustments so as to keep the economy on a full-employment track. To do this successfully you would have to know ahead of time exactly whether the economy was going up, thereby threatening inflation, or down, thereby threatening higher unemployment. You would therefore have to have an accurate forecast of economic activity for the next calendar quarter. Beyond that you will have to convince Congress to act promptly on the basis of your forecast.

Forecasting is a very inexact art.[2] One reason for this is that the economy is constantly being peppered by quite random and unpredictable shocks that your forecasting procedure, no matter how sophisticated, cannot take into account. And the thought of getting Congress to commit itself to a fiscal change on the strength of a forecast is unrealistic. Shortly after the Carter administration took office in 1977, the President's economic team arrived at the Capitol to request a tax cut because they believed the economy was weakening. Only a month or so later they returned to say that more recent

2. Although economists have no choice other than to make forecasts, asking economists to predict the future is very much like asking your doctor when he expects you to get cancer.

information had caused the administration to change its mind. It's not difficult to see why the administration quickly lost credibility and why its efforts at fiscal fine tuning were ridiculed.

Sometimes there is a very solid basis for a forecast. During the mid 1960s President Lyndon Johnson secretly ordered an escalation of the Vietnam war effort at a time of full employment. When his economic advisers subsequently learned of this they told him that a tax increase would be needed to prevent inflation. President Johnson resisted the advice for a time, thereby alarming the Federal Reserve and prompting the Fed to intervene with a restrictive monetary policy that had the effect, in the fourth quarter of 1966, of reducing spending in the economy to levels well below those that had been anticipated by business.[3] The mistaken sales forecasts produced a very sharp pile up of business inventories which subsequently led to production cuts as business filled orders from its over stocked shelves. The result was a mild slump during the first half of 1967.

It was obvious to the President's advisers and to anyone else who understood the situation, that once the surplus inventories were worked off, production would snap back and the economy would be on its way into an inflationary boom. Finally convinced of the need for a tax increase, President Johnson asked Congress for the legislation just before the advent of the anticipated boom. The subsequent scene at hearings of the House Ways and Means Committee was truly memorable. Brandishing a copy of economic indicators in his fist, Chairman Wilbur Mills marched down the list of indicators from beginning to end, demanding to know where the inflationary boom was. Did the administration think he was crazy enough to commit himself on the basis of its forecast? Made by a bunch of ivory-tower economists no less? How would he and the Congress look if the forecast proved to be wrong?

Is it any wonder that the tax increase was not enacted until a year later, long after the inflationary boom had become a reality?

The fact that fiscal fine tuning is unworkable doesn't mean that discretionary fiscal policy is of no value. When the economy is well

3. In the next chapter we'll explain exactly how the Federal Reserve conducts monetary policy and how this affects the economy.

below full employment, as it was when President Kennedy asked for a tax cut in 1963, the direction in which the economy and fiscal policy needed to be headed was obvious. The same has been true recently. With a mammoth gap of some $300 billion in 1987 prices between actual and potential GDP in 1992 we hardly needed a forecast to tell us that the economy would have benefitted from an expansionary shot in the arm.

Public Investment and Borrowing

Critics of deficit spending often claim that deficits crowd out private investment and thereby reduce economic growth. It is important to recognize that such categories of expenditure as government purchases and grants in aid have an *investment* content which contributes importantly to economic growth. The Federal highway program results in the construction of interstate highways that have created a transportation network which has greatly reduced transportation costs, made markets far more accessible to each other, and enabled suburban residents to drive to work. Government assistance to the educational system is vital for the creation of *human capital* that enables people to be more productive. Even some defense spending has investment content. The training of military recruits in computer use and electronics often enables military personnel to be more productive in subsequent civilian life, and some technologies developed for defense in areas such as communications and aerospace have important civilian applications.

In fiscal year 1992 federal non-defense capital outlays came to $102.6 billion. At the same time the fiscal year NIA deficit came to $288.8 billion. Therefore, if it were decided that government investment outlays ought not to be considered as part of the current deficit, or that they should be separated out from other sources of deficit into a capital budget and a current budget the deficit would have been reduced by 35 percent. This percentage would have been even higher had government investment in human capital such as expenditures on education, worker training and research and development been included. More important, a capital budget would focus attention on the fact that the economic infrastructure became increasingly starved during the 1980s. All major industrial countries spend more than the United States on public investment.

Japan, for example, puts about 5 percent of its national output into public capital. Japan's far higher economic growth rate over the past 50 years strongly reflects its attention to its infrastructure.

Before getting into the pros and cons of dividing the budget into a capital budget and a current or operating budget it is important to emphasize the importance of public investment. The Council of Economic Advisers has estimated that the costs imposed on the private sector of the economy by an inadequate economic infrastructure are so great that private profitability would have been 2 percent higher if non-defense public investment had remained at its level of 2.1 percent of GDP in the early 1980s instead of being permitted to fall during the Reagan and Bush Administrations.[4] Federal government direct investment in the economic infra structure declined from $18.9 billion in 1978 to $11.9 billion in 1988, a decline of 37 percent. Over the same period of time federal grants to state and local governments for highways and community and regional development fell from $15.4 billion to $5.9 billion, a mammoth decline of 61.7 percent. Bill Clinton isn't just whistling Dixie when he talks about the need for more infra-structure investment.

Business firms must have capital budgets, most state and local governments have them, and most foreign countries have them. The Federal government, however, lumps current and capital spending together. If a business kept its accounts the way the federal government does, it would immediately be in trouble with the Internal Revenue Service because, by including investment outlays as a current expenditure, it would understate its profits thereby reducing its corporate tax liability. Because of this the IRS insists that only that part of the cost of capital assets such as machinery, equipment, and buildings attributable to current operations may be deducted as a current cost. This current cost of capital is known as depreciation which must be figured according to schedules consistent with Treasury regulations. Economists think of depreciation as the loss of value of the capital caused by current operations, just as we think

4. *Economic Report of the President,* 1989, pp. 80-81.

5. This may not be entirely true. The IRS permits firms to depreciate their capital assets on an original cost basis. During a period of inflation, total depreciation is not likely to equal the dollar cost of replacing an original machine, even if the new machine is identical to the old one.

of the annual depreciation of a motorcar as equaling the reduction in the car's resale value after a year of operation.

How is investment in new capital assets financed? Depreciation allowances allow the replacement of fully depreciated capital goods to be financed internally.[5] But net additions to the capital stock must, in large part, be financed from outside the firm. In 1990 Net Private Domestic Investment came to $207.9 billion. Corporations were able to finance $63.3 billion of this through retained earnings. The remainder, however, had to come from outside business firms either through bank borrowing, bond issue, or stock issue. Indeed it is essential for business to be able to borrow. It enables business to pay *over time* for capital assets that are needed now, but that cost more than the money currently available. Should public borrowing for investment purposes be regarded in the same way? Most economists seem to think so.

Corporations must pay back their debt and so must the government when its obligations come due. But if a company is growing it will take out new debt and its total level of indebtedness is likely to increase in step with the growth of the company. When government obligations come due the holders of government bonds are paid and the government then simply retrieves the funds by issuing new debt that has nearly always been readily marketable. Private debt grows as the economy grows so it is not surprising that government debt also grows. The important issue is whether this growth is excessive. That is a question to look into in chapter 4.

Borrowing is justified for the purpose of financing investment. This is because investment in new assets such as machinery and equipment increases the profitability of the operation and, if the investment is sound, yields a return in excess of the amount needed to pay interest and repay principal. In the private sector the net return after principal and interest accrues to the investing firm. The bulk of the return from public investment differs in that it yields virtually no return to the government. Rather, it accrues to individuals and business in the form of higher income due to better education, cheaper and more rapid transportation, cheaper power and the like. Indeed infrastructure investment tends to be characterized by the fact that the returns it yields are spread over a long period of time, longer than would make such investment attractive to private parties. Nevertheless, it is vital if the economy is to grow and prosper.

These considerations suggest that the Federal government might do well to reform its budgeting practices by dividing the budget into a current budget and a capital budget. The former should be financed primarily by taxation, while the latter can appropriately be financed by borrowing. Some would go so far as to argue that inasmuch as infrastructure investment is vital to economic growth, such investment should be given priority over the government's current expenditures and should therefore be exempt from the budget cutting knife. Attention might then be focussed on the real sources of government waste--the federal farm program, national defense, spiraling Medicare costs, and that most sacred of all cows, the social security system.

Why then, doesn't the federal government follow the lead of state governments and introduce a capital budget? One reason often cited is that the federal government is a non profit organization that has no need to show a profit. More important, it is difficult to sort out public investment from other expenditures. Does military hardware contribute to economic growth? Do Medicaid payments increase the productivity of its recipients? Indeed, given the propensity to politicize the budgetary process, the division of the budget into a current and a capital budget would be likely to invite endless wrangling over how expenditure items should be classified, and huge opportunities for budgetary manipulation designed to lower the current deficit by shifting expenditure items to the capital budget.

The economic impact of government finance depends not only on the Federal budget but also on the budgets of State and local governments. Also, if the purpose is to make comparisons between the United States and countries that do not have a federal system, then surely a consolidated budget would provide a more suitable basis for comparison. For most of the time since 1972 state and local budgets have run surpluses and the consolidated deficits for all units of government were less than the Federal deficit. Moreover, these State and local surpluses have been substantially less than the federal grants to the state and local governments. Consequently, the effect of the grants to state and local governments is to bloat the federal deficit while allowing state and local governments to show a surplus. In 1991, for example, the Federal NIA deficit was $210.4 billion, the surplus of state and local governments was $17.1 billion, and the consolidated deficit was $193.3 billion. Federal grants in aid to state and local governments came to $153.3 billion. Had these grants been subtracted from the federal deficit and shifted to the state and local recipients, the federal deficit would have been reduced to $57.1 billion and state and local surpluses would have been converted into deficits of $136.2 billion.

It is important, especially when making year to year comparisons during a period of inflation, to take the effect of inflation on the deficit into account. Inflation automatically increases the dollar cost of existing government programs. It also raises revenues. Therefore, if it were desirable to compare the 1980 deficit of $35.3 billion with the 1990 deficit of $136.1 billion, it would be appropriate in making the comparison by holding prices constant at 1980 levels so that the *real* increase in the deficit can be assessed. Prices, as measured by the overall price deflator for GDP increased 57.9 percent over the period. Had there been no inflation the 1990 deficit would therefore have been $86.2 billion rather than $136.1 billion. Thus the *real* deficit in 1990 was 2.4 times higher than the deficit of 1980, a far smaller increase than in the *nominal* deficit which quadrupled.

A Balanced Budget Amendment?

During his eight years in office President Ronald Reagan rang up budget deficits that averaged $152 billion per year. Not to be outdone, President Bush's deficits came within a whisker of averaging $200 billion per year. Jimmy Carter's deficits averaged only $36.6 billion. Nevertheless, the fiction persists that Democrats are reckless spenders whereas Republicans practice fiscal frugality.

By some miracle of mystification and mental legerdemain both Reagan and Bush found it entirely possible to run up record deficits while simultaneously advocating a balanced budget amendment to the Constitution. The involuted logic, apparently, was that the Administration had no influence over the deficit which, with some aggressive rewriting of history, was blamed on congressional Democrats. Congress narrowly defeated a balanced budget amendment in 1993 and did so again in 1994. All past American Nobel Laureates in economics have stepped forward to oppose such an amendment; but Congress and some Presidents have persisted in playing Russian roulette with the economy. Although there are many different versions of such an amendment, they generally incorporate the requirement that the Federal budget must be balanced except during national emergency and/or if Congress suspends the requirement by a 60 percent majority.

Much of the public discussion of the balanced budget amendment has involved questions of political motivation and legal complications, while its economic considerations have been largely ignored. Either this means that Congress is not concerned with harm to the economy, or that it does not take the amendment seriously, or that it hasn't bothered to give thought to the consequences of placing the government in a fiscal straight jacket. To illustrate: There is the obvious danger that expenditures will already have equaled revenues prior to the end of a fiscal year. What is the treasury to do? Taken literally, the amendment requires it to default on its pre-existing legal obligations. This having occurred, there will immediately follow a flood of law suits against the government. The legal system will then be so hamstrung that it will be unable to perform its regular duties. Is it appropriate to permit Congress to abdicate fiscal policy decisions to the courts?

Alternatively, if the President and Congress ignore the amendment, the questions must surely arise as to why blatant violation of the Constitution is tolerated, and how it is possible for national politicians to have descended to a previously unimaginable level of irresponsibility. It is hard to escape the conclusion of critics of Congress that a vote for the amendment is no more than a device designed to convince naive constituents that they are doing "something" about the deficit, while, at the same time, dumping the problem onto others. It is hardly a wonder that opponents of the amendment insist on learning the specifics of how proponents expect to achieve the miracle.

The largely ignored economic issues are paramount, and the earlier analysis of the consequences of massive budget slashing should have made this clear. It has been seen that a draconian attempt to balance the budget will necessitate tax increases and expenditure reductions that greatly weaken the economy. Because of this, the cyclical deficit will rise and this, in turn, means that further budget tightening and further weakening of the economy will be necessitated if the Constitution is to be honored.

The major concern of the economist is that the automatic stabilizers that are so beneficial in moderating ups and downs in the economy will become destabilizers under a balanced budget amendment. This can be understood as follows: Suppose first that there are no income taxes or unemployment compensation. A weakening of the economy would then have no effect on the deficit and there would, in fact, be no cyclical deficit. No fiscal policy response would therefore be needed to comply with the balanced budget amendment. But in the presence of income taxes and unemployment compensation, weakening of the economy automatically creates a cyclical deficit. The government must then comply with the Constitution by raising taxes and reducing spending during a time of economic weakness. The economy will then be *worse off* than it would have been had there been no automatic stabilizers in the first place.

At the very least a balanced budget amendment must allow for cyclical deficits. This could be done by planning phased reductions in the *structural deficit* so as to reach structural budgetary balance at some time in the future. If, in the meantime, weakening of the economy increases the cyclical deficit, this would be permitted to occur without a restrictive budgetary response. In this manner progress towards a balanced budget could be made without an enormous immediate deflationary shock to the economy and without destroying the beneficial effects of the automatic stabilizers. A residual advantage of such an approach would be to force Congress, the Administration, and the general public to understand and appreciate the importance of the distinction between the structural and the cyclical deficits.

State and local governments have expressed the fear that the "contract with America" will merely have the effect of shifting the burden of many programs such as welfare and Medicaid away from the federal government and onto the states. If so it amounts to robbing Peter to pay Paul and the consolidated budget deficits of all levels of government will be largely unaffected. The Federal deficit declines while State and local deficits increase. Since State tax systems tend to be far less equitable than federal taxes, the implied shift in the tax burden will adversely affect the distribution of income.

The Gingrich plan to provide states with a fixed amount of income to supplement their welfare and other programs seems particularly harmful and naive. Suppose, for example, that a fixed amount is given to each state for foodstamps. If the money runs out after nine months are people expected then to starve? You might as well save more money by letting them starve sooner.

3

Deficit Financing, Money, and Inflation

If you are worried that budget deficits, especially increasing deficits, are inflationary, you are in very good company. The Board of Governors of the Federal Reserve system, acknowledged experts who control the nation's money supply, are so obsessed with the potential inflationary effects of the deficit that they seem determined to force the economy to stagnate for as long as it takes the President and Congress to cut the deficit down to size. Is inflation a legitimate fear? Does deficit spending mean that the government is printing money? Does it matter how the deficit is financed?

As discussed in the previous chapter, government expenditure and revenue policies have direct effects on total spending in the economy. Such policies also have significant indirect effects on spending because of their influence over interest rates, the supply of money and credit, and the level of financial wealth held by the non-bank private sector of the economy. These indirect effects are extremely important. Its not just that a rise in the deficit might be inflationary, its also the way in which the deficit is financed that helps determine the degree to which an increase in the deficit is inflationary.

When an increase in government expenditure is not matched by an equal increase in taxes the government must borrow. It can attempt to sell government bonds to the private sector of the economy and, if this is difficult or undesirable, as is sometimes the case, it puts pressure on the Federal Reserve to buy the bonds. The latter method of borrowing, which is equivalent to printing and spending money, is by far the most inflationary.

Money and Monetary Policy

Some very simple double-entry book keeping can help to identify the differences. Before getting into that it is important to be clear by what is meant by money and the money supply. The Federal Reserve (Fed) defines and keeps track of three monetary aggregates. To keep matters simple think of M_1 as coins, currency, and checkable deposits, and add savings and money market accounts to get M_2.[1] All aggregates refer to balances that are held in the non-bank private sector of the economy.

The money you hold is a *stock* magnitude the value of which you would enter into your personal balance sheet as an asset. Stocks held by business such as cash, accounts receivable, inventories, the value of plant and equipment, have the property that their value can be measured at a moment of time. Your income, on the other hand, is a *flow* of receipts that occurs over a period of time such as a month or a year. You won't find your, or a corporation's income, on a balance sheet. Rather you would find them in an income statement that records receipts and expenditures over an explicit time period such as a year. If I tell you that my income is $10,000 this information is of no value to you unless I also tell you whether I earned this income in a week, a month, or a year. However, if I tell you that I have $10,000 in my checking account this is useful information. You can always tell the difference between a stock and a flow by asking whether it is necessary to attach an explicit time dimension to make the information useful. If you do its a flow; if you don't it's a stock.

Confusing money with income is a common and dangerous error. We hear such confusion every day as when someone tells us that a tax cut will put more money in people's hands. A tax cut raises our after-tax incomes. It may have very little to do with money. You can have a high income without having any money if you pay all your bills on payday and then have nothing left in your pocket or your bank account. You can also have lots of money while having very little income if you are retired but have made a life-time habit out of stuffing dollar bills in a cookie jar or under a mattress.

---

1. To be precise, M_1 is the sum of currency, demand deposits, traveler's checks, and other checkable deposits. M_2 is a broader aggregate that includes M_1 plus overnight repurchase agreements, Eurodollars, Money Market Mutual Funds, all savings deposits and small time deposits. M_3, finally, equals M_2 plus large time deposits, term repurchase agreements, and money market fund balances held by institutions.

The Federal Reserve System (Fed) is the nation's central bank. The easiest way to think of the Fed is as a super bank into which both commercial banks and the federal government deposit their funds. It is therefore a bank for bankers and for the government. The Fed is an independent agency of the Federal Government. Its Open-Market Committee, which determines monetary policy, consists of thirteen members. Seven of these are the Fed's governors appointed by the President of the United States, and the other six are selected from among the presidents of the regional Federal Reserve banks.

In 1991 the Fed held about $260 billion in government securities. Such debt plays an essential role in the economy because its purchase and sale, by the Fed to and from private investors, enables the Fed to manage the nation's money supply. If the Fed wishes to stimulate business activity it purchases government securities from private investors. Such government security purchases by the Fed are known as *open-market purchases.*

Figure 3-1 traces the bookkeeping effects of an open-market purchase of 100. Shown in the chart are three consolidated balance sheets, or T, accounts for three entities--the Fed, a consolidated balance sheet for commercial banks, and a consolidated balance sheet for the entire non-bank private sector of the economy. The Fed purchases bonds from a member of the non bank private sector for which the recipient receives a check which he deposits in his commercial bank. Therefore, in the private sector bond holdings decline while deposits increase. Upon receiving the check the commercial bank credits the deposit accounts and makes a corresponding left-hand entry in its reserve account. Reserves represent bank money that commercial banks may use to make loans and purchase other earning assets. The commercial bank then sends the check back to the Fed which credits the account of the commercial bank. As can be seen in the chart, each positive left-hand entry is offset either by a corresponding right-hand increase, or by an offsetting reduction on the left hand. More important, it can be seen that the nation's money supply, defined as currency plus deposits in the hands of the non-bank private sector, has increased.

What are the likely economic effects of such a Fed-induced increase in the money supply? The Fed's action has increased the demand for government securities and has, therefore, tended to

Figure 3-1
Effect of A Federal Reserve Open-Market Purchase

Federal Reserve

U.S. Bonds +100	
	Member Bank Deposits +100

Commercial Banks

	Deposits +100
Reserves +100	

Non-Bank Private Sector

Deposits +100	
U.S. Bonds -100	

raise government bond prices while lowering their yields. Investors are then likely to sell some of their government securities from their portfolios in exchange for other lower priced and higher yielding bonds. Because of such portfolio readjustment the prices of such other assets rise while their yields fall, so that all interest rates tend to fall. Since bond prices have been raised and interest rates have fallen, businesses that need financing can borrow by issuing bonds on more favorable terms. Business can also increase its borrowing from commercial banks because the increase in bank reserves means that there is more money available to lend, and the terms of the borrowing are apt to become more favorable as banks lower their lending rates to compete with other banks for borrowers.

Inasmuch as the Fed's open-market purchase of government bonds has reduced the cost and increased the availability of credit, business borrowing to finance capital investment is likely to increase. Therefore, investment spending in the economy rises, production and incomes rise, and this has further multiplier effects as higher incomes induce additional consumption spending. The hoped for result is a rise in real GDP and an increase in employment.

Its important to realize, as well, that a rise in GDP will cause the cyclical deficit to decline. Therefore, bear in mind that expansionary monetary policy can influence the budget deficit in a favorable way. Expansionary fiscal policy cannot do this because it increases the structural deficit. Although the cyclical deficit will decline, the overall budget deficit will increase.

A third possible beneficial effect of expansionary monetary policy is that it could cause the international exchange value of the dollar to fall. Because of the fall in interest rates, higher yielding foreign assets become more attractive to investors who therefore take steps to shift their portfolio holdings away from domestic to foreign financial assets. To buy these assets they must convert dollars into foreign currencies and this causes the dollar to depreciate relative to other currencies. American importers then see that it takes more dollars to buy foreign commodities and this causes spending to be shifted away from imports towards domestically produced goods and services. Realizing that the cost of foreign travel has increased, vacationers change their plans and go to Disney World. At the same time foreigners find that their currencies buy more dollars and that they can buy U.S. exports more cheaply. Because of these developments there is a further rise in GDP as domestic production replaces imports and as export industries enjoy increased activity.

This sounds like a very attractive story. For the outcome to be this favorable it would have to be the case that production and employment could easily be expanded. This would be the case if unemployment were high and business were operating at less than full capacity. But if it's not easy to expand output because production is at capacity and additional labor is not readily available, competition for workers drives up wages, and the additional spending by business and consumers is then largely wasted in inflation. In fact, for the purposes of this chapter let's assume that the economic situation is one in which there is no GDP gap so that the primary effect of additional total spending would be to generate inflation. But bear in mind that what we have to say pertains only to such situations.

Financing an Increase in the Deficit

In order to study the financial effects of deficit spending a fourth balance sheet in the form of a T account for the U.S. Treasury is added. The entries in Figure 3-2 labelled with an **a** show the bookkeeping effects of an increase in spending by the treasury. This could take the form of a pay check to a government worker, a social security check, or any of the other myriad things for which the government spends money. When the treasury sends you a check and you deposit it in your bank account, you record an increase in your assets in the form of money. At the same time you recognize that the check represents a transfer of financial wealth from the government to you. On the right hand side of your balance sheet you therefore record an increase in net worth.

When your commercial bank receives the check it credits your deposit account and also adds an equal amount to its reserve account. The check is passed on to the Fed which, on seeing it, knows that its deposit liabilities to commercial banks have increased while deposit liabilities to the treasury have decreased. It therefore adds +100 to its member bank deposit account while subtracting the same amount from its U.S. deposit account. The treasury, finally, recognizes that its deposits with the Fed have declined and that it has transferred wealth to the private sector.

Again all bookkeeping entries are offsetting. It's important to notice that the government expenditure has increased both the money supply and the financial wealth of the private sector.

At some point the treasury will have to take steps to replenish its account. One way to do this is to print government bonds and sell them to the non-bank private sector. The accounting effects of this are shown by the entries labelled **b**. Beginning with the treasury, note that the treasury has increased its liabilities in the form of an increase in its U.S. bonds outstanding, but at the same time the treasury has received a check in payments for the bonds. The increase in bond liabilities is therefore offset by an increase in the treasury's deposits with the Fed. In the private sector individuals have an increase in their bond holdings offset by a reduction in their bank deposits. The commercial banks, finally, lose both deposits and reserves.

It is apparent, after both transactions have been made, that the treasury has gotten back the money it had spent. There is, therefore, no increase in the money supply. What is different, however, is that the private sector has received an increase in financial wealth in the form of an increase in its holdings of government bonds. Even though it is not true that this increase in the deficit increases the money supply, it nevertheless has an expansionary effect on the

Figure 3-2
Financing Government Spending: Bond Sales to the Private Sector

U.S. Treasury

U.S. Deposits -100 a +100 b	U.S. Bonds Outstanding +100 b Net Worth -100 a

Federal Reserve

	U.S. Deposits -100 a +100 b Member Bank Deposits +100 a -100 b

Commercial Banks

Reserves +100 a -100 b	Deposits +100 a -100 b

Non-Bank Private Sector

Deposits +100 a -100 b U.S. Bonds +100 b	Net Worth +100 a

Figure 3-3
Financing Government Spending: Bond Sales to the Fed

U.S. Treasury

U.S. Deposits -100 a +100 c	U.S. Bonds Outstanding +100 c Net Worth -100 a

Federal Reserve

U.S. Bonds +100 c	U.S. Deposits -100 a +100 c Member Bank Deposits +100 a

Commercial Banks

Reserves +100 a	Deposits +100 a

Non-Bank Private Sector

Deposits +100 a	Net Worth +100 a

economy. The increased government spending adds to the economy's spending stream, and the increase in financial wealth is likely to have some positive effect on consumer spending.

Under certain circumstances it will be advantageous for the treasury to replenish its account by selling its bonds to the Federal Reserve. The financial effects of this are shown in Figure 3-3 by the transactions labelled **c**. Notice first that all the **c** transactions are confined to the T accounts of the treasury and the Fed. The Fed receives the bonds and gives the treasury deposit credit. The treasury assumes an additional liability in the form of bonds outstanding for which it receives deposit credit from the Fed. Inasmuch as commercial banks and the private sector are unaffected by the transaction, their T accounts stay just as they were after the **a** set of transactions. Therefore, after all is said and done, bank deposits have increased and that means the money supply has increased. Once again the non-bank private sector enjoys an increase in financial wealth, but this time the increase is in the form of greater bank deposits whereas previously it was in the form of government bonds. Notice, finally, that the increase in the money supply and the increase in private wealth would have been exactly the same had the treasury simply printed dollar bills and spent them. Therefore, borrowing from the Fed is the practical equivalent of printing and spending money.

The generic term for an institution such as the Fed is central bank. Financing deficits by borrowing from the central bank is more inflationary than borrowing from the private sector. The reason is that when the treasury borrows from the private sector this tends to raise interest rates and slow investment spending. However, when it borrows from the Fed this has no effect on the government bond market so that interest rates, instead of rising, tend to fall because of the increase in the money supply. Investment spending could, therefore, rise rather than fall.

It is now helpful to introduce a concept called the *government budget restraint.* It has been seen that a dollar of government borrowing must be reflected either in an increase in the money supply and/or an increase in government bonds held by the private sector. This allows us to write the expression,

$$\Delta M + \Delta B = E - T$$

where $\triangle M$ stands for a change in the money supply, $\triangle B$ stands for a change in government bond holdings, E is government expenditure, and T is government tax revenue. Therefore, E - T is the budget deficit. To isolate the factors that cause the money supply to change, subtract $\triangle B$ from both sides of the expression. This gives,

$$\Delta M = E - T - \Delta B$$

and it can therefore be seen that there are only two ways in which the money supply can be increased. The first is through a budget deficit, and the second is through the destruction of bonds. Destruction of bonds is what takes place when the Fed buys bonds from the private sector and replaces the bonds with money.

The budget restraint shows that a budget deficit need not raise the money supply provided bond holdings in the private sector increase by the amount of the deficit. It also shows that if it is not possible for the government to sell bonds to the private sector, $\triangle B = 0$, so that there is then a direct connection between the deficit and the money supply. In that case,

$$\Delta M = E - T$$

As will be seen, this is a situation that frequently characterizes developing countries.

Notice, finally, that the budget deficit need not increase in order to raise the money supply and private financial wealth. If there is a budget deficit of $100 billion in one year, the money supply and private bond holdings must increase by that much during the year. Then, in the next year, if the identical deficit is run, these magnitudes will increase another $100 billion.

When deficits are financed through money creation this is called *monetization* of debt. Since this is the most expansionary way of financing a deficit, why would governments ever choose this route? In the first place, monetization may be in the interest of the economy. This would certainly be true during recession when it is desirable for deficit increases to be as expansionary as possible. If the government borrowed from the private sector this would lower bond prices, raise interest rates, and crowd out investment. To prevent the crowdout it would be appropriate to prevent the rise in interest rates by having the Fed buy enough of the bonds to prevent interest rates from rising.

As explained in Chapter 9, monetization of debt is also appropriate when it is desirable to minimize the shocks that fiscal and monetary policies send to other countries. When the structural budget deficit increased sharply between 1983 and 1985 this drove up interest rates in the United States and this made government bonds attractive to foreign investors. To buy American bonds they had to convert their own currencies into dollars and this caused the international value of the dollar to rise. This, in turn, made imports less expensive and it made exports harder to sell. Consequently a considerable portion of the expansionary effect of the fiscal policies was transmitted to other countries. Americans spent their tax cuts, but largely on imports. You could say that fiscal policy worked but in the wrong places. To avoid that, good-neighbor macroeconomic policy would have attempted to prevent the interest-rate escalation by combining the expansionary fiscal policies with expansionary monetary policy designed to hold down interest rates. In other words, monetization of the increase in the deficit could have prevented the expansionary shock to foreign countries.

Government borrowing from their own central banks may be necessitated by the exigencies of war-time financing. Such borrowing is also often necessitated in developing countries where the government is forced to borrow from its central bank if it hopes to continue to finance its badly needed investments in the economic infra structure. These issues are discussed in the sections to follow.

War and Inflation: The Disequilibrium System

It would be extremely difficult to conduct a major war effort without suffering inflation. Governments need additional resources which must be gotten from the private sector. Some of these resources can be obtained through increased taxation. But usually governments find it impossible to raise taxes by an amount equal to their increased military spending. At the same time the civilian labor force declines as the armed forces increase, and it is therefore difficult to expand production to satisfy both military and civilian needs. The usual outcome is inflation.

During the Civil War so many confederate greenbacks were printed that inflation quickly wiped out their value. Prices doubled in the United States as the result of World War I. However that was less than the 150 percent increase in the price level of Great Britain and the 250 percent increase experienced by France. The hyper inflation that engulfed Germany totally wiped out the value of German money and financial wealth. For the U.S. World War II brought remarkably little inflation with it in large measure because of the excellent economic planning that accompanied the war effort.

Table 3-1 shows federal government receipts, outlays, and deficits, covering the World War II period, expressed as a percentage of Gross National Product (GNP).[2] Federal government outlays increased steadily from 12.1 percent of GNP in 1941 to 45.2 percent in 1944. How was this mammoth increase in government spending to be financed? As seen in the table, taxes increased sharply from 7.7 percent of GNP in 1941 to a maximum of 21.7 percent in 1944. This is the highest that federal taxes have ever gotten. After World War II federal taxes, as a percent of GNP, have never exceeded 20.1 percent. Despite the enormous increase in taxes, this was not nearly enough to match the increased outlays. The budget deficit jumped from only 4.4 percent of GNP in 1941 to 31 percent in 1943. Compare this with 1992 when the budget deficit was 5 percent of GNP and notice, as well, that 5 percent isn't much bigger than the 4.4 percent registered in 1941.

Let's go back to the spring of 1941 and join an imaginary meeting that President Roosevelt might have had with some of his advisers. Among those present are the Secretary of the Navy, the Secretary of War, the Secretary of the Treasury, the Chairman of the Federal Reserve, and yourself, Chairman of the Council of Economic Advisers. Never mind that the position had not, at that time, been created. As is customary with Council Chairmen, you have been recruited from an academic institution and everybody calls you professor. The financial press has already labelled you an ivory-tower crackbrain not to be taken seriously.

Like most meetings at that time the atmosphere was somber in the extreme. Hitler's troops had already overrun much of Europe

2. Until fairly recently our most common measure of aggregate economic activity was Gross National Product (GNP) which measures the total value of all final goods and services produced in the economy during a given year. The difference between GNP and GDP is that GNP includes receipts by U.S. residents of interest, dividends and reinvested earnings of foreigh affiliates of U.S. corporations. This had the effect of causing GNP to exceed GDP by $10.7 billion in 1990. Switching emphasis from GNP to GDP has helped the U.S. national income and product accounts to become more consistent with national accounting practices in other countries.

and it looked as if Great Britain was in serious danger of invasion. At the same time the formidable Japanese were terrorizing the Far East. Almost everyone thought that U.S. entry into the war was inevitable. President Roosevelt favored entry but believed that the country and the Congress were not ready for it. Some major provocation, such as the subsequent attack on Pearl Harbor, would be needed to overcome the isolationist forces in Congress.

Table 3-1
Federal Government Receipts, Outlays and Deficit
(Percent of GNP)

Year	Receipts	Outlays	Deficit
1941	7.7	12.1	4.4
1942	10.3	24.7	14.4
1943	13.7	44.7	31.0
1944	21.7	45.2	23.5
1945	21.3	43.6	22.4
1946	18.5	25.9	7.5

Source: Office of Management and Budget, *Historical Tables: Budget of the United States Government,* Fiscal Year 1992.

The Secretaries of the Navy and War briefed the group with respect to the magnitude of the coming military effort. As much as one half of the nation's production might be needed for an indefinite number of years. Every able bodied man would have to be drafted into the military and their loss to the labor force would have to be offset by strenuous efforts to recruit youngsters, women, older people, and whoever else it was possible to find, into the civilian labor force.

After a lengthy discussion of mobilization, the meeting turned to the issue of how all that additional spending was to be financed. There was general agreement that taxes would have to be raised, the question, however, was by how much. The Secretary of the Treasury reminded the group that the country was still reeling from the loss of income and wealth caused by the nightmarish depression and that per capita GNP had been only $754 in 1940, about the price of a new Buick. Nevertheless, he thought it might be possible to get taxes up to 20 or so percent of GNP once the defense effort raises incomes, provided a payroll deduction system of tax collection were introduced. It would, he said, make it far easier to collect taxes if they were withheld from weekly and monthly paychecks rather than if they continued to be collected on a quarterly basis. He also expressed concern that very high tax rates would create incentives for people to conceal income and cheat on or evade taxes. Taxes reach their limit, he said, when these incentives begin to override patriotism.

Asked for your opinion, you indicate your agreement with the secretary that at some point higher taxes are likely to become counter productive. You add that very sharp increases in marginal tax rates would probably have very adverse incentive effects on labor effort. Because we wish to maximize labor effort, we would have to be very careful not to raise taxes by too much. Besides, you ask, wouldn't it be better to reward workers for their hard work and patriotism by giving them government bonds instead of taxing them to death?

The points you and the treasury secretary have made are well taken and it is agreed to introduce automatic payroll deduction and to raise taxes to about 20 percent of GNP. The remaining 20 or 25 percent would have to be financed by borrowing. The Secretary of the Treasury is then asked if he thinks it would be possible to borrow that much. "I really don't know," he says, "all I can tell you is that when we sell government bonds in the bond market this depresses their prices and raises interest rates. We certainly don't want to increase the cost of borrowing for defense industries. We also want to be able to market the bonds. If people know that these deficits are going to continue they will quickly realize that government bond prices are going to drop steadily so they won't buy them in the first place. Its obvious that we can't do it without lots of help."

"Where can we get the help Professor?" asks the President turning to you.

"Well Mr. President, I certainly agree with the Secretary that it is important for the defense effort to prevent interest rates from rising. It probably would be possible to market large volumes of debt provided we guarantee to the public that the market value of their bonds won't fall."

"How do we do that?"

"We could enlist the cooperation of the Federal Reserve by

having the Fed guarantee to support the government bond market. By that I mean, have the Fed stand ready at all times to buy enough of the bonds to prevent their prices from falling and interest rates from rising."

"Sounds like a great idea." says the President. "I could announce that its going to be a two and a half percent interest rate war and that the Fed will guarantee it. That way bond buyers won't have to worry about the value of their bonds."

Now visibly agitated, the Chairman of the Fed asks: "Do you realize what the professor is proposing? We have been talking about increasing defense spending by $75 billion per year; paying for less than half of it with taxes; and leaving another $40 billion to be financed by borrowing. Even if we only have to buy 15 percent of the newly issued debt to support the government bond market, we'll be lucky if the money supply doesn't increase by 20 percent a year. You can't avoid inflation when that's going on, and inflation gets more uncontrollable the longer it goes on."

After a deep breath the chairman continues. "You might protect the nominal values of the bonds you sell to people by pegging their prices, but you can't prevent inflation from eroding their purchasing power value. So who are we kidding when we support the bond market? We could issue bonds that are indexed for inflation, but that would just tell people that we've given up on inflation control. We can't do that."

The Secretary of Labor, who joined the meeting belatedly, reminded the group that 14.6 percent of the labor force remained unemployed in 1940. Although unemployment was declining rapidly in 1941, there was still a good deal of manpower and industrial capacity that could be tapped before inflationary pressures took hold.

"Thank you Madam Secretary. That's a useful reminder. Do we nonetheless agree that inflation is going to become a major problem?" Everyone concurred. "Do we agree that all of the policies we've been talking about today are going to be necessary?" Again, there was general agreement with the Chairman of the Fed nodding very grudgingly.

"How," persisted the Fed chairman, "are we going to prevent inflation? All that enormous government spending combined with rapid monetary growth. For the last decade we've been obsessed with the depression and we've thought we could increase public spending without worrying about inflation. Those days are almost over and we now have to refocus our minds on inflation, and let me tell you, nothing can demoralize a population faster than uncontrolled inflation. All you have to do is look at the post Civil War South and Germany in the 1920s to get the picture. What do you think gave rise to Hitler? All Germans aren't stupid; they must have been pretty demoralized to make the likes of Hitler their leader."

"Yes, yes," says the President, "Don't have a fit. Explain to us why inflation is such a problem."

"As prices rise wages will have to rise and as wages rise prices will have to rise again and we'll be caught in an endless spiral. People will stop saving and spend all their income to beat price increases. And that's the last thing we want. On top of that government bonds won't be marketable and the Fed will just have to increase its bond purchases and accelerate growth of the money supply. We could easily be asking for hyper-inflation. If that happens everything breaks down. No one will accept money in payment for goods and services, including labor services, and we're then likely to have to force business and labor to produce at gun point. I don't see how we can avoid a disaster. We can preach sacrifice. But reliance on patriotism can't be stretched too far."

Visibly shaken by this testimony, the President turns to you again. "What do you think, Professor?"

"What we are talking about here amounts to trying to hold together a vast disequilibrium system. Push it in one place and it pops out somewhere else. It seems clear to me that, in addition to what we've talked about, we'll need rationing and comprehensive price controls."

"My God, won't that mean creating another massive bureaucracy? Where are we going to get these people and where are we going to put them?"

"Yes, that's certainly a problem, but with the young people going off to war, we'll be able to recruit a lot of ivory tower types such as myself. Many of us wear thick glasses and have flat feet so we couldn't pass an army physical anyway."

The President looks at the ceiling and breaks into a smile: "What a sight, an agency full of professors who've never met a payroll trying to run the economy. I can just picture it, floor after floor of academic bureaucrats playing with toys trying to decide how much a teddy bear should cost.[3] Wait until Congress gets wind of that."

"With all due respect sir, do you have a better idea?"

"Listen Prof, why do we need rationing? Wouldn't price controls do the job?"

Delighted to get teddy bears out of the picture you reply: "We need rationing to make price controls workable. The idea behind rationing is to make people buy things using two different currencies--money which is going to be too plentiful, and ration tickets that we'll dole out sparingly. When people run out of ration tickets they can't buy any more no matter how much money they have. Because their expenditures will be held down by the shortage of ration currency they'll be forced to save more, and they'll buy more government bonds, and that's what we want. We won't be producing cars and durable goods for civilian use anyway, so we need to encourage people to think ahead to the end of the war when they'll need lots of accumulated savings to replace their worn out cars and other things when civilian production resumes."

"Won't price controls and rationing cause black markets?"

"Sure they will, but you can't have everything. Let's just hope that most people will be patriotic enough to comply with the program. Besides, law enforcement isn't my department."

Although the tale is somewhat fanciful, it pretty well sums up the policies that were adopted in preparation for and during World War II. Good to his word, President Roosevelt announced that it would be a two and a half percent interest rate war, and that's what it was.

---

3. It's no joke. The teddy bear became a symbol of some of the frustration that workers in the Office of Price Administration (OPA) had to endure. If the government froze the price of the teddy bear you were marketing, you simply discontinued this line of production. You then put the black ring around the bear's left eye instead of its right eye, thereby introducing a new product to which OPA would have to give a new, usually higher, price. If you were a distiller you would stop producing your brand of bourbon, come out with some cheap rot gut, and ask OPA to let you sell it at the same price for which your previously sold your bourbon. Civilian smokers couldn't find a Lucky Strike except on the black market. Yet stores were full of all sorts of low grade substitute cigarettes that would almost kill you if you took a drag.

By 1945 the federal debt was almost 5 times as large as it had been in 1941, and the Fed had increased its holdings of federal debt 10 fold. Not surprisingly the M_1 money supply increased 113 percent, or 20.9 percent a year. Although the armed forces increased by 10 million, the civilian labor force declined by only 2 million persons. Despite this decline, total production increased 34.7 percent, and the average annual rate of growth was a remarkable 7.7 percent. During the pre-war years 1935-1940 households had saved an average of 4.1 percent of their after tax (disposable) income. During the war years from 1942 to 1945 they saved an astonishing 23.4 percent. Partly because of this, prices, as measured by the GNP deflator, increased only 26.4 percent. This implied an average annual rate of only 6.0 percent during a period of acute shortages. Wholesale prices were held down to an average rate of 4.9 percent a year, and consumer prices rose 5.1 percent per year. Not until 1946, when price controls were dismantled, did inflation accelerate above 10 percent. In that year consumer prices jumped 14.1 percent and the GNP deflator increased 11.7 percent.

In summary: During a major war that uses up a large fraction of the nation's resources it's neither possible nor desirable to finance the entire increase in defense spending by tax increases. Borrowing is inevitable. Although borrowing from the Fed, which is what support of the government bond market amounts to, is the most inflationary way to finance public spending, this can't be helped if you hope to keep interest rates down and if you hope to be able to market government debt. Unless you also introduce effective rationing and price controls you will have a lot of inflation and that, ultimately, will be very harmful to the war effort.

When the war finally ended in 1945 many economists predicted that, with sharp reductions in defense spending, the economy would tumble right back into depression. Most of these predictions were based on multiplier analysis of the effects of reduced defense spending on declining income and consumption. They failed, however, to take into account the fact that when people own large quantities of financial assets as a result of high war-time saving, this enables them to sustain consumption spending even when their incomes decline. Isn't hindsight the most sensational thing ever invented?

Inflation and Economic Development

The United States and other industrial countries are very fortunate to have highly developed financial markets. Such markets greatly ease government financing problems and permit central bank open-market operations to go forward smoothly. In fact, we tend to take this for granted. There are, however, innumerable countries in the world that are not so fortunate.

In the poorest countries families have so little income that they are largely incapable of saving. The savings of a rural family often consist only of the grain that is saved for the next year's planting. Beyond that such a family will attempt to accumulate physical assets such as additional land and items appropriate for a daughter's dowry. Imagine trying to sell a government bond to such a family.

Because savings are low, illiteracy is high, and a large fraction of national economic activity is in the home, it is virtually impossible for governments to raise revenues other than what they receive from customs duties and luxury taxes. Since the government is powerless to raise taxes or to sell bonds it must hope for foreign financial assistance and, if such assistance is inadequate, it has no choice but to borrow from its central bank. The central bank grants the government a line of credit; the government then spends the money; and inflation is the outcome. There is, in such countries, a direct link between the government's budget deficit, growth of the money supply, and the rate of inflation.

In contrast to the United States, where the Chairman of the Federal Reserve is easily the country's most powerful economic official, central bank governors in developing countries often have very little influence over monetary conditions. They are forced to provide lines of credit when the government demands it, and they are often forced to make loans to government corporations and private borrowers. Any of these extensions of domestic credit carry with them equivalent increases in the money supply. Since the central bank cannot engage in open-market purchases and sales of government securities, its ability to control the money supply depends largely on its ability to restrain borrowing by the government and others.

Even in countries that are not considered poor, such as many of the Latin American countries, there is virtually no market for government bonds. The ongoing inflation that plagues these countries long ago convinced savers to shun government bonds, whose values are quickly eroded by inflation, in favor of physical assets such as land and precious metals. When they do invest in financial assets, this will be in a foreign country that enjoys price stability. The country's own government is viewed as unreliable and as a terrible credit risk.

Inflation has been an ongoing plague for many of the world's "developing" countries. This is true for Africa and it is especially true for Latin American countries. Just look at those ghastly inflation rates for the Western Hemisphere developing countries shown in Table 3-2. These countries include all the countries in the hemisphere except Canada and the United States. During the 1970s consumer prices in these countries increased at an average annual rate of 32.4 percent, and in the 1980s the annual rate of increase accelerated to 154.7 percent. Inflation rates were not only high, but continued to accelerate and have shown little sign of slowing. Prices increased 143.6 percent in 1991, slightly less than the average for the 1980s. Among the more important of the Latin countries inflation reached 2,134 percent in Argentina in 1990, 2,938 percent in Brazil, 7,482 percent in Peru, and 40.8 percent in Venezuela.

Table 3-2
Consumer Prices: Indexes and Annual Rates
(1985 = 100)

	1970	1980	1990	Average Annual Rates 1970-80	Average Annual Rates 1980-1990
Industrial Countries	31.8	73.5	119.5	8.7	8.0
Developing Countries	5.2	23.2	873.4	16.1	43.7
Africa	12.6	43.4	225.2	13.2	17.9
Asia	35.0	70.2	147.8	7.2	7.7
Western Hemisphere	0.2	3.3	36,499.4	32.4	154.7

Source: International Monetary Fund, *International Financial Statistics: Yearbook*, 1992

In the developing part of the world there is a clear cut connection between government budgets, growth of the money supply, and the rate of inflation. Money supply indexes are shown in Table 3-3. To interpret the indexes note that money supply levels receive an index value of 100 for 1985. Therefore, since the index for the Western Hemisphere was 0.2 in 1970 and 4.9 in 1980, this must have meant that the money supply was 24.5 (4.9/0.2) times as large in 1980 as it had been in 1970. This implied an average annual rate of growth of 37.7 percent. The average annual rate of growth between 1980 and 1987 accelerated to 91.7 percent, and after that monetary growth rates became so astronomical that some are not even reported by the IMF.

Between 1970 and 1990 money supplies in the industrial countries grew at an average annual rate of 8.6 percent, in Africa they grew at a rate of 17.6 percent, and in the developing countries of the Western Hemisphere they grew at a rate of 57.8 percent up to 1988 when data become sketchy. In 1990 the money supply grew 1,628.6 percent in Argentina, and in Peru it grew at a rate of 4,633.6 percent. Bolivia and Mexico registered monetary growth rates of 39.5 and 47.1 percent respectively. In Chile monetary growth was reduced to 11.8 percent in 1990 but it then picked up to 43.2 percent in 1991. Such erratic rates are typical. Although countries sometimes make progress in reducing their monetary growth rates, this never seems to last long.

Table 3-3
Indexes of Money Supplies
(1985 = 100)

	1970	1980	1987	1990
Industrial Countries	27.4	68.5	122.6	143.1
Developing Countries	2.0	23.1	189.6	594.1
Africa	6.3	40.8	121.5	209.2
Asia	8.2	48.6	135.1	216.3
Western Hemisphere	0.2	4.9	465.9	NA

Source: International Monetary Fund, *International Financial Statistics: Yearbook,* 1992

At the annual meetings of the International Monetary Fund (IMF or Fund), which every other year occur in Washington, D.C., you run into an old friend from graduate school days. You remember him as an excellent student and a personable young man of great charm and humor. In both speech and appearance he bears a strong resemblance to the late actor Raul Julia. After graduate school he returned to his home country in South America where he very quickly became an important government official. His latest promotion placed him among the elite since he is now governor of the central bank. When you run into him while standing in the hallway (everyone stands in hallways at professional meetings) you are distressed at how rapidly he has aged and how he has lost the habitual smile that once graced his face.

"Hey gringo," he says warmly, "What are you doing here?"

"Just hoping to stumble into the likes of you." you reply, "Congratulations on your appointment. Everybody at the old school is very proud of you."

"The old school," he laughs, "Remember how we used to talk about improving the human condition? Its been all down hill in my country since then."

"Are you going to the session on Latin inflation?"

"Are you kidding? I'm an expert on inflation. I live it, eat it, breathe it, and am accused of causing it every day. Besides these sanctimonious bozos never say anything new. Your treasury secretary is going to spout a bunch of crap about the need for hemispheric cooperation. The Managing Director of the Fund is going to go through his usual belt tightening ritual. And my own finance minister is going to blame the gringos for the debt crisis and everything else he can think of. Who needs it? Is that nice bar over on 18th and H still there?"

After finding a booth in the watering hole, he says: "Trying to run that central bank is the worst job in the world. Your Fed chairman is the most powerful economic official in your country. But me, I'm just a flunky for the finance minister. He walks into my office, dumps a load of that worthless debt paper of his onto my desk, and demands a line of credit which I'm forced to give him. He spends the money and we get more inflation. I also have to lend huge amounts of money to our banks and the government contractors that build the roads and the schools. Pushing out money and generating inflation. That's my life."

"Why do you have to do it?"

"Because we've got a five year development plan that we've got to move forward; because we haven't got enough revenue to pay for it; and because your commercial banks won't lend us dollars the way they used to. We'll never get out of the hole unless we build schools and raise the literacy rate. Recently we had a foreign ship run aground because one of our harbors hadn't been dredged in years. People can't get their goods to market because the roads are terrible and there aren't enough of them. And we can't get our manufacturers to increase their operations because they can't get enough electricity. Do you know how much it costs to build a dam? We have to keep spending. We don't have any choice. I fantasize about getting the Chinese to build a railroad for us, the way they did for Zambia, but those days are over. And anyway our generals wouldn't let communists in."

"You're not a poor country. Why don't you raise taxes to finance some of that spending?"

"We do tax a lot. Back in 1985 we took 20 percent of the GDP away in taxes. But its hell collecting them. We can't find enough people that are honest enough or well trained enough to staff an agency such as your IRS. Half the people in the country can't read and write and can't fill out a tax return. Everybody cheats on his taxes and knows nothing will happen to him if he gets caught. The government tries to get the cheats out of the woodwork by forgiving back taxes but that just encourages the cheating. The unions finally got mad about tax withholding when everybody else was chiseling so the government backed down and cut taxes so we're only getting 13 percent of GDP in taxes lately."

"How big is your deficit?"

"The deficit isn't all that huge. What's causing the problem is all that lending we have to do. Government expenditures plus lending came to 28 percent of GDP in 1985. You can imagine what all that lending does to the money supply. We had an increase of over 2,000 percent in the money supply in 1989 and considered ourselves lucky to get it down to around 1,000 percent the next year."

"I don't mean to belabor you with stupid questions, but is it at all possible for your finance minister to sell his debt paper to the private sector?"

"With the inflation rates we've been having lately we've given up trying to raise money by borrowing. It used to be possible to borrow, but only at short term. Nobody wanted to lend for more than 30 or 60 days because of inflation and even then it took astronomical interest rates to get anybody to lend. A few years ago our treasury bill rate was almost 500 percent. Now we don't even have a bill rate and I'd hate to think what it would be if we had one. Inflation has destroyed the incentive to save, and those who do save either get their money out of the country as fast as possible, or they put it into physical property. Lot's of people just buy gold. The last thing they want to do is lend to the government."

"What is inflation doing to the economy?"

"It's killing us. Nobody wants to work because the money they're paid is worthless. The business people I have lunch with tell me that its impossible to plan ahead since they don't know if prices are going to be 100 percent higher next week or 200 percent. They can't even plan this week's production, let alone determine if an investment in plant expansion is going to pay off. They smile pleasantly and ask why I can't pull off a miracle and stop the inflation. It's amazing. The real size of our economy tripled from 1950 to 1970. Since then its been going backwards. We've had negative per capita growth rates for most of the last fifteen years."

"What's happened to per capita income and employment?"

"Don't ask. Population's been growing at 2.5 percent and output hasn't been growing. You figure it out. Droves of people keep coming into the cities from the countryside in search of jobs; but there aren't any. To employ them we'd have to be able to give them tools to work with. But with the drying up of foreign credit we can't borrow enough to finance the capital goods imports we need. We tax the hell out of consumer goods imports so most of our imports are capital goods. But it isn't nearly enough. Last year our official unemployment rate was 18 percent; but I think its much higher than that when you count all of the under employment."

"So what are you going to do?"

"What can I do? Sometimes I think I ought to just pack it in and ask if you have a professorship for me at that nice college you teach at in the States."

"It's a nice life for sure; but you won't get rich that way."

"No but at least I won't have to keep being a stooge for the finance minister."

"Don't be discouraged. You're not the first central banker who had to take orders from the government. Its even happened in the U.S., and I sure wish somebody would tell Bill Clinton that. He still thinks the Fed is an independent agency."

"FDR, Harry Truman, and LBJ could have told him a thing or two about that."

"Yes, and have you ever noticed how much faster the money supply grows during presidential elections years?"

"No, I hadn't noticed that. Do you think the Fed was trying to get George Bush reelected in 1992?"

"Maybe its just a coincidence. Let's have another drink."

4

The National Debt: Burdens and Benefits

In this chapter attention shifts from the annual federal deficit to the cumulative national debt. Along with this comes a natural shifting of attention to longer range economic issues. The national debt is the cumulative sum of all past deficits minus all past surpluses. The chapter begins with a review of some pertinent information about the debt and continues with such issues as the burden of the debt. The debt burden has both a domestic and a foreign component. This chapter looks at the domestic component. The foreign component is discussed later on within the context of international economic issues.

How Much and Who Owns It?

Table 4-1 provides a time-series of information on the Gross Federal Debt and some of its subcategories, as well as the value of the debt expressed as a percentage of GDP. Between 1960 and 1980 the gross debt grew at an average annual rate of 5.9 percent. This growth rate accelerated sharply to 15.1 percent between 1980 and 1987, and then slowed to an annual rate of 10.2 percent from 1987 to 1993. Perhaps the most significant fact about the gross debt is that, measured as a percentage of GDP, it nearly doubled between 1980 and 1993, rising from 34.4 percent in 1980 to 68.3 percent in 1993.

Table 4-1 also shows that roughly one-fourth of the federal debt is held by various accounts owned by governments including the federal government. Examples of such accounts are the Social

Security and Medicare trust fund accounts. When such intra-government debt is subtracted from the 1993 gross debt of $4,351.2, the *net* debt, held by the public, is the substantially smaller amount of $3,247.2 billion. If debt held by the Federal Reserve System were classified as intra-government debt, the net debt would have been reduced by another $325.6 billion.

Table 4-1
Federal Debt
(Billions of dollars, end of FY)

Year	Gross Debt	Held by Government Accounts	Held by the Public (Net Debt)	Held by Federal Reserve	Other	Gross as Percent of GDP
1980	908.5	199.2	709.3	120.8	588.5	34.4%
1981	994.3	209.5	784.8	124.5	660.3	33.5
1982	1,136.8	217.6	919.2	134.5	784.7	36.4
1983	1,371.2	240.2	1,131.0	155.5	975.5	41.3
1984	1,564.1	264.1	1,300.0	155.1	1,144.9	42.3
1985	1,817.0	317.6	1,499.4	169.8	1,329.6	45.8
1986	2,120.1	383.9	1,736.2	190.9	1,545.3	50.3
1987	2,435.6	547.5	1,888.1	212.0	1,676.1	54.7
1988	2,600.8	550.5	2,050.3	229.2	1,821.1	54.1
1989	2,867.5	678.2	2,189.3	220.1	1,969.2	55.4
1990	3,206.2	795.9	2,410.4	234.4	2,176.0	58.6
1991	3,598.3	910.4	2,687.9	258.6	2,429.3	67.1
1992	4,001.9	1,003.3	2,998.6	296.4	2,702.2	66.3
1993	4,351.2	1,104.0	3,247.2	325.6	2,921.6	68.3

Source: Department of the Treasury

It is sometimes naively asserted that it would be easy enough to repay the federal debt because we "owe it to ourselves." Therefore, simply raise taxes by the current value of the net debt and then quickly give the $3.2 trillion back to bondholders in exchange for the outstanding bonds. Notice, however, as Table 4-2 makes clear, that only 10.3 percent of the debt held by the public in 1991 was held by individuals. Far larger shares were held by financial institutions, state and local governments, and foreign owners. Consequently, the people who would have to pay the taxes are not likely to be the same people that receive the debt repayment. Although some of the receipts may trickle down to the average taxpayer, the conclusion cannot be escaped that debt repayment would produce a revolution in the distribution of wealth.

Table 4-2
Ownership of Privately Held Federal Debt in mid 1993

	Value (Billions)	Percent of Total	Annual Rate 1980-1993*
Total	2,938.4	100.0	13.6
Commercial Banks	305.9	10.4	9.1
Individuals	303.0	10.3	7.6
Insurance Companies	208.1	7.1	22.2
Money Market Funds	72.2	2.5	22.3
Corporations	206.1	7.0	23.0
State and Local Governments	553.9	18.9	15.5
Foreign	568.2	19.3	12.8
Other**	717.0	24.4	15.9

* Mid-year over mid-year

** Includes savings and loan associations, credit unions, nonprofit institutions, mutual savings banks, corporate pension trust funds, dealers and brokers, certain Government deposit accounts, and Government-sponsored agencies.

Source: Department of the Treasury.

But suppose you, and each of our 200 million citizens, had paid his share of net debt of about $1,450 and that this exactly covers the government bonds you turn over to the treasury. If you then looked at your personal balance sheet after the transactions had been completed, you would find that you are poorer by this amount because you have lost your government bonds and have gained nothing in return. A lot of trouble could therefore have been saved by just passing a law that either forced everybody to burn their government bonds, or required them to be used as wall paper. Empirical research by economists has confirmed that such a loss in financial wealth depresses people's consumption spending. The effect of the debt repayment would therefore be hugely deflationary and throw the economy into a severe recession, if not a depression.

Or look at debt repayment another way. In Chapter 2 it was seen that eliminating the current deficit would be severely deflationary. Repaying the debt, even if done gradually, would mean going even farther because to do so would require the federal government to run a surplus. Is there really any good reason to punish the economy in such a destructive manner?

The Interest Burden of the Debt

In what sense is the national debt a burden and how does this burden harm the economy? One way the debt could be regarded as a burden is that growth of the debt has produced very rapid growth in federal interest payments. As can be seen in ***Table 4-3*** these payments have risen from $25.1 billion in fiscal year 1976 to $181.3 billion in 1993. This increase implies an average annual rate of growth of 12.3 percent, as compared with the average rate of growth of nominal GDP of 8.1 percent. Thus the growth of interest payments has outstripped the growth of GDP by a wide margin.

Tax payers are liable for the interest on the debt whereas bond holders are recipients of the interest income. Although it would be extremely difficult to estimate just exactly how this transfer of income affects the distribution of income, it is generally thought that the average beneficiary of federal interest payments has a substantially higher income than the average tax payer, inasmuch as the largest beneficiaries would be stock holders in corporations, financial institutions, and also foreigners. Therefore, a rise in federal interest payments, relative to GDP, implies that the debt causes income to be regressively redistributed. Call this the income redistribution burden.

The last column of ***Table 4-3*** shows the non-interest deficit, that is, what the deficit would have been had there been no interest payments. It is significant to note that there would actually have been a surplus in the budget in 1989 and 1990 had there been no interest payments. Since there was no cyclical deficit in 1989, this fact implies that the non interest structural deficit was negative, and it could easily be shown that this would be true for several other years if the cyclical deficits estimated in Chapter 2 were subtracted from the non interest deficit.

It appears, then, that it is the rising interest costs that are largely

Table 4-3
Federal Debt and Interest Costs

Fiscal Year	Net Debt (Billions)	Net Interest	Average Interest Rate (%)	Non-Interest Deficit
1976	477.4	25.1	5.26	31.9
1977	549.1	28.5	5.19	13.2
1978	607.1	33.1	5.45	1.0
1979	639.8	40.2	6.28	-25.3
1980	709.3	50.1	7.06	-1.1
1981	784.8	66.1	8.42	-9.2
1982	919.2	81.8	8.90	23.2
1983	1,131.0	89.6	7.92	93.2
1984	1,300.0	107.5	8.27	56.1
1985	1,499.4	125.2	8.35	50.7
1986	1,736.2	130.5	7.52	73.4
1987	1,888.1	133.6	7.08	18.3
1988	2,050.3	143.8	7.01	-0.5
1989	2,189.3	160.5	7.33	-46.2
1990	2,410.4	175.1	7.26	-17.2
1991	2,687.9	183.2	6.82	4.6
1992	2,998.6	189.7	6.63	80.7
1993	3,247.2	181.3	5.58	53.9
Annual Rate of Growth, %				
1976-1993	11.9	12.3		

Source: Department of the Treasury; Department of Commerce.

responsible for the bulging structural deficits of recent years while the rest of the budget has remained reasonably well under control. Interest costs have been accounting for an increasing fraction of federal spending that puts an ever increasing squeeze on the various programs in the federal budget. This squeeze continues every year even if the deficit doesn't grow. If the deficit is $200 billion and interest costs on this additional debt are $14 billion, continuation of a $200 billion deficit in the next year adds another $14 billion to interest costs. Therefore, additional revenue sources or expenditure reductions in this amount will be needed just to keep the deficit from widening.

The ability of the economy to handle public debt comfortably grows as the size of the economy grows. It is therefore customary to focus attention on the ratio of the net debt to some measure of aggregate economic activity such as GDP. This ratio remains constant when both are growing at the same rate, and when the debt grows more rapidly than GDP, it increases. It is possible to partition changes in the value of this ratio into the part attributable to interest payments and the part attributable to the non-interest portion of the annual deficit. ***Table 4-4*** provides the pertinent information and the accompanying footnote shows the basis for the calculations.[1]

Since the average rate of interest paid on the debt represents the rate of growth of interest payments, the ratio of interest payments to GDP rises if the *average rate of interest exceeds the rate of growth*.

---

1. Let the new debt in year t be designated as D_t and let Y_t stand for GDP. The change in the debt is the difference between D_t and the debt at the end of the preceding year, D_{t-1}. The debt increases because of interest payments during the year and because of an excess of non-interest expenditures over tax receipts. This can be expressed as,

$$D_t - D_{t-1} = iD_{t-1} + NIE_t - T_t$$

where i is expressed as a decimal and represents the average rate of interest paid on the debt, NIE_t is non interest federal expenditure and Tt is the level of tax receipts. NIE_t - Tt is what the deficit would be if there were no interest payments.

D_{t-1} may be added to both sides of the expression without changing anything. It would then be written,

$$D_t = (1+i)D_{t-1} + NIE_t - T_t$$

The final step is to divide both sides of this expression by Y_t to obtain the ratio of debt to GDP. This year's GDP may be expressed as the value of last year's GDP multiplied by 1 plus its growth rate during the year. For example, if GDP were equal to $1 trillion in the preceding year, and if it grew at an annual rate of 8 percent during the year, the next year's GDP would be $1.08 trillion, namely (1+.08) multiplied by $1 trillion. Consequently, we can write,

$$Y_t = (1+g)Y_{t-1}$$

When this growth relation is used to divide D_t by Y_t, we get the expression we are looking for, namely the ratio of debt to income partitioned into an interest component and a non-interest component,

$$d_t = \frac{(1+i)d_{t-1}}{(1+g)} + \frac{NIE_t - T_t}{Y_t}$$

It can be seen that the ratio of debt to GDP increases if the average rate of interest paid on the debt exceeds the rate of growth of nominal GDP. This is the interest part of increaes in the debt burden. The remainder would then result from an increase in the ratio of the non-interest deficit to GDP.

of the economy. It also rises when the non-interest deficit rises relative to the level of GDP. Columns 1 and 2 of ***Table 4-4*** show the average interest rate paid on the net debt and the rate of growth of nominal GDP. Column 3 shows the ratio of debt to GDP and column 4 shows this ratio as a percent of the previous year's ratio of debt to GDP. When a value in this column is less than 1.0, the ratio of debt to GDP has decreased from the previous year. When the value is greater than 1.0 it has increased. Column 5 shows the effect of interest payments on the change in the debt/GDP ratio and column 6 shows the effect of the non-interest deficit. It can be seen in column 4 that the interest burden declined throughout the 1970s, but increased fairly steadily beginning in 1982. The 1970s were characterized by rapid inflation and therefore high rates of nominal GDP growth relative to interest rates. This situation was reversed in the 1980s. Note also that the increase in the interest burden was

Table 4-4
Interest Burden of the Net Debt

Year	(1) Interest Rate	(2) Growth Rate	(3) Debt/GDP Ratio	(4) Change in Debt/GDP	(5) Interest Burden	(6) Non-Interest Burden
1976	5.26	11.51	0.27	1.08	0.94	0.07
1977	5.19	11.63	0.28	1.04	0.94	0.02
1978	5.45	13.10	0.27	0.96	0.93	0
1979	6.28	11.46	0.26	0.96	0.95	-0.04
1980	7.06	8.82	0.26	1.00	0.98	0
1981	8.42	11.91	0.26	1.00	0.97	-0.01
1982	8.90	3.93	0.29	1.12	1.05	0.03
1983	7.92	8.11	0.33	1.14	1.00	0.08
1984	8.27	10.97	0.34	1.03	0.98	0.04
1985	8.35	7.06	0.37	1.09	1.01	0.03
1986	7.52	5.69	0.41	1.11	1.02	0.04
1987	7.08	6.36	0.42	1.02	1.01	0.01
1988	7.01	7.94	0.42	1.00	0.99	0
1989	7.33	7.15	0.42	1.00	1.00	-0.02
1990	7.26	5.62	0.43	1.02	1.02	-0.01
1991	6.82	3.19	0.47	1.09	1.04	0
1992	6.33	5.51	0.50	1.06	1.01	0.03
1993	5.58	5.56	0.51	1.02	1.00	0.02

less in 1992 and 1993 than in 1991. This is because declining inter-estrates more than offset the effects of higher deficits.

Inspection of column 5 shows that in four of the years there are negative values and that the positive values never get above 0.08. Therefore changes in the non-interest burden are generally small and, in some cases, negative.

Another informative way to study the changing interest burden of the debt is to compute the tax rate necessary to pay the interest on the debt. The interest on the debt is the product of the rate of interest (i) and the value of the debt (D). Let the potential tax base be the level of nominal GDP (Y), and recognize as well that the interest paid on the debt is itself taxable income. Since the required tax rate is the ratio of interest payments to the tax base we may write,

$$\tau = \frac{iD}{Y + iD}$$

where τ is the tax rate. When numerator and denominator are divided by D, we obtain,

Formula 4-1

$$\tau = \frac{i}{Y/D + i}$$

It can therefore be seen that the tax rate depends upon the rate of interest and, once again, the ratio of debt to GDP, but this time turned upside down. The tax rate rises when the rate of interest rises and when the ratio of debt to GDP rises.

Formula 4-1 shows that the tax rate could never exceed 100 percent no matter how large the debt. Suppose the debt becomes 100 times as large as GDP. The ratio, Y/D, would then equal 0.01. If the rate of interest is 5 percent (0.05 in decimal form), the tax rate would be,

$$\tau = \frac{0.05}{0.01 + 0.05} = 0.83$$

or 83 percent. It is, therefore, always possible to pay interest on the debt because the interest on the debt is itself taxable income. It will be a long time before we have to concern ourselves with such an astronomical tax rate. But just imagine what might happen to the distribution of income in response to a sharp increase in the ratio of debt to GDP. As ***Table 4-5*** shows the tax rate needed to pay interest on the debt has never gotten higher than 3.1 percent.

Table 4-5
Implicit Tax Rates for Public Debt Interest

Year	(1) Interest Rate (decimal)	(2) Debt-GDP Ratio	(3) Tax Rate Decimal	(4) Tax Rate Percent
1970	0.050	0.287	0.014	1.4
1971	0.049	0.288	0.014	1.4
1972	0.048	0.281	0.013	1.3
1973	0.051	0.268	0.013	1.3
1974	0.062	0.245	0.015	1.5
1975	0.059	0.261	0.015	1.5
1976	0.053	0.270	0.014	1.4
1977	0.052	0.278	0.014	1.4
1978	0.058	0.272	0.015	1.5
1979	0.063	0.257	0.016	1.6
1980	0.071	0.262	0.018	1.8
1981	0.084	0.259	0.021	2.1
1982	0.089	0.292	0.025	2.5
1983	0.079	0.332	0.026	2.6
1984	0.083	0.345	0.028	2.8
1985	0.084	0.371	0.030	3.0
1986	0.075	0.407	0.030	3.0
1987	0.071	0.416	0.029	2.9
1988	0.074	0.418	0.028	2.8
1989	0.073	0.417	0.030	3.0
1990	0.073	0.435	0.031	3.1
1991	0.068	0.470	0.031	3.1
1992	0.063	0.497	0.030	3.0
1993	0.056	0.509	0.028	2.8

Both Formula 4-1 and ***Table 4-5*** show that the tax rate increases when the ratio of debt to GDP increases. However, if the debt and GDP both grow at the same rate, and the rate of interest remains constant, the ratio (D/Y) would remain constant and so also would the tax rate. The table shows that the tax rate rose from 1.4 percent in 1970 to 1.6 percent in 1979. It accelerated sharply in 1980 and 1981 because of rising interest rates and a widening cyclical deficit. It escalated again during the period 1982-1986 because of sharp increases in the structural deficit. From 1985 onwards there has been a leveling off. Despite a large increase in the deficit in 1993, the tax rate fell because the increase in the debt/GDP ratio was offset by lower interest rates.

Effect of the Debt on Interest Rates

Interest costs rise as the debt rises. Conversely it may also be true that rapid growth of debt puts upward pressure on interest rates. The interest rate, or yield from lending is a price, just like any commodity price, and, like most prices, is determined by conditions of supply and demand. The price at which quantity demanded equals quantity supplied is called the equilibrium price. One way of looking at the equilibrium interest rate is to think of it as the rate at which the demand for money balances equals its supply. Another, and equivalent, way is to think of it as the rate at which the demand for bonds equals the supply of bonds. If you suddenly decide that you have more cash on hand than you need for various purposes such as conducting your day-to-day business activities, you might take the surplus cash and purchase interest-earning financial assets. This will be reflected in an increase in the demand for bonds and a simultaneous reduction in the demand for money. It therefore raises bond prices and lowers interest rates. Or, you may simply deposit the cash in a bank. When lots of banks receive extra deposits they have more available to lend, and to encourage business firms to borrow, they will cut the rates charged to borrowers. Either way interest rates tend to fall.

The federal debt and the deficit affect interest rates through their effects on the supplies of money and government bonds. When the treasury borrows from the private sector to finance its deficit, it sells government bonds. Because this increases their supply, government bond prices fall and their yields increase. The lower prices and higher yields increase the attractiveness of government bonds relative to other financial assets, so investors sell some of these other assets to buy the more attractive treasury instruments. This then lowers the prices of the other financial assets and the yields on all financial assets therefore tend to rise in unison.

Since the total national debt affects the supply of government bonds, the longer-term trend in interest rates is likely to be affected by the rate at which the debt grows. To see the connection, just think about how you arrange your own financial portfolio, presuming you are lucky enough to have one. If you are like the vast majority of investors, you will hold a diversified portfolio of many different kinds of assets. The assets will differ with respect to the return you expect to receive on them as well as with your perception of the riskiness of the assets in terms of the probable magnitudes of anticipated capital gains and losses. Unlike the addicted gambler who enjoys risk for its own sake, you consider risk costly and would be ready to pay for a reduction in risk by sacrificing a part of your return. You are, therefore, *risk averse* and you regard risk and return as *imperfect substitutes*. This means that you require increasing amounts of return for each successive unit of risk that you take.[2] These characteristics cause you to be a *portfolio diversifier*. If asset A is riskier than asset B, you will hold some of A only because you expect to earn a higher rate of return on it. At the other end of the spectrum, you may hold a fraction of your financial wealth in the form of a virtually riskless asset such as a bank account on which your return is very low.

A rise in the yields that you receive on your financial assets raises your potential earnings relative to your risk. You therefore find it in your interest to accept more risk in order to take advantage of the higher yields. Put differently, the higher yields compensate for part of your risk aversion. You therefore increase the proportion of your

2. If you regard risk and return as perfect substitutes you would always be willing to take an additional unit of risk for an addition unit of return. Therefore, if the return on the first unit of risk justifies taking the risk, this would be true for all units up to the limit of your portflio. You would, therefore, put all of your portfolio into the risky asset. However, if interest rates fall so that the return on the first unit of risk no longer justifies the risk, this would be true for all units and you would therefore shift your entire portfolio in such a way as to minimize your risk. You would, therefore, be characterized as a *plunger* who either takes maximum risk combined with maximum return or minimum risk with very low return.

portfolio invested in risky assets while reducing the fraction held in low risk assets such as money. Economists describe such a portfolio shift by saying that a rise in interest rates reduces *liquidity preference.*

Suppose now that you reap a windfall gain. Your rich uncle unexpectedly distributes some of his wealth while he is still alive and sends you a bundle of 10 year negotiable federal government bonds having a current market value of $50,000. Do you simply add the bonds to your portfolio?[3] You might if brokerage costs are high. But if not, and if you are a rational risk-averse investor who wishes to attain an efficient portfolio, you will take part of the bonds and trade them in for some assets that are riskier than the 10 year bonds as well as some that are less risky. You will, in other words, sell off part of the bonds so as to bring the assets of your portfolio roughly back to the proportions in which you held them prior to receipt of the windfall. Therefore, an increase in your financial wealth increases your demand for all financial assets *including money.* It is important to remember, both now and for future reference, that the amount of money people wish to hold as a portfolio asset tends to rise as their total financial wealth increases.

How will your portfolio adjustment affect various yields? Since you are selling 10 year bonds while purchasing other assets, the 10 year bonds tend to fall in value while the prices of the other assets will tend to increase.[4] Consequently, the yields on the 10 year bonds will rise. This is *exactly what would happen* if the supplies of all government bonds increased at a faster rate than the supplies of other financial assets such as privately issued bonds, stocks, and money.

The growth of the money supply is determined by the Fed which therefore plays an important role in determining portfolio composition and yields. The growth of the value of privately issued bonds

---

3. If your portfolio is efficient it is not possible for you to increase your return without also increasing your risk by rearranging the composition of your portfolio. You cannot therefore make yourself better off by portfolio readjustment. If your portfolio is inefficient this means you can make yourself better off simply by rearranging the composition of your portfolio since you can either increase your earnings without increasing risk, or reduce risk without lowering earnings.

4. Here we are ignoring the effects of the portfolio readjustment that your uncle might make when he gives away the bonds.

and the value of stocks depends on how rapidly the economy is growing. It then follows that there should be no steady upward or downward pressure on interest rates if the economy and the federal debt grow at roughly the same rates, and if the Fed expands the money supply at this same rate. Put differently, portfolio balance tends to be maintained when the supplies of all financial assets grow at roughly the same rates. Since the federal debt grew more rapidly than the economy during the 1980s while monetary policy was, on the whole, conservative, it is not surprising that interest rates were substantially higher during the 1980s than they were during the 1970s.

Investment Crowdout: The Growth Burden

If growth of the ratio of public debt to GDP has put long-term upward pressure on interest rates it could also have had the effect of reducing the share of GDP that the economy puts into plant, equipment, and industrial and commercial structures. Increases in interest rates discourage borrowing for these purposes. Therefore, a prolonged period of high interest rates could find the economy with less productive capacity, and therefore with less potential output, than it would have had if interest rates had not risen.

This is one of the major ways in which growth of public debt can place a burden on future generations. Unless a future Congress and President completely lose their minds, future generations will not have to pay back the debt, but if they have less capital stock on hand because of current debt accumulation, their potential GDP will be lower and their per capita income and living standards will be reduced.

Some aspects of investment crowdout were discussed in earlier chapters. Only a few additional notes are needed here. While government borrowing tends to raise interest rates, this can be offset by Federal Reserve action. Treasury bond sales tend to raise interest rates while open-market purchases by the Fed lower them. When government borrowing is accompanied by open-market purchases the Fed is, in fact, financing part of the deficit, and in the process it is increasing the money supply. As emphasized in Chapter 3 the important question is whether such monetizing of the debt is appropriate.

During periods of high unemployment when output is below its potential, there is no competition for resources between government and the private economy. Nevertheless crowd out could occur if the Fed permits interest rates to rise. Clearly, in such a situation it should be the Fed's responsibility to prevent interest rates from rising. The increase in the money supply that accompanies the Fed's action will then finance increased production rather than inflation.

The situation is radically altered when unemployment is low and output equals its potential. Additional government spending then creates competition for limited resources and this causes inflation because output cannot be sufficiently expanded to match the rise in spending. Rising interest rates help to moderate the inflationary pressures because they help to hold back investment spending. Monetizing debt by the Fed is then clearly inappropriate. Although the rise in interest rates caused by the added borrowing helps to moderate inflation, it will not be sufficient to prevent it. If it is undesirable to crowd out investment, the best way to prevent higher government spending from being inflationary at a time of full employment is to reduce private consumption by matching the added government spending with tax increases.[5]

A number of contemporary economists subscribe to the view that increased government spending does not cause interest rates to rise and investment to be crowded out. What gets crowded out, instead, is consumption spending. The argument is that when the government increases spending and finances this by selling bonds the increase in the supply of bonds to the bond market is matched by an equivalent rise in demand. This is because the rise in the deficit is believed to cause taxpayers to expect higher taxes in the future and

5. If the increase in government spending consists of an increase in federal purchases, an equal tax increase is not likely to neutralize the inflationary effects entirely. This is because the tax increase will not reduce consumption spending by as much as the tax increase. Although a large fraction of the tax increase is reflected in lower consumption, a portion will be reflected in lower saving. For example, if government purchases and taxes are both raised by $10, and if consumption declines by $8, there will be a net increase in total spending of $2. Taxes would therefore have to be raised by another $2.5 billion to offset the spending effect of the $10 increase in government purchases. It is important, therefore, to keep in mind that increases in government purchases have a more high-powered effect on the economy than equal tax increases. However, this would not be true if the increased government spending were in the form of transfer payments. When the government takes away $10 and this reduces your spending by $8, your spending will increase by that amount if the government then gives the $10 back to you.

this, in turn, reduces their consumption while raising savings. Higher savings imply increased demand for financial assets. Thus, the reduction in the demand for goods and services by private individuals offsets the government's increased demand that occurs in response to the rise in deficit spending, while the increasing supply of financial assets caused by higher government borrowing is matched by higher demand due to greater saving.

This hypothesis, which is sometimes called the Ricardian hypothesis, seems far fetched and yet empirical studies have failed to refute its predictions. This is probably due to the fact that the outcome depends on what people believe about the future. When President Bush said "read my lips" (no higher taxes) he implicitly promised to finance any additional spending by borrowing. Believing the President, people would not be inclined to raise savings. However, when President Clinton promised to reduce the deficit, this implied higher taxes and could quite easily have raised the fraction of disposable income saved.

What might be termed international crowdout is a second major consequence of high interest rates. This is an important issue that is discussed in Part III. In the meantime this chapter closes with a brief discussion of the constructive uses of federal debt, and adds a few notes on ways to increase economic growth.

Uses of Debt

In many ways the growth of national debt reflects the fact that its accumulation has often made the economy a lot better off. For example, the cumulative cyclical deficits from 1975 to 1993 added roughly $760 billion to the national debt (***Table 2-3***). This debt was created because the government financed anti recession programs such as unemployment compensation and because it absorbed part of the recession-caused income losses instead of forcing the private sector to absorb the entire loss. The economy would really have suffered, and continue to be suffering, had policy not been willing to create such debt.

The federal borrowing necessitated to improve the economic infra-structure has contributed to economic growth and has made the economy far better off. In fact, if policy hadn't been so stingy in supporting the infra structure, economic growth would have been greater and per capita income would have been higher. It can be argued that the same is true for the borrowing necessitate to finance grants in aid to state and local governments.

Government securities represent highly desirable earning assets in the portfolios of investors, and will continue to do so as long as inflation remains under reasonably effective control. U.S. government securities are often described as "gilt edged" since they are viewed as safe because the government's taxing authority stands behind them. There is, at nearly all times, a very brisk market for government securities, clear evidence that they are desirable assets. Domestic investors stock their portfolios with U.S. government bonds, and this is true for foreign investors as well. Although the government bond market did go into a severe decline in 1979-1980 because of the sharp escalation of interest rates, that was a most unusual event. If people didn't want government bonds, they wouldn't buy them. That is true in the many countries that suffer rapid inflation. But it's not true in the United States.

It has already been explained that an important use of federal debt is that it enables the Fed to manage the nation's money supply through the purchase and sale of government debt. Although the Fed could achieve the same monetary effects by purchasing and selling privately issued securities, questions would quickly be raised as to why the Fed is providing financial assistance to one company but not to another. Clearly, it's best to have government debt around so that the Fed can conduct the nation's monetary policy in a non-discriminatory manner.

A caveat with respect to the importance of public debt and monetary policy needs to be added. The Fed can also affect the money supply by raising and lowering the *rediscount* rate at which it makes loans to commercial banks. When it makes a loan to a commercial bank, the commercial bank receives reserves in exchange for an IOU to the Fed. When the commercial bank then makes a loan to a member of the non-bank private sector, a deposit is created, and the money supply is increased. When the Fed was established in 1913, it was thought that the primary purpose of the Fed would be to serve as a "lender of last resort." Except for the 1920s, however, borrowing from the Fed has never been a major factor in monetary policy. The Fed reserves the right to deny loans to commercial banks, and it is likely to send Mr. J. Pinkerton

Snoopington, one of its bank examiners, to look at the bank's books. Commercial banks that need additional reserves and want to avoid Mr. Snoopington can usually get them quickly in the "federal funds" market by borrowing them from banks that have a surplus of reserves.

Deficit Reduction and Economic Growth

Given the stagnant condition of the economy in recent years, the first order of business should be the restoration of full employment and potential output. This having been accomplished, it will then be appropriate to consider a growth strategy designed to raise the rate of growth of potential output. Since potential output increases when the stock of productive capacity increases, discussions of economic growth nearly always place heavy emphasis on raising the ratio of investment to GDP.

To get more investment interest rates need to be reduced. Since both budget and monetary policy affect interest rates, these policies play an important role in determining the real economic growth rate. Policy action on both fronts is, in fact, essential. Suppose the economy has attained full employment and it is then suggested to shift resources into investment by getting the Fed to increase the money supply in order to lower interest rates. Although it is desirable to lower interest rates, such Fed action is inflationary. The inflationary pressures, however, could have been avoided had the expansionary monetary policy been combined with tightening of the budget. This would reduce both the shares of national output going to government and to consumption and would therefore make room for the non-inflationary expansion of investment. And notice, finally, that both policy steps have the effect of lowering interest rates.

As seen above, an effective growth strategy implies the need for a change in the *mix* of monetary and fiscal policy. Monetary policy must become more expansionary whereas fiscal policy must become more restrictive. People often don't understand the purpose of mix changes, tending to think that the policies are just neutralizing each other and are therefore working at cross purposes. But, as seen above, mix changes are sometimes the key to solving a major economic problem.

Per capita income cannot grow if labor productivity, output per man-hour, fails to grow. During the 1960s productivity in the United States grew at an average annual rate of 3.2 percent, but productivity growth has been far short of that level since then. Despite the productivity slump, many families became better off during the 1970s because large numbers of married women entered the labor force. During the 1980s many people thought they were better off because of generous tax cuts and because foreigners were willing to finance their car purchases and other imports. Where is the next windfall to come from? Obviously, it will be necessary to concentrate on raising productivity.

Productivity growth depends on capital, both physical and human. Productivity grows when workers lose less work time through accident and illness, and when workers at all levels become better trained and educated. Productivity grows when workers have more and better machinery and equipment to work with. To get the new equipment it is necessary to set aside part of the economy's current production and use these resources for investment in the modernization and expansion of the capital stock. In other words, room must be made for investment by saving more and consuming less.

Government can help to make room for investment by reducing its claims on current output. This is a major reason why, viewed from a long range perspective, it is important to reduce government dissaving by gradually lowering the structural deficit. The same is true for individuals and households who could be encouraged to save more by changing the tax system. Senator Sam Nunn, a Georgia Democrat, and Senator Pete Domenici, a New Mexico Republican, have suggested a plan designed to attain both ends. The two pronged plan calls for phased budget reductions that would gradually reduce dissaving by the federal government. The second part of the plan calls for tax reform designed to raise private saving.

A long-standing complaint against the individual income tax is that it discourages private saving because savings are double taxed. When you earn $50,000 you are taxed on your entire income. If this leaves you with $35,000 and you save and invest $5,000, the interest and dividends earned on the $5,000 are again taxed in subsequent years. Had you spent all your income and saved nothing in the first place, you would have avoided the future taxes.

Economists have frequently toyed with the idea of dealing with this problem by replacing the taxation of income with the taxation of expenditures. Senators Nunn and Domenici have included this proposal in their plan. At first blush the proposal sounds like a sales tax and you would immediately have to wonder if it would be necessary to carry a ledger around to make entries every time you bought a pack of cigarettes or a candy bar. Fortunately, you wouldn't have to do this. To implement the plan it would be necessary only to change your income tax form. When you fill out your tax return you begin by adding up your beginning year total net worth--money, stocks, bonds, real property and the like--minus your debts. People that have an interest in their personal finances do this as a matter of routine and if they wish to borrow from a bank they will be forced to do it. Suppose this beginning net wealth comes to $200,000, and suppose that your end of year net worth is $210,000. Since your net worth has increased by $10,000 during the year this represents the year's savings. Then suppose that your income for the year is $50,000. Simply deduct $10,000 from your income and this gives you your expenditures of $40,000.

Under an expenditure-based tax the $40,000 in expenditures, rather than your income of $50,000 becomes the base on which your tax liability is figured. The effect of the expenditure tax, therefore is to exempt your $10,000 in savings from taxation. Had you not done any saving, your expenditure would have equaled your income and would therefore have been $50,000, and your tax liability would then have been higher. Surely, then, this change in the tax system would provide a far stronger incentive to save than you have at present. Although you will pay taxes in subsequent years on your interest and dividends, at least the savings are not taxed twice.

How does an expenditure-based tax differ from a sales tax? Sales taxes are regressive because lower income persons spend a larger fraction of their income on consumption than higher income persons. However, an expenditure based tax can easily be made progressive by creating expenditure brackets and applying rising tax rates to the successive brackets, in exactly the same way as this is done with the individual income tax.

5

Deficit Reduction and Economic Recovery

The Fiscal Policy Dilemma

To organize thinking about macroeconomic issues such as unemployment and inflation it is important to begin by specifying a list of objectives, or *targets,* for policy. Targets for the coming year might be to reduce the unemployment rate to 6 percent, to hold inflation to 3 percent, and to reduce the budget deficit by $80 billion. Having agreed to the targets, ways must then be found of using a limited number of available policy *instruments,* or tools, to achieve these targets. The primary instruments of macroeconomic policy are fiscal policy and monetary policy. It is important that the targets be consistent (jointly attainable) and that their numbers be kept as low as possible because there is only a limited number of policy instruments available to achieve the targets.

When a policy instrument is in a conflict or dilemma we mean that it is not possible to change the value of the instrument in a way that moves the economy closer to one major target without causing it to depart even farther from another. This is the situation in which federal fiscal policy found itself after 1989. Raising employment implies the need for expansionary fiscal policies such as tax cuts and expenditure increases. But such policies widen the budget deficit. Reducing the budget deficit necessitates restrictive fiscal policies such as tax increases and expenditure reductions. But these further depress the economy.

A dilemma leaves economic policy with very difficult choices. It is important, therefore, to be sure that making deficit reduction a primary goal of policy is essential enough to risk damaging the economy. And if it is decided that deficit reduction is of paramount importance, it is then necessary to consider how damage to the economy can be minimized. These are the issues that are addressed in this chapter.

The wisdom of hindsight teaches that the years 1985-88, when the economy was moving briskly towards full employment, would have been the appropriate time for reducing the structural deficit. However, because of rapid economic growth the cyclical deficit declined and the overall deficit therefore also declined. Since the deficit appeared to be righting itself, Congress and President Reagan felt little pressure to do much about it. Senators Phil Gramm and Warren Rudman did manage to get a deficit reduction plan enacted in 1985 but its effects were limited partly because it exempted such sacred cows as the bulk of defense and social security.

President George Bush inherited the Reagan deficits and appeared intimidated by them. Never in his administration was there consideration of an active fiscal policy designed to raise the economic growth rate to an appropriate level. Indeed, in agreeing to the Budget Enforcement Act of 1990, the President not only went back on his promise not to raise taxes, but endorsed a deflationary fiscal policy at a time of significant weakness in the economy. Bush also appeared to have been intimidated by the Federal Reserve and its Chairman, Alan Greenspan, whose conservative monetary policies were never seriously challenged by the Administration.

Not knowing what to do about the economy seemed to cause Bush to search for and dwell on statistics that indicated that the economy was not in bad shape. Most helpful to the President was the unemployment rate. He never stopped emphasizing that, until 1991, unemployment rates during his administration were nearly always within the neighborhood of the 5.5 percent that economists considered to be a natural rate of unemployment and, indeed, the data bore him out. When unemployment then began to rise he minimized this fact by asserting that unemployment rates showed that the economy was still in far better shape than it had been during the previous recession when unemployment reached 9.7 and 9.6 percent in 1982 and 1983, respectively. Therefore, by keeping his eyes firmly fixed on the statistical dashboard rather than the economic highway, President Bush was able to ignore the fact that the economy was getting into serious trouble.

President Bill Clinton and his advisers surely are aware of the dangers of a restrictive fiscal policy for the economy. That is probably why Clinton originally placed so much emphasis on the speedy enactment of his $16.3 billion stimulus package that included extension of unemployment benefits, a summer work program, a small amount of infrastructure investment, and an investment tax credit for small business. The hope, presumably, was that these measures would strengthen the economy so that it would be better able to absorb the effects of the deflationary deficit reduction measures to follow. Since the bulk of the stimulus package was torpedoed by a Senate filibuster in April 1993, it came as something of a surprise to see Clinton maintaining his public support for the budget cuts that he had originally proposed. He probably believes, and he is probably correct, that if you are going to cut the budget you will have to do so when the political climate permits it regardless of whether it is appropriate from an economic standpoint. The President, however, was taking a terrible gamble. The benefits of the budget cuts on future economic growth will not be felt until after his term of office, and in the meantime he risked being in charge of a far weaker economy than the already weak economy of 1993. Because weakening of the economy carries with it increases in the cyclical deficit, the President seemed not even likely to get the credit he deserves for his strenuous deficit reduction efforts. Fortunately, the economy exhibited stronger than anticipated growth in 1994 and that is the primary reason for the reduction in the deficit that we have been enjoying.

Interpreting the Unemployment Rate

President Bush dwelled on statistics, especially the unemployment rate, to justify his lack of domestic economic policy initiatives. Inasmuch as the unemployment rate is one of the economy's most important economic indicators, it is appropriate to pause to discuss the correct way to interpret the unemployment rate and especially why changes in the unemployment rate are usually quite small even while dramatic changes are occurring in the economy.

Despite its importance as an economic indicator, the unemployment rate is also one of the most potentially misleading. The civilian unemployment rate is the ratio of total unemployment to the civilian labor force, expressed as a percentage. Also, total unemployment is the difference between the civilian labor force and civilian employment. Therefore we may write,

$$\mu = \frac{U}{L} = \frac{L - E}{L}$$

where the unemployment rate is expressed as a decimal, U is total unemployment, L is labor force, and E is employment. When employment increases, unemployment declines, and the unemployment rate therefore declines.

Labor force, employment, and unemployment data are gathered on a monthly basis from an enormous sample that exceeds 50,000 families. An individual is asked by the Census Bureau whether he or she was employed during a particular week of the month. If the answer is yes, the person is counted as both employed and as in the labor force. If the answer is no, but the person is drawing unemployment compensation, he or she is counted as unemployed and as a member of the labor force. Jobless people who are not drawing unemployment compensation are then asked a number of questions designed to help the census taker determine whether the person was actively engaged in job search. Did you answer a want add? Did you register with an employment agency? If the answer to such questions is yes, then the individual is classified as unemployed and as a member of the labor force. However, if the answer is no, it is assumed that the person is voluntarily idle. He or she is therefore *not* counted as unemployed *nor* as in the labor force. The person is, rather, classified as not in the labor force. Yet that same person might return to job search and, hopefully, to employment when business activity improves.

It is well known to economists that only small increases in the unemployment rate are associated with large losses in output. There are several reasons for this. First, when the economy enters a slump and business cuts production, it usually does not lay off workers in the same proportion as it reduces output. Skilled workers are not easy to find and a business that tried to minimize its labor costs through lay-offs would just have to find and bear the cost of training new workers when demand revives. The drop in output is therefore partly reflected in a decline in labor productivity (output per worker) rather than a decline in employment.

A slump in the economy also forces some full-time workers into part-time occupations. Since the Bureau of Labor Statistics (BLS) does not distinguish full from part-time employment when it computes the unemployment rate, the unemployment rate does not recognize that the number of full-time jobs has declined. Total employment would therefore be lower and unemployment would be higher if employment were corrected to a full-time equivalent basis.

But by far the most important reason for the fact that the unemployment rate does not fluctuate as much as output is that labor force participation for many groups in society varies with the business cycle, declining when employment declines and rising during periods of rapid job growth. The primary cause of this is so-called *discouraged worker* effect. Some of the persons who have been laid off and have exhausted their unemployment compensation simply drop out of the labor force because they are too discouraged to look for work. This is especially true for teenagers but it is also true for adult males. When that happens they are no longer counted as unemployed.[1]

To illustrate the effects of cyclical variations in labor force participation, suppose that the economy loses 1,000 jobs. If the labor force remained constant, measured unemployment would increase by 1,000. However suppose, as recent research strongly indicates, that when 1,000 jobs are lost about 460 people become discouraged and drop out of the labor force.[2] Measured unemployment then drops by only 540 even though 1,000 jobs have been lost. Clearly, then, the unemployment rate rises when the economy deteriorates, but by far less than it would have risen had the labor force remained constant.

In 1992 the civilian labor force was 127.0 million persons, employ-

1. Discouraged workers drop out of the labor force when employment conditions deteriorate. However, "secondary" or "additional" workers come in. A housewife, for example, may be forced to enter the labor force when her husband suffers a prolonged period of unemployment.

2. Dernburg, Thomas F. and Victor Ukpollo, "Hidden Unemployment in the United States: Has It Been Getting Worse?" September 1992. Unpublished manuscript.

ment came to 117.6 million, unemployment was 9.4 million, and the unemployment rate was 7.4 percent. If labor force remained constant as employment expands, it would require an increase in employment of 2.4 million jobs to reduce the unemployment rate to 5.5 percent. However, we estimate that if the unemployment rate were 5.5 percent, the labor force would be 2.7 million higher. The number of additional jobs required to achieve a 5.5 percent unemployment rate would therefore be 4.3 million rather than 2.4 million.

Counting the potential labor force entrants among the unemployed implies unemployment of 11.4 million, rather than the official count of 9.4 million. The implied unemployment rate is 8.8 percent. Since the actual unemployment rate was 7.4 percent, the addition of what might be termed *hidden* unemployment adds 1.4 percentage points to the unemployment rate. However, the really important fact is that the economy needs almost 2 million more jobs to attain a satisfactory unemployment rate of 5.5 percent than is indicated by a crude look at labor force and unemployment statistics.

This discussion is not meant to be critical of U.S. government economic statistics. Indeed, most knowledgeable persons consider our data to be among the best in the world. It simply means that, in the case of some of the data, it is necessary to be very careful about how to interpret them.

Developing a Systematic Economic Plan

To develop an intelligent economic plan for the coming fiscal year you would first need to spell out a quarterly time path of the values of your objectives or targets. You might therefore establish a target path for the unemployment rate or the level of real GDP, the rate of inflation, and, if you are heavily concerned with economic growth, the ratio of investment to GDP or the size of the structural budget deficit.

Your next step would be the development of a quarterly *baseline* forecast of economic activity. The baseline forecast is your best estimate of unemployment, GDP, the budget deficit, and other target variables *assuming the continuation of current policy* such as current monetary and budget policy.

The third step would be to compare the target values with the baseline forecast and to measure the gaps between your targets and your forecast. These gaps would then permit you to see the amounts of the shortfalls and that, then, would serve as a guide for policy.

You might be surprised to learn that a procedure of this sort was specified in the Budget Act of 1974 which created the congressional budget committees as well as a professional staff known as the Congressional Budget Office (CBO). The plan called for forecasts of economic activity by the administration and the Federal Reserve. Relevant testimony would then be supplied to the budget committees, the banking committees, and the Joint Economic Committee for use in planning the budget and other aspects of economic policy for the coming fiscal year.

The gaps serve as directives for policy. But should the GDP gap be closed by monetary policy or by fiscal policy? Perhaps it is possible to close one gap, but not the others. How should thinking about the use of policy tools be organized? The first thing to bear in mind is that if there are two objectives, or targets, these targets can be met only if there are at least two policy instruments available. Monetary policy, for example, could be used to lower unemployment. Or monetary policy could be used to achieve a target rate of inflation. But it would be an accident if both could be attained using monetary policy alone. Therefore, equality of instruments and targets is a clear necessity.

Second, the policy instruments must be *independently effective*. One instrument cannot just be an exact substitute for another. For example, GDP could be raised by expansionary monetary policy, and the GDP effect could then be negated by tightening the budget. But this would not leave the economy where it started because both policies lower interest rates and therefore raise the ratio of investment to GDP. The policy tools are therefore independently effective. Alternatively, the Fed could increase the money supply by purchasing government securities or it could increase the money supply by increasing its loans to commercial banks. It hardly makes any difference. Therefore open-market policy and rediscount policy are not independently effective and do not qualify as independent instruments.

Third, in order to achieve more than one target, it is necessary to coordinate policy changes so as to achieve the correct policy *mix*. To illustrate, suppose there are two major targets--eliminating the gap between potential and actual GDP, and attaining a target level of budget deficit. The policy instruments are the structural budget deficit and the money supply.

You may have noticed that we have gotten this far without drawing any of those frightful diagrams with which economists torture their students. However, it's now time to draw one. Take our word for it; it greatly simplifies matters. Therefore, have a look at ***Figure 5-1***. The horizontal axis measures the money supply which is assumed to be under the control of Federal Reserve policy. The vertical axis measures the structural budget deficit which is the responsibility of the President and Congress. As previously explained, the actual deficit differs from the structural deficit because of the presence of a cyclical deficit caused by the failure of the economy to reach its potential GDP target.

Let the QQ curve that slopes downward and to the right represent the combinations of structural deficit and money supply that achieve potential output, that is, the maximum output attainable without accelerating inflation. A decline in the structural deficit, for example, would reduce spending and output below potential; but this

Figure 5-1

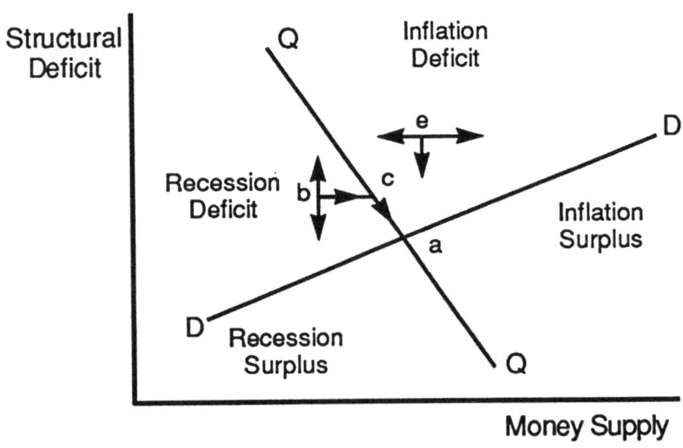

could be offset by an increase in the money supply. Points to the left of QQ imply that output is below potential. The zones to the left of QQ are therefore labelled recession. Similarly points to the right of QQ imply that total spending is excessive so that these zones are labelled inflation.

Let the DD curve specify the combinations of money supply and structural deficit that achieve the current politically determined deficit target. The DD curve slopes upwards and to the right. A decrease in the money supply would lower GDP thereby causing the cyclical deficit to increase. Since the overall budget deficit would now be greater than the target deficit, the target deficit could be reached by reducing the structural deficit. Consequently, points above and to the left of DD imply that the actual deficit is greater than the target deficit whereas points below and to the right of DD imply that the actual deficit is below the target deficit. Zones above and to the left of DD are labelled deficit and zones below and to the right are labelled surplus.

The curves intersect at point *a* which is the only combination of structural deficit and money supply at which both targets are attained. The objective of policy, therefore, is to reach point **a**. For the past several years the economic situation has implied a point such as **b** in which the economy is well below potential real GDP and the budget deficit is regarded as excessive. At point **b** fiscal policy can be seen to be in the conflict, or dilemma, situation previously noted. If the structural deficit is increased to raise output and employment the actual deficit will increase. If the structural deficit is decreased to move towards the target deficit, the economy will move farther away from potential output.

Monetary policy, on the other hand, is *not* in a dilemma. Expansionary monetary policy stimulates the economy and raise output and employment. Since GDP rises while unemployment falls, the expansionary monetary policy also reduces the cyclical budget deficit. It would, therefore, move the economy towards *both* of its targets. The directive for policy is clear: Divert attention away from fiscal policy while using expansionary monetary policy in an effort to reach point **c**. Once there the dilemma for fiscal policy is removed. Point **a** can then be approached by combining further monetary expansion with simultaneous reduction in the structural budget deficit.

Note that movement from point **c** to point **a** necessitates a change in the policy mix; monetary policy must become more expansionary while fiscal policy must become more restrictive. Consequently the same change in the policy mix needed to attain the short run targets of deficit reduction and potential output is exactly the same as the mix change, discussed in Chapter 4, needed to attain the longer term target of achieving a more rapid rate of economic growth.

In summary: The first rule of economic policy is that if there are two targets of economic policy, at least two independently effective policy instruments are needed if both targets are to be achieved. Second, when a policy instruments is in conflict, the policy instruments that are not in conflict should be viewed as the primary instruments of policy. Finally, an orderly and efficient transition from a point such as **b** to **a** implies the need for policy coordination. It's far too expensive for the economy to permit policy instruments to go their separate ways or to work at cross purposes.

Finally, note that the role of the policy instruments would be reversed in the event that the economy were perceived as being at a point such as **e** where the deficit is too high and total spending is excessive and therefore inflationary. Monetary policy now has the dilemma. Expansionary monetary policy reduces the deficit but worsens inflation. Restrictive monetary policy slows inflation but widens the deficit. Fiscal policy is no longer in a dilemma because a reduction in the structural deficit reduces both inflation and the budget deficit. Fiscal policy therefore should become the primary instrument of policy. As seen in the next section, this is exactly the way the Federal Reserve views the economy, and it clings to this view on a continuing basis, impervious to the actual facts of the economic situation.

Monetary Muddle: What's Wrong With the Fed?

It is now abundantly clear that it would be a huge mistake to cut the deficit without, at the same time, substantially accelerating the rate at which the Federal Reserve increases the nation's money supply. However, the Fed has not done its part despite the deficit reduction program enacted in 1993, and in the spring of 1994 its restrictive actions sent shock waves throughout the economy as the Fed created an inflation false alarm. Why, then, does the Fed

Table 5-1
Real Monetary Growth and Interest Rates

Year	Real Rates of Growth		Nominal Interest Rates		Real Rates
	M_1	M_2	3 Month	10 Year	10 Year
1976	0.22	6.98	5.0	7.6	1.3
1977	1.14	3.44	5.3	7.4	0.5
1978	0.29	0.06	7.2	8.4	0.5
1979	-1.69	-0.78	10.0	9.4	0.8
1980	-2.44	-0.54	11.5	11.5	2.0
1981	-2.94	-0.01	14.0	13.9	3.9
1982	2.37	2.56	10.7	13.0	6.8
1983	5.58	7.61	8.6	11.1	7.0
1984	1.56	4.13	9.6	12.4	8.1
1985	8.21	4.37	7.5	10.6	6.9
1986	13.82	6.65	6.0	7.7	5.0
1987	0.31	0.38	5.8	8.4	5.2
1988	1.01	1.56	6.7	8.9	5.0
1989	-3.33	0.59	8.1	8.5	4.1
1990	-0.31	-0.92	7.5	8.6	4.2
1991	4.65	-0.85	5.4	7.9	3.8
1992	10.95	-1.43	3.5	7.0	3.5
1993	7.44	-0.91	3.0	5.9	3.3

Sources: Department of Commerce and Board of Governors of the Federal Reserve System

continually put the economy through a monetary squeeze and why does the country put up with it?

Table 5-1 shows monetary growth and interest rate data beginning with 1976. Shown are the average annual rates of growth of real M_1 and M_2. To get these figures actual money supply data were divided by the price deflator for GDP, and the growth rates of these real magnitudes were then computed. Real monetary aggregates are important because the real monetary growth rates provide information pertinent to the question: Is the money supply growing fast enough to finance a suitable rate of growth of real output? In the past real GDP and real M_2 have tended to grow at roughly the same rate. Therefore, a good rule of thumb is that if 3.5 percent is a desirable real GDP growth rate, that is roughly the rate at which the real quantity of money ought to be growing.

The monetary growth data show that the Fed has not been meeting its responsibility for financing the real growth of the economy. Indeed the economy has been going through a monetary wringer throughout much of the period since 1987. Real M_1 growth was negative in 1989 and 1990 and real M_2 has been consistently negative for the past four years. There was a sharp pick up in the growth of M_1 in 1992 when, it appears, the Fed was motivated to assist President Bush's reelection campaign. There was, however, a significant slowing down in the rate of monetary growth during the first half of 1993.

Although short term interest rates have come down sharply since 1989 long term rates, as measured by the yield on 10 year government securities, had dropped by only about 2.7 percentage points since 1986. The drop in long term rates has been less than one percentage point when the real cost of borrowing, measured by subtracting the rate of inflation from the nominal interest rate, is calculated.

A quick summary of what was said in Chapter 3 serves as a useful reminder of the effects of expansionary monetary policy in an economy that is below potential output. Specifically expansionary monetary policy would:

1. Provide the economy with the liquidity it needs to restore rapid growth. It would lower interest rates thereby stimulating borrowing by business for investment in plant expansion and modernization. This yields multiplier effects that raise real GDP and create jobs thereby reducing unemployment.

2. Because of lower unemployment, unemployment compensation payments drop, and because of higher payrolls, personal incomes, and profits, the yield from Federal taxes rise. Therefore, whereas expansionary fiscal policy widens the budget deficit and raises inter-

3. It is true that generating domestic employment via currency depreciation is a beggar-thy-neighbor policy because it steals employment from abroad. Foreign countries are not likely to thank us for this. However, they can offset the loss by expanding their own money supplies. In the present state of the world economy such policies would be most welcome. If the German Bundesbank complains about our monetary policies, that is their problem. They should be lowering their own interest rates rather than trying to get us to raise ours.

est rates, expansionary monetary policy lowers the budget deficit and reduces interest rates.

3. Lower interest rates cause capital to flow abroad in search of higher yielding foreign financial assets. The dollar therefore falls in value relative to other currencies. The depreciation of the dollar makes the cost of exports lower as seen by others, thereby raising export demand and GDP. At the same time imports become more expensive in terms of dollars. Producers and consumers therefore are provided with an incentive to use domestic sources of supply in place of imports.[3] This too raises economic activity in the United States and this, in turn, reduces the cyclical deficit.

4. Lower interest rates directly reduce the interest cost of servicing the national debt. In addition, all of the other reductions in the deficit reduce the rate of growth of the national debt thereby slowing the growth of interest payments.

Why then the reluctance to move aggressively on the monetary front? Undoubtedly reluctance arises from a fear of renewing inflation and from the false notion that tight money is needed to prevent the budget deficit from being inflationary. Some suspect, as well, that the Fed wishes to keep pressure on Congress to reduce the deficit. If interest rates are reduced by monetary policy, this might give Congress an excuse not to lower interest rates by cutting the deficit.

It is true that periods of rapid economic expansion are sometimes accompanied by increases in the inflation rate. But under the economic circumstances of recent times this risk was minimal. The economy had available to it ample unemployed labor and ample underutilized capital stock. In addition, real defense purchases were continuing to fall, and the severe recession being suffered by other industrial countries continued to depress exports. It was therefore safe to assume that increased total spending would primarily raise output and employment with little or no adverse inflationary effect. Even the Fed had to concede that by mid 1994 there had been no visible evidence of higher inflation.

It seems clear that the Federal Reserve has been using growth of the Federal deficit as an excuse for its failure to support recovery. From July to December 1991 M_1 growth mysteriously tailed off to almost nothing while real M_2 became sharply negative. It is hardly surprising that this coincided with sharp increases in the budget deficit that came to about $100 billion during the year. The increased deficit was caused by the continuing deterioration of the economy and was therefore largely an increase in the cyclical deficit. The rise in transfer outlays was exceptionally large.

It has already been explained that increases in the cyclical deficit cannot possibly be inflationary because such increases in the cyclical deficit are caused by declining spending. Such spending reductions cause inflation to fall rather than to rise. Is it possible that Federal Reserve officials do not understand the difference between the inflation effects of an increase in the cyclical deficit as opposed to an increase in the structural deficit?

Inspection of monetary statistics such as those provided in Table 5-1 makes one wonder if there is any rhyme or reason to Federal Reserve monetary policies given the erratic and often destabilizing monetary growth rates recorded in the data. One reason for this lies in the Fed's unwillingness to assume responsibility for primary economic targets. Relevant primary targets for monetary policy should be the rate of growth of GDP, the unemployment rate, and the inflation rate. However, the Fed knows that attainment of these targets is complicated by the fact that the outcome also depends on fiscal policy as well as unanticipated shocks. Therefore if the Fed accepts responsibility for achieving such primary targets, it is likely to be blamed for failures not of its own making.

Because of unwillingness to accept responsibility for primary targets, the Fed has chosen to aim for the attainment of proximate targets, such as interest rates, that it can control. In addition, legislation, which it has found easy to circumvent, has attempted to make the Fed concentrate on achieving target rates of monetary growth.

Throughout much of its history the Fed practiced a policy which was known as "leaning against the wind" designed to stabilize interest rates. Such policies work in a stabilizing manner when the primary shock that drives the economy is a monetary shock such as a change in liquidity preference or a financial innovation that reduces the demand for money. For example, if people suddenly decide to readjust their portfolios to hold more money, they will sell some of their bonds. This depresses bond prices and raises interest rates. By open-market purchases the Fed can prevent the rise in interest rates thereby preventing higher interest rates from reducing spending.

Unfortunately much of the time the predominant shock that affects the economy is a real shock such as a change in fiscal policy, a change in investment demand, a change in export demand, and the like. In such a case monetary policy that stabilizes interest rates destabilizes GDP. For example, GDP and employment decline if export demand declines. The demand for money and credit therefore declines and interest rates decline. If the Fed is committed to leaning against the interest-rate wind, she will embark on a restrictive monetary policy that then adds further deflationary pressure to the economy.

The most conspicuous example of such perverse behavior was the Fed's response to the economic collapse between 1929 and 1933. As the economy declined the demand for money and credit declined and interest rates would therefore have tended to fall. However, rather than permitting the decline in the demand for money to lower interest rates, the Fed embarked on a program of "mopping up excess liquidity". This prevented interest rates from declining so that the Fed's policy served to add to the deflationary forces that were causing the collapse of the economy. From 1929 to 1933 real GNP dropped 30.1 percent, M_1 and M_2 were permitted to drop 25.2 and 30.9 percent, respectively, and all the while interest rates remained virtually constant.

Times, unfortunately, have not changed very much. Despite the requirement of the Budget Act of 1974 that obliges the Fed to harmonize its policies with those of the administration and the congressional budget committees so as to achieve agreed to employment, growth, and price level targets, the Fed continues on its own merry way by targeting the Federal Funds rate[4] and by ignoring its own monetary growth targets, targets that it is obliged to announce as prescribed by legislation.

---

4. The federal funds rate is the rate of interest that commercial banks charge each other for the loan of reserves

5. A closed economy is an economy that lives in isolation. It neither engages in international trade nor in international payments. It is a figment of the imagination of economists designed to simplify exposition. Regrettably it leads to horrendous errors.

Who's In Charge?

With rare exceptions the Fed Chairmen of the last thirty years have been the sort about whom the financial press could say, "Their appointment meets with the warm approval of the financial community." When the Wall Street Journal says that, you can be sure its a code phrase for tight money and high interest rates. A further translation might be: "Prevent inflation at all times and never mind if the consequences are a sluggish economy and high unemployment."

In 1975 the economy was flat on its back in the wake of the first major OPEC oil price increase. More concerned about inflation than unemployment, Fed Chairman Arthur Burns took every opportunity to play monetary blackmail by telling congressional committees that if they passed the tax cut that was being contemplated, he would see to it that the expansionary effects of the tax cut would be neutralized by restrictive monetary policy. Congress was left with the chilling thought that its efforts to raise employment would come to nothing with only a bigger budget deficit and higher interest rates to show for it.

Paul Volker, who was appointed by President Jimmy Carter in 1979, promptly stepped so hard on the monetary brakes that he threw the economy into its worst collapse since the Great Depression of the 1930s. Apparently educated by the old macroeconomics textbooks which treated the U.S. economy as a closed economy,[5] he seemed totally unaware of the enormous impact that restrictive monetary policy would have in the new world of flexible exchange rates and nearly perfect international capital mobility. Thus, and as will be explained in Chapter 9, when the Fed began its monetary tightening in late 1979 interest rates in the United States reacted by rising sharply. This produced a huge capital inflow as foreign investors, seeing far higher yields in the United States, converted their domestic financial assets into currency which they then used in the foreign exchange market to buy dollars so as to buy the higher yielding U.S. financial assets. The resulting increase in the demand for the dollar caused it to appreciate. Because this lowered the domestic cost of imports, imports rose sharply, and because it raised the foreign currency cost of U.S. exports it caused exports to stagnate. This produced a huge trade deficit which had an enormously deflationary impact on the economy.

Alan Greenspan, the present Chairman of the Fed, is cut from the same cloth as most of his predecessors. Although less openly arrogant and contemptuous than Arthur Burns, and allegedly a better economist than Paul Volker, he too is a product of the banking-Wall Street mentality. Watching him in action, during Senate testimony when he served as Chairman of the Council of Economic Advisers and later, it was obvious that he opposed just about everything that the moderate and liberal Senators thought might be good for the country. He was vehemently opposed to the Federal loan guarantee that helped to save the Chrysler Corporation from bankruptcy and saved the jobs of its workers. It was clear, as well, that he had a genius for making phoney arguments sound plausible if this served his purpose. As the data reported in Table 5-1 clearly show, he is a firm believer in monetary strangulation while claiming this to be necessary for the achievement of a nebulous goal that he calls "sustainable growth."

His remarkable ability to befuddle congressional committees has served him well in recent years. On his frequent trips to Capitol Hill Greenspan has been urged by members of the Banking Committees to accelerate monetary growth in order to lower interest rates. Greenspan has often replied that while it is important to get interest rates down it is more appropriate to do this by reducing Federal borrowing than by having the Fed engage in open market purchases. The latter increases the money supply and risks the rekindling of inflation. Deficit reduction runs no such risk. This is certainly true; but it is quite irrelevant. Expansionary monetary policy is an expansionary policy and therefore creates the risk that some of the monetary growth will be wasted in the financing of higher prices. This risk is absent when interest rates are lowered by deficit reduction because deficit reduction represents restrictive fiscal policy that lowers output and employment, and puts downward pressure on inflation. This fact, however, fails to interest the Chairman who surely must know that his argument is designed to be misleading. One suspects, also, that Greenspan resorts to the argument so as to keep pressure on Congress to reduce the budget deficit. More subtle than Arthur Burns, to be sure, but monetary blackmail nonetheless.

Greenspan understands that it has been hard to convince anyone that there has been a serious threat of inflation in recent years. He therefore resorts to the argument that, even though there is little danger of inflation, a rise in monetary growth rates will nevertheless raise inflationary expectations. Therefore expansionary monetary policy could actually raise long term interest rates. It sounds preposterous, yet there is a grain of irrelevant truth in it.

It is true that an increase in the expected rate of inflation will cause nominal interest rates to rise. You wouldn't, for example, continue to lend money at 6 percent if you thought the rate of price increase would suddenly jump from zero to an annual rate of 6 percent. If you did, your real return would be zero because the interest you earn just cancels the reduction in the purchasing power value of your loan.

The relevant question, however, is whether such a rise in interest rates will slow investment spending. This, in turn, depends on whether the real cost of borrowing rises or falls. Both economic theory and empirical research support the proposition that the real cost of borrowing *declines* in response to an increase in the expected rate of inflation. The real cost of borrowing is the difference between the nominal rate of interest and the anticipated rate of inflation. For example, if you earn 10 percent on a loan, but you expect inflation to be 4 percent, you recognize that it takes interest earnings of 4 percent to offset the 4 percent reduction in the purchasing-power value of the loan. Therefore, your expected real rate of return is 6 percent. You could write the simple expression,

$$\mathbf{r = i - x}$$

where r is the real cost of borrowing, i is the nominal rate of interest, and x is the expected rate of inflation.

Economists of an earlier generation believed that the real cost of borrowing depended on slow to change "fundamental" real factors such as the productivity of investment and the savings habits of the population--productivity and thrift as they put it. Their hypothesis therefore implied that a rise in the expected rate of inflation from zero to 4 percent would raise the nominal rate of interest by 4 percentage points, but would leave the real rate of interest unaffected.

Empirical research has generally failed to support this hypothesis. It suggests that a rise in the expected rate of inflation of 4 percent, will raise nominal interest rates but by less than 4 percent, *thereby causing the real rate of interest to decline.* These empirical findings are supported by the modern theory of portfolio choice discussed in Chapter 4. Recalling that discussion, it was seen that most investors are risk averse and that risk and return are viewed as imperfect substitutes by them. From these assumptions it followed that these investors are portfolio diversifiers who hold a wide variety of assets that differ with respect to risk and return. One of the assets held in such portfolios will be money which is riskless and yields no return.

A rise in the expected rate of inflation will cause portfolio substitution away from money because when the inflation rate is positive the real purchasing-power value of the money declines. Investors therefore shift their portfolios into higher yield and higher risk assets to avoid the penalty of the negative interest rate on money. The portfolio substitution, however, raises the prices and lowers the yields on the riskier longer term assets. It therefore follows that a rise in the expected rate of inflation lowers the real rate of return that lenders are willing to accept so as to avoid the penalty associated with money holding. A rise in the expected rate of inflation therefore reduces the real cost of borrowing.

Seen from this perspective, a rise in anticipated inflation has a positive effect on investment expenditures, rather than the negative effect implied by Chairman Greenspan, because it lowers the real cost of borrowing. The fact that nominal interest rates may rise is irrelevant. Greenspan surely understands this but his congressional audience does not, and he is therefore able to use the threat of higher interest rates as a device for befuddling and intimidating the Banking Committees. All the hocus pocus in the world cannot alter the fact that expansionary monetary policy has an expansionary effect on investment and the economy.

Why Does Bill Clinton Cater to the Fed?

Someone ought to have told Bill Clinton when he entered office that the single most important step he could take on behalf of the economy would be to get rid of Alan Greenspan with his bankers' and Wall Street priorities and replace him with a businessman or economist who has shown serious concern for the jobs and welfare of ordinary working people, the profitability of productive business enterprise, the growth of the economy, and the appropriate coordination of monetary policy with the fiscal policies of the Administration and Congress. The appointee must also be unimpressed by Wall Street propaganda which asserts that the first priority for monetary policy is the stability of the habitually neurotic financial markets. Yet, instead of searching for such a person Clinton has talked a great deal about reassuring the financial markets and, at his State of the Union Message of 1993, he conspicuously sat the First Lady down next to the Fed Chairman. Indeed he has been giving every indication that he is taking Greenspan's continued presence for granted, that he has little understanding of the important role of monetary policy in a program of recovery, and some have gone so far as to assert that Clinton's budgets have really been Greenspan's budgets.

It is true that the Fed Chairman's term of office has not expired. Yet in the past Federal Reserve Chairmen have generally been gracious enough to step down when a new President arrives in Washington, especially when the Chairman was appointed by a President from a different party. It is always possible for the President to help this process along by offering the incumbent a juicy plum. Jimmy Carter, for example, got rid of Arthur Burns by appointing him ambassador to Germany.

It is true that the Fed is technically an independent agency of the Federal government. However, this does not exempt it from the responsibility to harmonize its monetary policies with other economic policies. It is hard to imagine how World War II could have been financed had President Roosevelt not insisted on Federal Reserve cooperation. After the war, wanting to maintain low interest rates to facilitate post-war reconversion, President Harry Truman insisted on the continuation of war-time interest rate policy. Although many thought such policy ill advised, Truman nevertheless forced the Fed to comply. During the 1960s, alarmed at rising interest rates caused by monetary restriction, President Lyndon Johnson hauled Fed Chairman William McChesney Martin down to his Texas ranch where, in full view of a battery of TV cameras, he dressed the Chairman down and demanded that he lower interest rates.

There is plenty of precedent for insisting on Federal Reserve cooperation with government policy. It's a good thing too. Given its importance, the President just can't let monetary policy go its own way. Left unrestrained, the Chairman of the Fed is our most powerful economic official. When the Secretary of the Treasury wants to raise your taxes, he has to convince the President and the Congress of the need for it. When the Fed chairman wants to destroy your job because of a morbid fear of inflation, he can just do it with impunity.

The recent financial crisis of Mexico which found the peso falling precipitously has prompted the Fed to purchase pesos with dollars. The result has been a welcome increase in the U.S. money supply that has prevented the Fed from continuing to force up interest rates. It remains to be seen how the Fed responds when the tax cuts proposed by the new Republican Congress become a reality. In early 1995 the economy was in pretty good shape, hardly a good time for a tax cut and a defense spending increase. The deficit is sure to widen again, the Fed could easily become panicky about inflation again, and interest rates would then shoot up precipitously both because of the higher deficit and the Fed's likely restrictive monetary response to it.

Part II
Cutting the Deficit

6

Cutting the Deficit: Social Insurance

Evaluating Public Expenditures

Do you know how to cut government spending? What specifically do you propose? This and the subsequent two chapters provide some grist for your decision-making mill. You're the tax payer. Are you getting an adequate return for your tax dollar?

Tax increases cut into purchasing power while the benefits of government spending are not always clearly visible. Most people therefore react more favorably to the prospect of cutting the deficit by means of expenditure cuts than by tax increases. However, to make such judgements thoughtfully rather than simply as reflexive reactions, we would have to be able to assert that the last dollar spent in the private economy does more for economic well being than the last dollar spent in the public sector. We would also have to examine all of the functional expenditure categories in the budget to make an informed judgement about whether the allocation of federal spending between the categories is appropriate. Do we have the knowledge and the patience to sort these things out? Can we reach agreement with respect to private and public spending priorities?

Congress and the administration are supposed to do this sorting for us and, to be sure, Congress expends a lot of time and energy on the budget. But when it comes to doing something significant about cutting the budget the results are generally disappointing, and it's curious that critics of government spending rarely get down to specifics. Like former Senator William Proxmire, some of them get their jollies by unearthing trivial examples of waste in the budget, on which they bestow "golden fleece" awards, while accomplishing very little except to waste the time of their congressional staffs.

Does Congress have the time to review and restructure all of the major programs effectively on an annual basis? Obviously not. That is one reason why rhetoric vastly exceeds action. The other main reason is hardly a secret. You don't have to be a political scientist to know that Congressmen represent regions whose economic interests differ from the national interest. Congressmen from Texas will oppose tax increases harmful to the oil industry. Congressmen from southern California will oppose defense cuts. Congressmen from North Carolina will oppose cuts in the federal tobacco program. Congressmen from Florida will oppose cuts in social security. Everybody knows this. Nevertheless, despite nearly universal aversion to tax increases, such increases are sometimes easier to legislate than spending cuts. It's possible to raise taxes in a way that imposes only a small burden on the average taxpayer whereas expenditure cuts have major adverse effects on the members of powerful special interest groups. An obvious example is social security. Instead of containing expenditures by rationalizing the social security benefits structure, thereby antagonizing an important and powerful special interest group, Congress has time and again found it far easier to raise social security taxes.

Assessing the efficiency of the budget is facilitated by asking two major questions:

1. Are the resources preempted by the government more socially useful than their alternative private use?

2. Is the division of public expenditure between different functional categories – health, national defense, agriculture and the like – such that social welfare is maximized?

Economists try to get at the answers to these questions by resorting to the all important *marginal principle* which they apply to a myriad of problems. For example, if a firm wishes to maximize its profits it should raise output up to the point where the additional (marginal) revenue obtained by selling one more unit of output just equals the additional (marginal) cost incurred in producing the next unit. Similarly, if a firm wishes to minimize the cost of producing a given level of output it has to decide how much labor and how much physical capital stock to use. Costs are minimized when the extra (marginal) output that can be obtained by spending one more dollar on labor just equals the extra (marginal) output obtained by spending one more dollar on capital stock. Finally, a household maximizes its well being when it distributes its income over various commodities so that the added satisfaction (marginal utility) of all commodities, relative to their prices, is equal.

The same principle should be applied to issues of public finance. Therefore, when the government adds a program that preempts resources from the private sector, the program is in the social interest if the *marginal social benefit* of the last dollar spent on the program exceeds the marginal cost to society of transferring resources from private consumption and investment to the government. Similarly within the federal budget the tax dollar is optimally distributed when the last dollar spent on each functional category yields the same social benefit.

Although marginal social benefit is often difficult to estimate, thinking in these terms greatly helps to define problems. A public investment project is in the social interest when the social rate of return on the project exceeds the rate of return that would have been obtained had the resources been invested in the private sector. An increase in government consumption is in the social interest if the marginal social benefit of the expenditure exceeds the marginal social cost of taking the resources away from private consumption.

Deficit spending during recession is clearly in the social interest. Lower taxes and higher transfer outlays, for example, raise private consumption at a time when there is no competition for resources. That is to say, when the economy is below potential output, the effect of the increase in deficit financing is to mobilize resources that would otherwise have been idle. In such a situation the additional government activity, be it in the form of tax cuts or expenditure increases, provides a net benefit to society because it costs the private sector nothing. The same reasoning applies to expansionary monetary policy during recession. By lowering interest rates and stimulating private investment resources that would otherwise have been idle are mobilized. The economy enjoys an increase in its stock of productive facilities that enables it to produce more in the future.

The marginal principle calls immediate attention to the inefficiency of present budgetary procedures. First hand experience with the Senate Budget Committee suggests that Congress rarely thinks in terms of the marginal principle. Put differently, when Congress contemplates the expansion of a specific program little thought is given to the question of whether the added resources could more beneficially be used elsewhere. Budget cutting efforts are invariably inefficient. For example, in 1985 Congress passed the Gramm-Rudman deficit reduction plan which attempted to phase the deficit down over a number of years so as to reach budgetary balance. However, the act exempted most of defense as well as social security from the budget cutting knife. This meant that Congress adopted the principle that the last dollar spent on defense and social security *always* yields more social benefit than the last dollar spent on the non-exempt categories.

Only a moment's reflection suggests that this sort of budgeting is irrational. If the first dollar spent on social security is given to the most needy person while the last dollar is given to the least needy person, it is obvious that the last dollar yields very little social benefit because it is paid to the retiree who has ample outside income and does not need a subsidy from the government. The marginal cost to the tax payer vastly exceeds the marginal benefit to the recipient. Obviously, then, it makes no sense to single out certain programs and insulate them from overall budgetary considerations. President Ronald Reagan apparently believed that the marginal social benefit of added defense spending exceeded the marginal social benefit of expenditures on other programs. The result was to starve many of these programs thereby adding to low-income housing shortages, aggravating urban problems, accelerating the deterioration of the economic infrastructure, and contributing to the continuing deterioration of public education.

Table 6-1 shows how federal government expenditures are distributed over the various functional categories. The table reports expenditure levels for the years 1981, 1987, and 1993. It also shows average annual growth rates over the periods 1981-87 and 1987-93. The table tells a very incomplete story. For example, the table indicates that government outlays for commerce and housing credit have been modest. However, the federal government makes huge housing subsidies to individuals by permitting them to deduct mortgage interest and property taxes from their taxable income. Such hidden subsidies are called tax expenditures. In the housing area this subsidy came to $177 billion in 1993 with the owners of mansions being the primary beneficiaries. If all tax expenditures were added to federal outlays they would have added $408 billion to total federal expenditures in 1993.

The areas in the budget of greatest concern are the budget busters whose growth outstrips the growth of the total budget, and the categories in which marginal social benefit is low. Total federal expenditures grew at an average annual rate of 6.3 percent over the period 1981-1993. Among the budget busters are interest on the public debt and health care. The latter is particularly troublesome because of the enormous acceleration of the growth rate in the most recent period. Social security does not appear to be a budget buster. Yet the social security system is inequitable, inefficient, increasingly burdensome to business and the working population, and likely to encounter severe problems in the absence of reform. This chapter looks at these problems.

Federal health expenditures have been rising at an alarming rate. From 1981 to 1987 health expenditures including Medicaid rose at a rate of 6.84 percent. But this rate accelerated to 17.5 percent during 1987-93. And Medicare expenditures have been rising at rates close to 10 percent. A review of the way the health care industry operates makes clear that expenditures are unlikely to be contained in the absence of complete reform of the health care system. Analyzing the economics of the health care industry is the task of Chapter 7.

The rate of increase of outlays on defense has declined sharply in the more recent period and, measured in constant prices, defense purchases have actually declined. This creates major problems of readjustment involving the transfer of resources out of defense into alternative productive activities. Tax expenditures, such as the housing subsidy, are a source of waste and inequity because, as a rule, the wealthy benefit disproportionately from itemized tax deductions. Little social benefit accrues from the federal farm program. These issues are discussed in Chapter 8.

The Growing Burden of Social Insurance

The most important social insurance programs are unemployment insurance (UI), retirement under social security, hospital insurance for elderly persons (HI) under Medicare, Medicaid which provides medical benefits to the indigent, Federal Disability In-

Table 6-1
Federal Outlays by Functional Categories
Fiscal Years 1981, 1987, and 1993

	1981	1987	1993	Annual Growth,% 81-87	Annual Growth,% 87-93
Total Outlays	$678.3	1,003.9	1,408.2	6.9	5.8
National Defense	157.5	282.0	291.1	10.2	0.5
International Affairs	13.1	11.7	18.8	-1.9	8.2
General Science, Space, and Technology	6.5	9.2	17.0	6.0	10.8
Energy	15.2	4.1	4.3	-19.6	0.8
Natural Resources and Environment	13.6	13.4	20.2	-0.3	7.1
Agriculture	11.3	26.6	20.4	15.3	-4.3
Commerce and Housing Credit	8.2	6.2	-22.7	-9.5	x
Transportation	23.4	26.2	35.0	1.9	4.9
Community and Regional Development	10.6	5.1	9.1	-11.5	10.1
Education, training Employment and Social Services	33.7	29.7	50.0	-2.1	9.1
Health	26.9	40.0	99.4	6.8	16.4
Medicare	39.2	75.1	130.6	11.4	9.7
Income Security	99.7	123.3	207.3	3.6	9.1
Social Security	139.6	207.4	304.6	6.8	6.7
Veterans Benefits and Services	23.0	26.8	35.7	2.6	4.9
Administration of Justice	4.8	7.6	15.0	8.0	12.0
General Government	11.4	7.7	13.0	-6.3	9.1
Net Interest	68.8	138.7	198.8	12.4	6.2

Sources: Department of the Treasury and Office of Management and Budget.

surance (DI), and Aid to Families with Dependent Children (AFDC).

When President Franklin D. Roosevelt signed the social security retirement program into law in 1936 he did so to help the millions of impoverished elderly people that had no other visible means of support. The clear objective of the law was to alleviate acute poverty among the elderly.

Were President Roosevelt alive today he would be amazed at how far his social security program has strayed from its initial intention. He would wonder why retirement benefits are being paid to many people that don't need them and why benefits are taxed at a lower income tax rate than other income. Since he himself worked until the day he died, he might find it curious that the system provides incentives for people to prefer idleness, at huge cost to the economy and the taxpayer, rather than productive activity, especially when it is well known that for many mature people inactivity dulls the mind, induces depression and other health problems, and often promotes premature death. He would also be saddened to learn that social security has not eliminated poverty among the elderly.

President Roosevelt would really be astonished by the enormous cost of running the entire social insurance system. The original payroll tax rate imposed to pay for social insurance was one percent. Today it is 7.65 percent. That amounts to tax increases of 665 percent since the inception of the system. In 1981 retirement benefit payments came to $139.6 billion. In 1993 they came to $304.6 billion, more than a doubling, implying an annual average rate of growth of 6.7 percent.

The increasing economic burden of social insurance programs is attributable to a number of factors. Over the years the relative number of persons covered by social security has increased while benefits have become more generous. In the mid 1960s, under President Lyndon Johnson's "Great Society" program, federal disability insurance (DI) was added and hospital insurance (HI) under Medicare was also introduced. A second reason for the growing burden is that in 1972 Congress provided for the automatic increasing of retirement benefits to offset the effects of inflation. This single act made massive inroads against poverty among the elderly. A third reason is that, with the exception of Medicaid, social insurance programs are financed by payroll taxes and that the growth of payrolls began to slow during the 1970s because of lower rates of productivity growth than those experienced during the 1950s and 1960s. Because of this the growth of revenue slowed unexpectedly and this has been offset by sharp increases in payroll tax rates. The recessions of the mid 1970s and the early 1980s were far deeper and protracted than any recession since World War II and that has necessitated increases in the payroll tax rates that employers must pay for unemployment insurance.

But by far the most important reason for the increasing burden of social insurance has been the ageing of the population. This development has raised the cost of both the retirement and the Medicare systems. In 1945 each retiree's social security income was contributed by over 45 active workers. Because the 65 and over age group has, and will continue to be, the nation's fastest growing age group, that number has dwindled steadily to where it is now in the neighborhood of 3 workers per retiree. In the January 1993 *Annual Report of the Council of Economic Advisers* it was estimated that by the year 2030 there will be only 2.3 workers per retired person. That means that each active worker and his employer will have to provide 43.5 percent of the social security income received by a single retired person.

Financing Social Insurance: The Payroll Tax Explosion

In reviewing specific programs it is first important to be familiar with their method of financing. The factors cited above have led Congress to legislate sharp increases in the payroll tax rates that finance social insurance programs. The tax rate applied to employee payrolls in 1937 was 1 percent. By 1970 the rate had risen to 4.8 percent. It rose again to 6.13 in 1980, and by 1990 it was 7.65 percent, an increase of 25 percent in the space of 10 years. In 1993 employees paid at a rate of 6.2 percent up to a maximum taxable base of $57,600 to finance the retirement program. They contributed an additional 1.45 percent for Medicare up to a maximum taxable base of $135,000.[1] Thus the combined rate is 7.65 percent. Employers pay the same rate. Employers also pay payroll taxes to finance unemployment insurance. Although UI rates vary between businesses

1. Tax rates in 1994 are the same as in 1993. However, the tax base for social security has been raised to $60,000 while the medicare base has been eliminated.

and between states, it is estimated that the average UI tax rate is about 3 percent of payrolls. This brings the typical employer's contribution to almost 11 percent of his labor costs. Self-employed persons pay the full freight of 15.3 percent.

What's wrong with payroll taxes? All taxes have unpleasant consequences. They reduce purchasing power and have the potential for slowing the economy. However, compared with most other taxes, payroll taxes are a very poor way to raise money. The payroll taxes paid by employers represent heavy additions to labor costs. The employer may be able to pass part of the cost back to his employees in the form of lower wages. In that event the taxes reduce consumer spending in the same way as income taxes do this, albeit in a regressive manner.[2] But if it is not possible to shift the entire burden to lower wages, the payroll taxes increase production costs thereby reducing output and employment while also causing the price level to rise. Because payroll tax rates have been increasing steadily and will undoubtedly continue to increase, employer payroll taxes act as a persistent drag on the economy causing the economy to lose output and employment while simultaneously adding to inflation.

A second major problem with heavy reliance on payroll taxes is that the taxes charged to employees and self-employed persons are exceedingly unfair and inequitable. During the 1980s income tax relief was granted to upper bracket incomes. These tax cuts were of little benefit to low income workers who, paying very little in income taxes to begin with, could not benefit from income tax cuts. In the meantime, however, the payroll taxes that these workers paid continued to rise. Indeed payroll taxes now rival the individual income tax as a source of Federal revenue. In 1992 the Federal government collected payroll taxes of $489.7 billion while individual income tax collections amounted to $474.1 billion. Twelve years earlier in 1980 payroll taxes yielded only 72.9 percent as much revenue as the individual income tax, whereas now they yield roughly the same. This increasing reliance on payroll taxes has produced an enormously regressive effect on the distribution of national income.

Payroll taxes also have adverse income distribution effects be-

2. When a tax is regressive this means that the low income taxpayers pay a larger *percentage* of their income in taxes than high income taxpayers.

cause non payroll sources of income are not subject to social insurance taxation at all. Dividends, interest, rents, royalties and capital gains escape social insurance taxation. Also, since the retirement tax is a flat rate up to a maximum taxable base of $60,000, any labor income in excess of this amount completely escapes taxation. A highly paid person with a salary equal to double the maximum tax base pays at an effective rate of only one-half the rate paid by lower income workers.

Although the evidence is not conclusive, a third major problem with payroll taxes is that many workers appear to view the social security taxes they pay, and that are contributed on their behalf by employers, as a substitute for retirement saving. It is likely, also that knowledge of the availability of unemployment compensation causes workers to save less because the nest egg needed to survive a spell of unemployment is perceived to be smaller. If these claims are true the economic growth prospects of the economy are seriously impeded by social insurance programs. When a person puts his savings into a private retirement fund (a provident fund as this is called) the funds are invested in stocks and bonds and are therefore made available to business for investment in plant expansion and modernization. However, social insurance taxes do not finance investment. Each tax dollar that goes into the retirement system is either immediately spent for consumption by currently retired persons or lent to the federal treasury. Social security, and the other social insurance systems, are pay as you go systems as opposed to provident funds. This fact argues strongly for the eventual conversion of social security into a genuine provident fund that could be either publicly or privately established.

The existence of a maximum taxable base for social security is unfair and it is also extremely expensive because labor income above the base escapes taxation. To raise more revenue the first order of business should be removal of the cap. That, it is estimated, would yield at least another $25 billion in revenue, revenue that could be used to reduce taxes, lower the budget deficit, or provide benefits sufficient to raise *all* elderly persons out of poverty and improve their health care.

What is the purpose of the cap? The curious logic that justifies it is that, since millionaires should not receive larger benefits than other people, the millionaires should be taxed at a lower rate. In other words the cap is needed to maintain the dubious principle that a person's benefits should reflect his contributions.

The link between contributions and retirement benefits is extremely tenuous. In the early days retirement benefits vastly exceeded contributions. And despite a lot of complex mumbo jumbo to the contrary, the taxes paid today have very little to do with the benefits received during retirement. They are, rather, geared to the need to provide benefits to those who are presently retired. It is time to get honest about maximum taxable bases recognizing that the link between benefits and contributions is an indefensible fiction and recognizing, at the same time, that the cap is both expensive and a source of unfairness.

A major myth that needs to be destroyed is the myth that because social security has been running a surplus it is not a burden on the Federal budget. According to the propaganda put out by the American Association of Retired Persons, AARP, the retirement system is not part of the Federal budget at all. This is true in a technical sense because social security is classified as "off-budget" in the administrative budget, but comes as a surprise to those who note that in the National Income and Product Accounts Budget contributions for social insurance are included as a revenue source while social security benefits are included in transfer outlays. Both obviously affect the overall deficit. Why, indeed, is social security off budget whereas medicare is not?

The social security surplus is invested in government bonds which earn interest income. The system is therefore subsidized by other revenue sources and by government borrowing. The fact that the social security system runs a surplus is due to the fact that payroll tax rates for the retirement program have been sharply raised. If medicare taxes had been raised by comparable amounts medicare would be running a huge surplus. But that would hardly support the argument that medical expenditures are not out of control or that the money is wisely or efficiently spent. By the same token the social security surplus in no way indicates that social security benefits are not out of control relative to the economy's ability to bear the burden, or that the benefits are distributed fairly and efficiently.

Retirement Benefits: Welfare for the Well-to-Do?

Two essential facts stand out with respect to the payment of social security retirement benefits. The first is that many people who receive social security retirement benefits scarcely need them because they have ample outside income and wealth. The second fact is that social security has not eliminated poverty among the elderly. In 1989 11.4 percent of persons 65 and over received incomes below the Federal poverty standard, a figure that compares favorably with the 13.0 percent for persons under 65. Noteworthy, however, is the fact that the poverty percentage among the elderly rises rapidly with age. Whereas 8.2 percent of persons between the ages of 65 and 69 were below the poverty level, this percentage jumps to 13.5 percent for persons 75 to 79, and to 18.4 percent for persons 85 or older. It is not entirely clear why this is the case. One reason is that as spouses die survivors receive inadequate survivors benefits. As spouses die the private pension funds of survivors decline or are lost entirely.

One of the principles to which most Americans would subscribe is that productive work is desirable and that it would be far better to have potentially productive persons earn income and contribute taxes than to have them be idle and dependent on government checks. However, the social security benefit structure is in sharp violation of this principle. It encourages people to retire rather than providing them with incentives to continue working and contributing to the economy. And that includes paying social insurance taxes.

People under the age of 70 who work are penalized by benefit cuts. Benefits are taxed at a lower rate than other income making a social security dollar worth more than a dollar of other income. Those who continue to work continue to pay payroll taxes whereas those who do not work draw benefits and pay no taxes.

A rational plan for paying benefits recognizes that need should be the primary consideration. Put differently, social security benefits should be paid so as to eliminate poverty among the elderly, not to pay benefits to well-to-do people. But at present social security is the only Federal income maintenance program that is not income tested. To change this it would be necessary to accept the fact that there is no justification for sustaining the fiction of a link between benefits and contributions.

Table 6-2 provides hypothetical examples of benefit schedules that would accomplish what social security ought to accomplish. Specifically, the plan would:

1. Save money by using an income test for the receipt of benefits. The principle is that well to do elderly people should not receive benefits paid for by the average working taxpayer.

2. Recognize the fact that the incidence of poverty rises sharply with age and therefore restructure benefits so as to eliminate poverty for all elderly persons.

3. Adopt the principle that those who are able and willing to continue working past 65 should be rewarded rather than penalized for doing so.

The hypothetical schedules shown in the accompanying table represent an attempt to meet these criteria. To keep matters simple the illustrations are confined to persons with no dependents.

Table 6-2
Illustrative Tables for the Payment of Retirement Benefits

	Schedule 1		Schedule 2		Schedule 3	
Other Income	Benefit	Total Income	Benefit	Total Income	Benefit	Total Income
0	10,000	10,000	12,500	12,500	15,000	15,000
5,000	9,000	14,000	11,500	16,500	14,000	19,000
10,000	8,000	18,000	10,500	20,500	13,000	23,000
15,000	7,000	22,000	9,500	24,500	12,000	27,000
20,000	6,000	26,000	8,500	28,500	11,000	31,000
25,000	5,000	30,000	7,500	32,500	10,000	35,000
30,000	4,000	34,000	6,500	36,500	9,000	39,000
35,000	3,000	38,000	5,500	40,500	8,000	43,000
40,000	2,000	42,000	4,500	44,500	7,000	47,000
45,000	1,000	46,000	3,500	48,500	6,000	51,000
50,000	0	50,000	2,500	52,500	5,000	55,000
55,000	0	55,000	1,500	56,500	4,000	59,000
60,000	0	60,000	500	60,500	3,000	63,000
65,000	0	65,000	0	65,000	2,000	67,000
70,000	0	70,000	0	70,000	1,000	71,000
75,000	0	75,000	0	75,000	0	75,000

Schedule I: This is the basic proposed rate schedule for a person who retires at age 65. Just to pick a round number we establish the principal that no person 65 and over should have a total inflation adjusted income of less than $10,000 per year. The rate schedule is then calculated so as to eliminate benefits altogether for persons whose incomes from other sources are $50,000 or more.

These figures are arbitrary and are picked purely for illustrative purposes. It can be seen that no person has a retirement income less than $10,000. To reach a cut off at $50,000 of total income, it is necessary to reduce benefits by $1,000 for every $5,000 of non social security income. There is, therefore, an effective income tax rate of 20 percent applied to other income, but, at the same time, no retired person suffers a reduction in income. The savings from such a change would be enormous. Eliminating benefits for those with other incomes of $50,000 or more is estimated to save $25 billion. Reducing benefits as other income rises adds additional billions in savings.

Schedule II: This proposed schedule would apply to persons 70 years of age who retire at age 65. The purpose of such a schedule is to raise retirement income with age thereby eliminating the distressing circumstance that poverty increases sharply with age for the 65 and over age group. The schedule therefore raises the basic minimum retirement income by $500 during each additional year of life. Therefore a retired person aged 70 receives a minimum income of $12,500 whereas a retired person age 65 receives $10,000.

Schedule III: This proposed schedule would be applied to persons who work until age 70. The idea is to reward the postponement of retirement by adding another $500 to the basic benefit for every year by which retirement is delayed. Therefore the person who retires at age 70 receives another $2,500 because he is five years older than the 65 retiree, and an additional $2,500 as a reward for continuing to contribute to the economy. His minimum benefit therefore is $15,000.

According to the mortality tables published by the Department of Health and Human Resources the average male who reaches the age of 65 can expect to live another 15 years. If he reaches the age of 70 he can expect another 12 years of life. Assuming that neither person has outside income, the person who retires at 65 will draw benefits under Schedules I and II totalling $220,000 whereas the person who retires at age 70 will draw $234,000 in cumulative benefits. Although this represents an increase of $14,000, this is less than the payroll tax gain due to postponement of retirement. At existing tax rates a person who earns an annual income of $30,000 would pay $11,475 into the system during the five year period of delayed retirement and his employer would contribute an equal amount for a total of $22,950. There is, therefore, a net saving of $8,950 for each person who selects this option.

The benefits from introducing these changes would be enormous. The budget cost of social security would be far lower and the savings could be applied to deficit reduction or permit payroll taxes to be reduced. The latter would raise wages, employment and output and have a beneficial inflationary effect as well. Since retired persons are consumers, while workers are both producers and consumers, providing incentives that encourage productive people to postpone retirement would increase per capita income, thereby raising living standards, and increasing the base for *all* taxes as well. The marginal social benefit of social security would then be vastly greater than at present and might not exceed its marginal social cost.

The suggestion has frequently been made to cut social security benefits by raising the retirement age under social security from 65 to 70 years. The alternative suggested here recognizes that many people do not enjoy their work, are eager to retire, and that there is little reason why they should not be permitted to do so. If you want to retire and go to Florida when you reach age 65 go in good cheer and in good health, but if you enjoy working and can carry your own weight we'd be happy to have you contribute to the economy and to the revenues of the Federal government.

Schedule III shows how this goal, which relies on incentives rather than compulsion, can be achieved. Under this proposal people who delay retirement are rewarded with higher benefits and the more productive of them, as measured by other income, would benefit from an increase in the cut-off point from $50,000 to $75,000 of other income.

It is important to emphasize that these hypothetical schedules make no allowance for inflation. But inflation correction would seem to be appropriate. Otherwise the value of benefits received by retired persons would be arbitrarily eroded by inflation. Indeed, the idea purveyed by President Clinton and others to effect budget savings by temporary suspension of inflation adjustment of benefits is one of the least desirable of the many options available for effecting social security savings.

Summary of Suggestions

To summarize, consider the following list of ways to improve and economize social insurance programs:

1. Eliminate the maximum taxable base of $60,000 for social security thereby raising substantial additional revenue and improving the distribution of income.

2. Cut at least 5 percentage points off the combined employer-employee payroll tax rate of 15.3 percent on the presumption that there is no justification for using payroll taxes to finance Federal disability insurance and Medicare. These programs would then be financed by income taxes and other alternative sources of revenue. The effect would be to improve the distribution of income, increase national savings thereby lowering interest rates and stimulating economic growth, while reducing the drag that rising payroll costs place on production and employment. Ideally, Congress and the President ought to rid the economy from the burden of payroll taxes altogether.

3. Restructure social security retirement benefit schedules to reward rather than penalize work, to income test benefit payments by reducing benefits as non social security income rises, and to eliminate the rising age incidence of poverty for those over 65.

Its time to get honest about social insurance. This means a return to Franklin Roosevelt's principle that the purpose of social security benefits is to eliminate poverty among the elderly, and Lyndon Johnson's conviction that adequate health care for the elderly and the indigent is a social responsibility. Retaining income maintenance programs that are not income tested really does represent the ultimate in irrational policy--budgetary, economic, and social.

Budgetary Cosmetics: The Trust Fund Hoax

Budgetary gimmickry cannot alter the fact that the budget deficit is the difference between government expenditure and tax revenue.

However, the creation of so called Federal trust fund accounts has provided opportunities to pretend otherwise. Payroll taxes are not called taxes but rather "contributions for social insurance." Revenues are deposited in the Social Security and Medicare trust fund accounts and benefits are paid from them. Social security, moreover, is classified as "off budget" a favor that, for some reason, has not been bestowed on Medicare.

Recently trust fund gimmickry has been elevated to a fine art. Senator Sam Nunn, an old hand on the Senate Budget and Armed Services Committees, suggested that all savings from reduced defense spending should go into a *deficit reduction trust fund* account. Taking up the same theme, President Clinton floated the idea of putting all the added revenues from tax increases into such an account and in August 1993 he issued an Executive Order to that effect. What is the point of establishing such a trust fund? Will it reduce the deficit or is this just budgetary window dressing as Republican critics have asserted?

When the revenues paid into a trust fund exceed the benefits paid, the trust fund enjoys a surplus. The accumulated surplus is then considered to represent savings that, in the case of Social Security for example, are regarded as a nest egg that insures income for future retirees. However, the surplus does not simply sit there. Rather, it is turned over to the general fund of the Treasury in exchange for government bonds that earn interest for the trust funds. The Treasury then is free to spend the money so there is, in fact, no nest egg at all.

If the Treasury spends the revenues borrowed from the trust fund, the trust fund surpluses are exactly balanced by government spending. If the Treasury needs to engage in further borrowing, there will be an overall deficit. The magnitude of this deficit is independent of the presence or absence of the trust funds. Indeed a trust fund surplus changes nothing except to reassure people, often falsely, that there will be enough money available to pay for their retirement and health care. If the trust funds ran deficits they would then have to borrow from the Treasury unless legislation were passed that reduces outlays or increases revenues.

Exactly the same would be true in the case of the deficit reduction trust fund. Increased revenues stemming from a rise in tax rates would be deposited in the fund which would then transfer the revenues to the general fund of the Treasury in exchange for government bonds. The effect on the overall budget deficit would then depend entirely on whether the Treasury spends the money or whether it uses it to reduce its borrowing. The overall deficit would still be exactly equal to the difference between the Treasury's total spending and its tax receipts from all sources.

Suppose, for the sake of argument, that this particular trust fund is prevented from lending its receipts to the Treasury. Being denied the funds while having to pay its bills, the Treasury could simply sell an equivalent amount of bonds to private parties instead of to the trust fund. The deficit continues to be the difference between the Treasury's total outlays and total tax receipts. The only difference is that the Treasury borrows from the private sector instead of the trust fund account.

A tax increase will reduce the deficit if government expenditures are not raised. If expenditures are raised by the amount of the extra receipts there will be no reduction in the deficit. The President and Congress can affect the outcome by legislation that changes tax laws and expenditure programs. They cannot affect or control it by creating trust funds.

Suppose the increased taxes go into a trust fund and are unaccompanied by higher spending so that the deficit initially declines by the amount of the higher taxes. The higher taxes destroy purchasing power and reduce consumption spending. This then has depressing multiplier effects on GDP. That, in turn, lowers tax receipts, raises transfer outlays, and widens the cyclical deficit. Who is supposed to pay for this addition to the deficit? Is it appropriate to take it out of the Treasury or should the money come out of the trust fund since it was the higher taxes that went into the trust fund that initiated the unfavorable revenue feedback? Should we engage in fiscal cosmetics or should we be honest about the budget?

Trust funds are highly useful for generating misinformation, raising false expectations, and obscuring real problems. Social Security is a prime example. The AARP, a very powerful organization that lobbies on behalf of the elderly claims, in its publications, that social security benefits do not add to the budget deficit because the trust fund account enjoys annual surpluses and because social security is an "off-budget" item. The implication is that social security benefits should never be slashed because they have no effect on the deficit.

In a recent issue of its magazine, *Modern Maturity,* Lovola W. Burgess, President of AARP wrote that:

> ...despite its important role in our society, Social Security is still misunderstood, especially as it relates to the federal budget deficit. Put simply Social Security does not add to the federal deficit. In fact Social Security has built a substantial reserve to help pay benefits to current and future retirees.[3]

It's a certainty that the experts at AARP know as well as the rest of us that a rise in social security benefits raises government transfer outlays and therefore increases the deficit. They also surely know that increases in payroll taxes add to federal revenues and reduce the deficit. Although it is good of AARP to protect the interests of its membership, including myself, I'm not at all happy that this has to be done by obfuscation. When I begin to receive social security benefits in a few years this will be a drain on the budget just as any other expenditure category, no more no less. By pretending that social security has been revealed from upon high to be sacred and untouchable, we merely obscure the fact that there are real problems that need to be addressed. I'm not at all sure that persons such as myself should receive social security benefits when we are likely to have plenty of outside retirement income, while many elderly people continue to live in poverty and poor children receive inadequate medical attention.

When any federal expenditure category is exempt from the budget cutting knife this exemption caries with it the assumption that the last dollar of expenditure on the favored program is always more valuable than the last dollar spent on other things. Thus exempting the program is bound to be inefficient and creates a misallocation of public expenditure funds.

Congress, in its infinite wisdom, has chosen to classify social security as "off-budget", a favor not bestowed on similar trust fund accounts such as Medicare. Does this mean that social security benefits do not add to the deficit while Medicare expenditures do, or does it mean that the off budget deficit is simply lower while the on budget deficit is higher by the same amount? It's time to cut through the smoke screen and quit trying to kid people into thinking

---

3. *Modern Maturity*, June-July, 1993, p. 5.

that there is plenty of money available for their retirement when that is not at all the case.

7

Financing Health Care

Unpleasant Facts About Health Care Finance

Federal health expenditures increased from $66.1 billion in 1981 to $229.7 billion in 1993, well more than a tripling in the space of twelve years. This implied an average annual rate of growth of 11.0 percent, a rate that has accelerated to 12.2 percent since 1987. Over this same ten year period the rate of growth of nominal GDP was only 6.4 percent. Health expenditures are not only gobbling up an increasing fraction of the federal budget, they are doing the same thing to State budgets, and they are also gobbling up an increasing fraction of national income. Some of these facts are shown in ***Table 7-1***.

Table 7-1
National Health Expenditures

	1970	1975	1980	1985	1990
Total (billions)	$74.4	$132.9	$249.1	$420.1	$666.2
% of GDP	7.0	8.3	9.1	10.5	12.2
Per capita	$346	$592	$1059	$1699	$2566

Source: Levit, K. R, et al. "National Health Expenditures," *Health Care Financing Review,* Fall 1991.

In 1990 Medicare and Medicaid costs accounted for 15 percent of all federal expenditures, while Medicaid costs accounted for 11 percent of all state expenditures.[1] As a percentage of GDP national health expenditures were 5.3 percent in 1960, 9.1 percent in 1980,

1. Newhouse, Joseph P., "Medical Care Costs: How Much Welfare Loss?" *Journal of Economic Perspectives,* Summer 1992.

Table 7-2
Health Expenditures in Selected Countries, 1989

Country	Percent of GDP	Per Capita in U.S. Dollars	Percent of U.S. Outlay
United States	11.8	2,354	100
Sweden	8.8	1,361	58
Canada	8.7	1,683	71
France	8.7	1,274	54
Netherlands	8.3	1,135	48
Austria	8.2	1,093	46
Germany	8.2	1,232	52
Switzerland	7.8	1,376	58
Italy	7.6	1,050	45
Norway	7.6	1,234	52
Ireland	7.3	658	28
Belgium	7.2	980	42
Finland	7.1	1,067	45
New Zealand	7.1	820	35
Australia	7.6	1,125	48
Japan	6.7	1,035	44
Denmark	6.3	912	39
Portugal	6.3	464	20
United Kingdom	5.8	836	36

Source: Schieber, George J., et al., "Health Care Systems in Twenty-four Countries, *Health Affairs,* Fall 1991.

12.2 percent in 1990, 14.3 percent in 1993 and, if present trends continue, are projected to come to 18 percent in the year 2000 and 26.1 percent in the year 2030. As can be seen in ***Table 7-2*** the United States spends far more both as a percentage of GDP and on a per capita basis than any other industrial country, many of which have far more comprehensive health insurance systems.

Table 7-3 shows how the health care dollar is allocated. The share of health care attributable to hospital costs and physician services has remained remarkably stable. However, the share allocated to program administration has risen 53 percent since 1980 while the share allocated to research and construction has dwindled by 52 percent. With the exception of these sharp changes it is evident that health inflation is general, covering all major health care categories.

Table 7-3
Allocation of the Health Care Dollar
(percent of total)

	1970	1980	1990
Personal care	87.2	87.7	87.9
Hospital	37.5	41.0	38.4
Physician Service	18.3	16.8	18.9
Dentistry	6.3	5.8	5.1
Drugs	11.8	.6	8.2
Nursing Homes	6.6	8.0	8.0
Administrative Cost of Insurance	3.8	4.9	5.8
Government Public Health	1.9	2.9	2.9
Research and Construction	7.1	4.5	3.4

Source: Levit, Katherine, et al., "National Health Expenditures 1990," *Health Care Financing Review,* Fall 1991.

The federal government finances hospital care for the elderly under the Medicare program and participates in the joint federal-state Medicaid program. Medicare is financed by payroll taxes and operates through the HI trust fund. If current trends continue the HI trust fund is projected to be exhausted in the year 2005, and it is estimated that payroll tax rates will have to be raised another 3.5 percentage points over the next 75 years to keep the trust fund solvent. The Supplemental Medical Insurance program, which finances physician services for the elderly, is financed in part by monthly premiums contributed by those eligible for Medicare and from general tax revenues. Projections indicate that these premiums are likely to rise from $46.10 per month in 1995 to $310.50 in the year 2020.[2] ***Table 7-4*** shows the effects of health care on the federal budget.

Table 7-4
Federal Health Care Expenditures
(billions of dollars)

	1980	1986	1990
Total Federal Outlays	590.9	990.3	1,393.0
Health Expenditures	72.0	132.8	195.3
Medicare	37.5	77.4	111.2
Medicaid	14.5	24.8	42.9
Veterans	6.2	9.9	11.4
Health as % of Federal Budget	12.2	13.4	14.0

Source: Congressional Budget Office, *The Economic Budget Outlook: Fiscal years* 1992-1996.

About 20 percent of the increasing cost of health care is attributable to increases in the quantity of health care consumed while 80 percent is simply inflation. Quantity has increased in part as the result of greater use of outpatient facilities owned by doctors. The number of cat scans rose 400 percent between 1980 and 1990. In 1980 only one in every 400 men aged 65 and over had availed himself of coronary by-pass surgery, whereas in 1990 one in every hundred men had done so.

As shown in ***Table 7-5***, medical inflation is the only component of consumer price inflation that had not declined since the inflationary 1970s. Medical inflation alone contributed about one percentage point to the annual increase in consumer prices in very recent years.

Macroeconomic Problems

When inflation in one component of consumer spending causes that component to encroach on others this retards economic expan-

2. Source: Health Technical Panel, "The Medicare Program: Projection and Options for Change, " *Report to the 1991 Advisory Council on Social Security,* July 1991.

Table 7-5
Consumer Prices
(Average Annual Rates of Growth)

	All Items	Food	Housing	Apparel	Medical	Energy	All Excluding Medical*
1970-80	7.8	8.0	8.3	4.4	8.2	12.9	7.8
1980-90	4.7	4.3	4.7	3.2	8.1	1.7	4.1
1990-92	3.6	2.1	3.4	2.9	8.1	0.4	2.6

* Author's estimates.
Source: Bureau of Labor Statistics

sion in the entire economy. Most gains in real labor compensation during the past decade have been gobbled up by rising health insurance premiums leaving consumers with relatively less income to spend on other things. When, as is presently the case, a large fraction of the health care dollar is supplied by employers, this raises labor costs, depresses wages, reduces employment, and raises the prices of goods and services. In 1991 health care costs to employers took as much as 14 percent of payrolls for all companies nationwide.[3] Medical inflation now represents the same sort of drag on the economy that energy inflation placed on it during the 1970s. With medical inflation accounting for one third of all inflation in the United States, with inflation serving as a principal obstacle to the use of expansionary monetary policies, and with rising premiums continually adding to labor costs, it is clear that medical inflation serves as a heavy source of unemployment and failure of the economy to attain potential output and rapid growth.

Industry Performance Criteria

Economists use the pure competition model as an ideal against which they evaluate the performance of an industry with respect to efficiency and the optimal allocation of resources. In this ideal model the industry produces a uniform product or service, it has many firms supplying the good or service, and no single producer is large enough to be able to influence price. If market price temporarily exceeds the average cost of production (including sufficient

3. Faltermayer, Edmund, "How to Close the Health Care Gap," *Fortune*, May 21, 1990.

return to the owner to reward him for remaining in the industry) the resulting extra profit margin attracts new suppliers and their capital into the industry. The added supply contributed by the new entrants then drives price down and eliminates excess profits. Because of these competitive conditions equilibrium in the industry is attained when price equals minimum average cost as well as marginal cost. Marginal cost is the cost of producing the last unit of output. When price and marginal cost are equal the last consumer to receive the product pays a price exactly equal to the cost of producing the unit.

This is a welfare criterion that economists apply to industry performance. The condition is violated when monopolistic elements--known as market imperfections--enable producers to charge prices that are in excess of marginal cost. When this is the case some consumers who are willing to pay a price in excess of the cost of production are rationed out of the market. This is certainly true in the health-care industry where the supply of doctors is sharply restricted by medical school admissions practices and by insufficient medical school capacity. The free entry criterion is violated and this is a major reason for the excessive costs and high incomes that characterize the medical profession.

A competitive environment rewards efficiency and punishes inefficiency because high cost producers are forced out of the industry. Thus a competitive environment provides strong incentives to produce at minimum cost, to introduce new technology, and to supply the product at the lowest possible cost to the consumer.

The American health care industry is woefully lacking when measured against the welfare criteria of economists. It is heavily monopolized because entry is restricted and because doctors, hospitals, and drug companies are permitted to engage in anti competitive practices. It is also very important to understand that one of the principal sources of economic inefficiency is the circumstance that, unlike other industries, hardly any of the participants in the industry--consumers, producers, middle men --have an *incentive* to cut costs and improve efficiency. Finally, and again in contrast to other industries, the services provided by the American health care industry are delivered in an incredibly uneven manner. For those that can afford it, the system probably provides the best care in the world. At the same time, although the U.S. is the only country that spends more than 10 percent of its GDP on health, life expectancy is lower and infant mortality is higher than in other industrial countries.

Incentives: The Consumer

In 1993 the Ford Motor Company reached a new collective bargaining agreement with the United Auto Workers. In that agreement the company undertook to provide comprehensive medical insurance for its employees. Employees would neither be responsible for deductibles nor co-payments. Health care is a free good for workers with such coverage--they can consume as much of it as they wish without this costing them a dime in out of pocket expenditures. Evidence suggests that the rapid growth of employer coverage has caused many people to view health care as a virtual freebie. They know that somebody has to pay for it, but since the level of benefits is not linked to the costs perceived by individuals, there is little reason to economize. Indeed employer-paid premiums are not taxable income to workers. Therefore a dollar paid in health insurance premiums on behalf of an employee is worth more to the employee than a dollar of wages.

That is a major flaw in health care financing--consumers overconsume health care because its out of pocket cost is low. In 1960 56 percent of medical costs were out of pocket payments made by the patient. Because of the growth of third party payments by employers and governments, this percentage declined to 23 percent in 1990. The decline in out of pocket payments has greatly reduced the patient's incentive to inform himself with respect to appropriate and economical treatment and permits him to consume as much expensive health care as he wants without considering its cost.

One controlled experiment disclosed that a group that was given comprehensive health insurance consumed 30 percent more health care than a comparable group that was given catastrophic health insurance plus a lump sum payment equal to the group's average estimated health care costs.[4] The second group had an incentive to economize so as to pocket as much of the lump sum payment as possible; the first group did not. This over-consumption, caused by what is known as *moral hazard* due to insurance and third-party

4. As described in the *Economic Report of the President*, January 1993, p. 142.

payment, is exacerbated because there is, at present, a tax subsidy to employers that encourages insurance coverage with low copayments and deductibles and encourages workers to accept health insurance coverage in place of wage increases.[5] The cost to the government of this subsidy has been estimated as roughly $75 billion per year. Also, because it is believed that insurance will cover the costs, expensive technologies are introduced even though it is not clear that they would be justified if consumers had to pay for them directly. Finally, a tendency on the part of insurance companies to cover hospitalization but not outpatient treatment has encouraged consumers to go to hospitals, even when this is far more costly than outpatient treatment, because that reduces the out of pocket payments that the consumer has to make.

These facts suggest that the incentives provided by the system to consumers is horribly perverse. Not only does the system encourage overconsumption of health care on the part of the insured, but, at the same time, it drives many people out of the health insurance network. The Census Bureau has reported that there were, in 1993, 39 million persons in the United States that lacked health insurance of any kind. Another disheartening fact is that this number has risen rapidly, increasing by 2 million in 1993 alone. These people are not all poor people. Some are denied health insurance by insurance companies by reason of age and prior medical history. Some, such as self employed people, are excluded from larger health insurance pools. Many of them, usually healthier and younger members of society, drop their medical insurance voluntarily when premiums rise. This dropping out, known as *adverse selection,* means that the remaining pool of insured persons is older and less healthy. Consequently the cost, per individual, of providing health insurance to the remaining insured increases as the healthier persons drop out and this means that insurance companies are forced to raise insurance premiums. As the premiums continue to rise, more people drop out and premiums are forced up again. The outcome of this vicious circle is excessively high premiums for the insured combined with rapid increases in the number of those that lack medical coverage.

---

5. Roughly speaking, moral hazard means that insurance coverage invites people to get sloppy. If you buy a new car and do not take out theift insurance you are likely to be very careful about locking your car when you park it. However, if you enjoy insurance coverage against theft you might sometimes forget to lock the car. Indeed you might not worry about theft at all if the insurance premiums were paid by someone else.

It is entirely conceivable that the process of adverse selection could continue to narrow the insurance pool to the point where only the rich can afford health insurance.

Some students of health insurance argue that the figure of 39 million uninsured vastly understates the problem of inadequate coverage. In the 1994 *Economic Report of the President* the Council of Economic Advisers points out that while the number of uninsured is 39 million, at least four times that many lack "health security" in the sense that they are uninsured at some time during the year. This is largely due to the fact that employers supply the health insurance. People that are laid off or in transit between jobs often lose their insurance. Because of the fear of losing their health insurance, people tend to cling to their jobs rather than seek new opportunities. This greatly impedes labor mobility and reduces economic growth, lowers job satisfaction, and causes people to remain in jobs for which they are overqualified. A health insurance system that gets employers out of the picture would appear to have many advantages.

The present system of health-care finance in the United States is clearly flawed. To guard against moral hazard individuals, rather than employers, must be made financially responsible for their health care spending decisions. To guard against adverse selection it is necessary to mandate that all persons must carry at least a minimum package of health insurance. These are the rock-bottom requirements of a rational system.

Incentives: Physicians

Physicians and hospitals are compensated on a fee for service basis rather than the estimated cost of curing a specific disease. This system provides no incentive for providers to introduce efficiencies, control costs, and stem the rise in fees. The cost of providing health care is also inflated because of the ability of doctors to engage in anti competitive practices. The supply of new doctors is sharply limited by inadequate medical school facilities and by the influence of doctors' lobbies such as the American Medical Association (AMA) over medical school admissions policies. It has been estimated that roughly 9 out of every 10 qualified medical school applicants are turned down. Doctors have learned that they can behave as regional monopolists by forming clinics, such as orthopedic clinics, to which all orthopedists in the region belong. This eliminates competition, allows doctors to charge higher fees, and be sloppy and inconsiderate of their patients. The only option available to the patient is for him to seek treatment in a larger city where regional monopolization is more difficult. Nearly every county in the nation has its own medical society. When a newly-minted physician goes into practice he is told what fees to charge. If he fails to comply he is blacklisted and charged with being "unethical". As shown in Table 7-6 the average fee received by doctors in the United States vastly exceeds the fees that Canadian doctors receive. And remember, Canada is the world's second highest per capita health care spender. Finally, doctors are able to exclude nurses and paramedics from performing services they could easily provide.

Not only are there not enough doctors, but the existing number of doctors is not optimally allocated between different medical fields. It is at the primary care level that diagnosis is done and preventive medicine is practiced. Governor Howard Dean of New Hampshire, himself a physician and a leader in the drive for health care reform, has pointed out that only 15 percent of the present pool of physicians is in primary care. He believes that a far more effective allocation of doctors would be to have 50 percent of them delivering primary care. The present incentive system, however, rewards doctors more handsomely for moving into specialized fields such as surgery and radiology.

Table 7-6
U.S. Physician Fees Versus Medicare and Canadian Fees, 1993

	Private	Medicare	Canadian
Intermediate Office Visit	$35	$31	$25
Follow Up Hospital Visit	53	45	15
Inguinal Hernia Repair	876	335	253
Cataract Removal with Lens Implant	2,021	941	440
Coronary By-Pass (Three Grafts)	4,791	2,225	1,129

Source: Urban Institute, *Policy and Research Report,* Summer 1993.

The fee for service payment system rewards doctors for providing costly services whether or not they are needed. In an attempt to economize on doctor and hospital fees Medicare has adopted the practice of compensating physicians with fixed fees for specific diagnostic categories. In other words doctors and hospitals are compensated for the cost of curing a disease rather than the number of tests and hospital visits they make. This method of providing compensation removes the reward that doctors and hospitals get by running up the number of inessential tests and procedures. Applied to hospitals such a fee system would create an incentive for hospitals and doctors to discharge patients as early as possible.

Malpractice

Doctors currently labor under the threat of malpractice litigation. Premiums paid by doctors for malpractice insurance have been rising at an annual rate of 15 percent, and the fees doctors charge include the premiums they have to pay. Because of the threat of malpractice suits doctors engage in so-called defensive medicine which means that they prescribe more tests and procedures than necessary. The estimated cost of defensive medicine in 1989 was $20 billion, or about 18 percent of physician fees. The threat of malpractice has also driven some doctors away from high risk treatment categories, and the resulting supply shortages have raised the costs of these categories.

The issue of malpractice must be addressed because it is a principal source of medical inflation. It raises insurance premiums and doctors' fees and primarily benefits the attorneys who run up their billings by spending enormous time attempting to prove or disprove negligence on the part of the doctor.

One potentially promising plan to reduce the cost of malpractice is known as enterprise liability. Under this plan the doctor continues to pay malpractice insurance premiums to his insurance company. However, in the event of a law suit the allegedly injured patient sues the insurance company rather than the doctor. The doctor is therefore indemnified against litigation and this permits him to discontinue defensive medicine. The plan also calls for no-fault malpractice insurance. This means that compensation is granted when the outcome of a procedure is significantly worse than normally expected without having to show that the outcome was the result of negligence or incompetence. The presence or absence of negligence on the part of the physician therefore no longer needs to be proved and this means that litigation becomes far less costly, time consuming, and complex.

Incompetent and negligent doctors will remain under pressure to improve their performance under this program because it is in the interests of the insurance companies either to increase the malpractice premiums of negligent doctors or to deny them coverage altogether. A doctor no longer able to retain coverage is then on his own. If he continues to practice he becomes personally liable. Hopefully, such doctors will be driven out of the profession as patients abandon doctors that have lost their malpractice insurance.

Incentives: Insurance Companies

Although it is in the interest of insurance companies to control costs, the incentive to do so is dulled by the fact that doctors control the boards of directors of private health plan groups, while medical society approval is required for membership on the boards of such groups. Thus the insurance carriers are controlled by the very doctors who benefit most from higher fees. Most insurance carriers pay for services provided by high-cost and low-cost doctors alike so that doctors' incentives to compete with respect to price are eliminated.

As entitlements under third party payers, both private and public, have expanded it has become far easier for doctors to increase their fees. This, along with exotic new technologies, has provided physicians with incentives to move into higher paid specialties. In part because of this the incomes of doctors have risen far more rapidly than the incomes of persons outside the medical field.

Efforts, on the parts of insurance companies and the government, to contain costs have had the consequence of bloating administrative costs. These expenditures, which amounted to $80 billion in 1991, are vastly greater than in other countries. Canada, which has universal health insurance, spends only one half as much as the United States on administrative costs per patient. These costs include the costs of premium collection, underwriting health insurance applications, verifying eligibility for benefits, preparing checks, and other administrative expenses. One student of administrative costs estimated that eliminating private health insurance would reduce administrative costs by enough to provide coverage for the 39 million Americans that presently lack health insurance.[6]

Incentives: Hospitals and Nurses

Hospital profits have been low and some 700 hospitals closed their doors between 1980 and 1990. Despite the pressure to economize it has been difficult for hospitals to do so. Hospitals must compete for doctors as well as for patients. To attract doctors they must offer attractive facilities and state of the art technology. This creates pressure for hospitals to buy expensive equipment and provide added bed capacity even when the hospital administration knows that the facilities will be underused and that duplicate equipment is available at nearby facilities.

Just as the cost-based fee system eliminates the incentive for doctors to reduce their fees, so also does the fee system eliminate the incentive to cut hospital costs. The system of compensation rewards hospitals with more revenue for providing more patient care as well as more expensive care.

There is little in the health care field that has not become more expensive. Nurses were relatively poorly paid in 1980. But in the subsequent decade nurses averaged a 25 percent increase in their real hourly earnings. Some of this was needed to attract persons into the nursing profession, and a significant part of it reflects the fact that the average hospital patient is sicker because the hospital stays for the less sick have become shorter, while much of the treatment of the less sick has moved to the growing number of outpatient facilities owned by doctors.

Drug Companies

In 1990 sales of the drug industry reached $67 billion or about 10 percent of the health care dollar. Drug prices zoomed upwards during the 1980s. As estimated by the Bureau of Labor Statistics the increase in 1991 was 9.4 percent, more than double the increase in all consumer prices. The rate of increase in drug prices slowed to

6. Weil, Thomas P., "Is It Time for NIH?"*Best's Review,* April 1990.

5.7 percent in 1992, but this was still almost twice as fast as the overall rate of consumer price inflation of 3.0 percent. Furthermore, and despite the overall slow down in drug inflation, the Senate Special Committee on Aging reported that eight of the thirty one leading drug manufacturers had raised their prices by more than three times the rate of inflation in 1992.

Do drug companies have an incentive to hold down drug prices? Unfavorable publicity may help, but the incentive system does not. Patients pay for expensive medications prescribed by their doctors without hesitation, especially when part or all of the cost is covered by insurance. The developers of new medications receive patent protection that grants them a monopoly that delays the appearance of inexpensive generic substitutes for an excessive number of years. Doctors are cultivated by pharmaceutical companies and, wishing to seem up to date, frequently prescribe the newer, more expensive, medications even though cheaper generic substitutes might do just as well.

The justification for patent protection is that without it there would be no advances in medical technology and in the development of new drugs. There certainly is truth in this as recognized by the founding fathers when they provided for patent protection in the Constitution. However, the exclusive rights granted to patent holders has been badly abused by people and companies that take out patents merely for the purpose of obtaining the right to litigate.

The exclusive right to market a new drug allows drug companies to charge prices for prescription drugs that bear no reasonable relationship to the cost of production. The justification is that without exorbitant profits the incentive to engage in research and development of new drugs would be dulled. Again there is a grain of truth in this although the stock market performance of drug companies taken as a whole indicates that their profits have been exorbitantly high.

A Rational Health-Care Plan

Despite its huge and growing cost, the health-care delivery system of the United States does not get the job done. It is far too expensive; its growing burden damages the economy; and many people overconsume health care while others underconsume it. Thirty nine million Americans lack health insurance of any kind and four times that many lack continuous coverage. Many of those who are covered would lose their insurance at least temporarily if they tried to switch to better jobs. Only 40 percent of those with incomes below the poverty line are currently covered by Medicaid, a percentage that has been *declining* despite rising costs, and 58 percent of the care provided to the elderly is by out of pocket expenditure despite Medicare coverage. Doctors are leaving high Medicaid density areas and hospitals are closing in such areas.[7] The supply of physicians is inadequate and the distribution of physicians is sub optimal both with respect to location and specialization. Last but not least, the specter of catastrophic illness threatens to wipe out life-time savings leaving survivors destitute. Those who would claim that the American health-care system is the best in the world should be asked to explain why infant mortality is higher and life expectancy lower than in many other countries.

Although Americans believe in providing a safety net for the indigent they also seem to believe that someone else ought to pay for it. Much of the treatment received by poor people is provided in the emergency rooms of hospitals. Such treatment is frequently very expensive because it is postponed until the illness has become acute. Hospitals generally retrieve the cost of ER treatment by raising fees to other patients and their insurance companies. This hardly represents an intelligent or equitable way to provide health care for poor people.

It would seem to be essential to replace the current hit or miss system by a system of mandatory universal health insurance. Such a system would encourage early diagnosis and would eliminate adverse selection. The per capita cost of health care would be substantially reduced. Nevertheless the total cost of health care would increase sharply if another 39 million persons were provided with insurance.

There are three ways to finance health care. The financial burden of health care can be placed on employers; it can be placed on individuals; and it can be placed on governments. The present system draws on all three sources of support. However, the balance

7. David Satcher, M.D., "Targeting the Underserved: The Urgency of Health Care Reform," *Tennessee's Business,* Volume 3, 1992.

has shifted over the years so that at present a smaller fraction is paid by individuals while larger fractions are paid by employers and the government. This trend has increased moral hazard and encouraged overconsumption of health care by the insured. Because health insurance is not mandatory it has promoted adverse selection thereby increasing the pool of the uninsured while raising the average cost to the insured.

The great advantage of placing the primary burden for health insurance on the individual is that it encourages him to economize on the use of the health care system. The disadvantage is that many individuals are unable to afford health care. Conversely the advantage of government responsibility is that coverage can be provided to the needy. The disadvantage is that, by freeing the individual from responsibility, overconsumption is encouraged.

Economic analysis suggests that the worst of all systems is a system that places heavy responsibility on employers. Although employers pay health insurance premiums in part out of funds that would otherwise have gone into higher wages, thereby in fact transferring a portion of the burden to workers, such a system creates the illusion that health care is a free good. Because health insurance is job dependent the system fails to cover those who do not, for one reason or another, enjoy employment. Because coverage lapses if a worker quits to seek a better job, workers are frozen into their existing jobs. As a result labor mobility is impeded, workers are less productive than they might be, and job satisfaction is reduced. Because rising premiums raise labor costs they tend to reduce output and employment and the resulting restriction in the supply of goods and services pushes up prices. Thus an employer based system is a severe impediment to economic growth and high employment.

These considerations suggest that a rational health care system would replace employer responsibility with a system that relies on individuals with the assistance of government in a way that maximizes the advantages of each while minimizing the disadvantages. The first order of business, then, would be to eliminate employer-paid health insurance. The tax breaks that employers currently receive should be transferred to individuals in the form of tax credits. The cost savings to employers would, in part, be passed on to workers in the form of higher wages thereby increasing the ability of individuals to finance their health care.

An effective individual-government system of financing health care might be as follows:

1. Have the federal government provide catastrophic health insurance to all persons to prevent their assets from being wiped out by catastrophic illness. Such insurance is characterized by the fact that all covered health-care costs are paid by the insurance subject to a very high deductible for which the patient is responsible. At present private catastrophic policies often involve deductibles as high as $50,000 but cover all additional costs with life-time coverage as high as $1 million. Such a program should be financed by contributions from all taxpayers through the federal income tax. The size of the deductible would vary with respect to individuals' income and wealth. Persons with low income and wealth would be entitled to a low deductible. The deductible would then rise for individuals with higher income and wealth.

2. Mandate that all individuals be required to purchase a minimum package of health insurance designed to assist in defraying the catastrophic deductible. Coverage by insurance companies must be provided by carriers regardless of health status, age, or previous medical history. Premiums must be established on a "community-rating" system. This means that different persons cannot be charged different premiums for identical policies. An income test should be used to provide coverage for the indigent under an expanded Medicaid program. Those who want more than the minimum package would be welcome to purchase additional insurance. Inasmuch as the individual is responsible for the catastrophic deductible and inasmuch as coverage is universal, both adverse selection and moral hazard are largely eliminated.

3. Retired persons would be covered by the catastrophic insurance program. This would permit other costs to be cut by eliminating Medicare and assisting elderly persons with the financing of the catastrophic deductible by increasing their social security benefits by an amount equal to their age group's average annual health-care costs. Because this provides incentives not to overconsume health care, health expenditures by persons 65 and over would be reduced.

4. To provide incentives for doctors and hospitals to cut costs, the fee for service system would be eliminated and benefit payments would involve fixed compensation for the treatment of specific diagnostic categories. It is very doubtful whether medical inflation can be stemmed without government action to alter the medical compensation system.

5. Improvements in the efficiency of health care consumption would be effected by the provision of more and better information to consumers. Therefore, follow the lead of Medicare by providing information on mortality rates for different hospitals. Also publicize information on local doctor, hospital, and drug prices, as well as with comparisons to other regions and alternative treatment options.

6. Take strenuous steps to alleviate supply shortages. The first order of business is to increase the number of doctors, providing new entrants into the medical field with incentives to select primary care. To do this provide a standardized federal admissions test for admission to medical schools together with stiff fines for schools that discriminate on the basis of other criteria. Supply a generous federal loan program to finance medical tuition. Make the loans repayable by public service in low income areas in need of primary care physicians. Hospitals and medical schools are important components of the economic infrastructure. Increased government investment in the infra structure would include the expansion of hospital and medical school facilities.

7. Reform the malpractice racket by mandating enterprise liability and adopting no-fault malpractice insurance. Also establish clear, tough, and uniform criteria to be used by the courts in determining health issues that qualify as suitable for litigation.

These are the basic ingredients of a rational system. The intention is to increase and reallocate supply, improve incentives to economize, provide universal coverage, eliminate defensive medicine, and insure individuals against financial ruin in the event of catastrophic illness.

8

Cutting the Deficit: Agriculture, Defense, and Tax Expenditures

Three additional budgetary issues are raised in this chapter. The expensive federal farm program provides a perfect example of how a federal program that was intended to serve a critical need at one time can become entrenched, do the opposite of what it was intended to do, and remain costly even after it has long since outlived its social and economic usefulness. The defense program provides a good example of the budgetary and economic problems created by a declining industry. Tax expenditures, finally, demonstrate the degree to which the federal government hides its influence over the economy and the extent to which it has abdicated its responsibilities by throwing tax breaks at people and corporations rather than defining a rational above board basis for its programs.

The Federal Farm Program: Bucolic Plague?

The anti smoking crusade in the United States has reached epic proportions. Nonetheless the Department of Agriculture busily lavishes subsidies on tobacco farmers. Almost 90 percent of the $20 billion the government spent on agriculture in 1993 was for what is euphemistically described as income "stabilization." To be accurate, it meant redistribution of income from taxpayers to farmers, primarily the more affluent echelon. As an average the subsidy amounts to roughly $6,000 per farmer. The taxpayer foots this bill and, in his role as consumer, pays about $6 billion more for every percentage point increase in the cost of food caused by price support programs.

In the summer of 1993 many mid-western states were beset by seemingly endless rainfall and flooding. Many farmers in Iowa, Illinois, and elsewhere lost large portions of their crops. One would hope that, at such a time, the federal farm program would come to the rescue of these unfortunates. Regrettably quite the opposite is true. Reduction in the supply of crops raises prices and this *reduces* federal payments to farmers at a time when the need for assistance is most critical. This is because assistance to farmers works through devices that boost prices. That only helps farmers that have crops to sell. It does not help poor farmers with little to sell, and it helps well to do farmers in a perverse way since the less they have to sell the lower their payments from the government.

Federal assistance to agriculture in the form of land grants, establishment of land grant colleges and agricultural extension services, dates back to the early 19th century. The expensive farm program that we know today, designed to regulate production and boost prices and incomes, dates from the early days of President Franklin Roosevelt's New Deal when rural poverty was widespread.[1] Its continuation even in the face of growing rural prosperity is variously justified on the grounds of preservation of the family farm and on the grounds that federal assistance is needed because agricultural prices and incomes are subject to sharp and unpredictable fluctuations.

Instead of making direct payments to poor farmers so as to alleviate rural poverty, the farm program attempts to raise farm income by interfering with the price system. Government interference with the price system is almost never a good idea and the farm program is living proof of that fact. The dubious theory that underpinned much of the New Deal's economic program was that recovery would be facilitated if prices could be jacked up to their previous prosperity levels. In the absence of demand increases, this

1. This is not completely accurate. Prior to the New Deal, during the administration of President Herbert Hoover, a Federal Farm Board was created to stabilize commodity prices. The idea was to establish a forecast or trend price. If market prices are below trend prices the board would purchase crops, if the price were above the trend the board would sell. Since the level of the trend price was politically influenced it was unrealistically high. The board therefore found itself in the position of always having to buy while never being able to sell. It therefore very quickly exhausted its "revolving fund."

could only be accomplished by restrictive practices designed to reduce supply. By 1933 prices had fallen some 30 percent below their 1929 levels. Real GDP had also fallen 30 percent. With the economy flat on its back, Professor George Warren, one of the deep thinkers in President Roosevelt's brain trust, reasoned that, since real output and prices had both dropped 30 percent since 1929, it stood to reason that if prices could be "reflated", then output and employment would recover. Looking for a radical solution, President Roosevelt embraced this bizarre notion. It found expression in the National Industrial Recovery Act (NIRA) which suspended the antitrust laws and encouraged business to form trade associations so that they could collude to restrict output and charge monopoly prices. It also found expression in a destructive attempt artificially to inflate farm prices by plowing under crops and slaughtering animals. How consumers were expected to buy the higher priced output was never made clear, nor was there any explanation for how employment could be raised by reducing production in agriculture and elsewhere.

Any reasonably competent student of introductory economics can explain that the factors making for *downward* stickiness of wages and prices during recession are obstacles to recovery. He should be able to explain that when wages and prices fall, the real purchasing power value of the nation's stock of money increases. Having more money than they need to conduct day-to-day business, people use the surplus to purchase earning assets such as bonds or they may just leave the surplus dollars in their bank accounts. In either case the effect is to lower interest rates, and this encourages borrowing by business for investment purposes. Also, when prices fall the money and government bonds that people hold gain in purchasing power value. Because this means that they enjoy an increase in real financial wealth, there is a tendency for people to increase their consumption spending.

Warren's theory flew in the face of such well-accepted analysis. It could, perhaps have been justified on the grounds that boosting or putting a floor to prices would break deflationary expectations. Such expectations tend to cause economic activity to be postponed as firms wait for wages to decline before increasing employment, and as consumers and business firms postpone purchases on the assumption that prices of consumer goods, raw materials, and capital goods will fall further. In the shell-shocked condition of the economy of 1933, such an interpretation would not have been entirely implausible.[2]

The notion that government price boosting and rigging would help the farm sector of the economy draws support from the fact that farm income is unstable and from the fact that the demand for most agricultural commodities is unresponsive to price change. Because food is a necessity of life and its consumption cannot be postponed, increases in the price of food tend to reduce consumption of food by a far lower proportion than the proportionate increase in prices. Because of this *price inelasticity* higher prices for agricultural commodities are often associated with sharp increases in farm income.[3]

The simplest and most effective way to alleviate rural poverty would be to provide income transfers to poor farmers just as social security provides income to the elderly. However, that implies subsidies, widely held to be morally destructive and bad for the rural character, whereas higher incomes through price rigging were held to be legitimately earned in the market place.

Has anything been accomplished by government interference in agricultural markets? Rural poverty has diminished largely because poor people have left farming, not because of higher prices. The bulk of the marketable crop is produced, not by small family farms, but by large agglomerates, the owners of which are anything but poor. When income is redistributed to the farm sector by boosting prices, this helps those with marketable crops to sell, not the poor farmers that have little to sell. Indeed those who have only a small amount to sell have been driven off the land because higher farm prices have led to the inflation of agricultural land values and to inflation in the cost of farm machinery. Because of this the poor farmer's ability to escape poverty by mechanization and expansion

2. Price flexibility is essential if the automatic market adjustments needed to restore prosperity are to be permitted to operate. As suggested in the text, flexibility of wages and prices tends to raise spending because of their effects on interest rates and financial wealth. Interest rates also fall during recession because the demand for money and credit declines. New Deal policy, however, worked against this. Price rigging was encouraged by government policy and, as detailed in Chapter 5, the Federal Reserve did its best to prevent interest rates from falling.

3. Inelasticity with respect to price underlies the old notion that bumper crops depress farm income. The increase in supply so depresses prices that, despite selling more, farmers earn less.

of his acreage has been greatly reduced. Rather than preserving the family farm, federal farm programs have helped to destroy it.

It is true that instability of farm income caused by price fluctuations is a serious problem. It is also true, because of seasonal production lags, that it is difficult to predict future market prices at the time at which production decisions are made. These problems can be inexpensively mitigated by a system of forward pricing for agriculture. Under such a system the government makes a price forecast for each commodity based on expected market demand and supply conditions. Then, prior to planting, it guarantees the forecast (forward) price to the farmer, thereby providing him with a set of prices that serve as a guaranteed basis for production planning. If the market price at harvest time turns out to be higher than the forward price, all is well, and since market conditions imply a brisk demand for the particular commodity, increased production in the next growing season is encouraged. However, if at the time the crop is marketed the market price is lower than the forward price, farmers may sell their crops to the government at the forward price. But the forward price guaranteed in the next year will then be reduced thereby discouraging production of crops that are in over supply.

The farm population of the United States has dwindled steadily to about three million farmers. More and more of our agricultural output is produced by large conglomerates rather than by family farms. Yet the flow of federal subsidies continues. One wonders if the marginal social benefit of the farm dollar in the federal budget and in consumer prices is not negative. Federal intrusion into agriculture adversely affects the distribution of income; it involves huge storage costs; its surpluses do a better job of feeding rats than poor people; it raises prices to consumers; and it causes resources to be badly allocated because price rigging encourages the use of more resources in the agricultural sector than are economically justified. Last but not least, since 1980 it has widened federal budget deficits by about $20 billion annually.

Defense Purchases: Down But Not Out

It would be presumptuous to discuss defense spending without having made study of defense a full-time occupation. Fortunately that is not the present purpose. The purpose, rather, is to cite the defense industry as an example of the problems that arise when an industry, for one reason or another, is in a state of decline. Indeed, when the defense budget is cut, the problems this creates for the economy are very similar to the problems that are caused when an industry contracts because of import competition, because of shifting consumer tastes, and because of obsolescence caused by technological change.

Table 8-1 shows the levels and annual rates of growth of federal defense expenditures beginning with FY 1981. To obtain a better idea of the real costs of national defense, it is useful to divide the nominal expenditure figures by the *price deflator* for defense purchases calculated by the Department of Commerce. These constant dollar values, measured in 1987 prices, are shown in the final columns of the table.

Defense purchases exhibited very high growth rates during the first half of the 1980s as President Ronald Reagan sought to beef up the nation's defense, but these rates have been tailing off since that time. With the exception of 1990 real defense spending has declined

Table 8-1
Defense Expenditures
(Billions of Dollars, Calendar Years)

Year	Expenditures		Price Deflator	Expenditures in 1987 Dollars	
	Level	Rates		Level	Rates
1981	167.5	17.4%	81.1	206.4	5.7
1982	193.8	15.7	87.6	221.4	7.2
1983	214.4	10.6	91.6	234.2	5.8
1984	231.1	7.8	94.8	245.8	5.0
1985	258.6	11.9	97.3	265.6	8.1
1986	276.7	7.0	98.6	280.6	5.7
1987	292.1	5.6	100.0	292.1	4.1
1988	295.6	1.2	103.0	287.0	-1.8
1989	299.9	1.5	106.8	281.4	-2.0
1990	314.0	4.7	110.7	283.6	0.8
1991	322.5	2.7	114.7	281.3	-0.8
1992	313.8	-2.8	120.1	261.2	-7.2
1993	303.6	-3.2	125.1	242.7	-7.1

in each year beginning with 1988. As a percentage of real GDP real defense outlays fell from 6.4 percent in 1987 to 4.7 percent in 1993. The claim over resources of national defense is clearly diminishing.

The tailing off of real defense purchases is one of the factors responsible for the sluggishness of the economy since 1989. This is not to suggests that defense cuts are bad, but rather to say that when such reductions are made provisions needs to be made for offsetting their adverse employment effects. To some extent defense purchases will be automatically replaced by investment because lower defense spending reduces federal borrowing and may therefore reduce interest rates. However, such automatic substitution, though welcome, cannot be sufficient to offset the loss of jobs in defense industries and in consumer goods industries adversely impacted by multiplier effects. Consequently, defense cuts are likely to cause substantial unemployment unless accompanied by tax cuts and/or increases in other government expenditures. Put differently, it would be very naive and destructive simply to breathe a sigh of relief on the easy assumption that the end of the cold war provides the magic wand that permits budget deficits to be eliminated.

President Clinton has spoken of his desire to use defense savings to provide medical coverage for the uninsured. That would fill a major national need and would, at the same time, prevent defense cuts from placing a drag on the economy. But simply switching expenditures from one function to another will not do the job. Since the resources utilized in defense industries cannot be quickly adapted to use in the health-care industry, switching of spending would merely cause unemployment in the defense industry while simultaneously causing even more rapid inflation in the health sector. Just imagine what would happen if 39 million more people suddenly obtained health insurance unaccompanied by any increase in the supply of doctors, nurses, and hospitals.

The United States is extremely fortunate to have a highly adaptable and mobile labor force. When the domestic auto industry went into decline during the last half of the 1970s, due to sharply higher fuel costs and import competition, many of the younger workers who lost their jobs in Michigan and other auto producing states quickly packed up and moved to Texas to work in the booming oil industry. Most other countries are not so fortunate. Traditional employer-employee relationships are often such that it is difficult to change jobs. In Europe if you see a job opportunity in another country you are likely to have to learn a new language and obtain a passport as well as a work permit. Despite such impediments as the lack of portability of health insurance, the U.S. labor market is highly adaptable. Frictional unemployment, which measures the number of people in transit between jobs, is far higher in the U.S. than in most countries. That is a very good thing because it means that our labor force readily accommodates itself to changing economic circumstances such as those caused by technological innovation, downsizing of declining sectors, and the like.

Nevertheless, effective policy would support the movement of resources, especially people, out of declining industries into expanding industries. President Kennedy, for example, obtained legislation that provided adjustment assistance for victims of increased foreign competition caused by tariff cuts. We need the same sort of relief for victims of defense cuts. This implies provision for retraining, financial assistance during periods of transitional unemployment, as well as relocation support. The severance pay received by those that have been discharged from the military is a huge help, as is the growing amount of resources that the military has been devoting to the retraining of personnel.

Regrettably, persons knowledgeable about these retraining programs give them very low marks because these programs do not adequately train military personnel for civilian occupations. The kinds of equipment, such as computers, used in the training programs are often not up-to-date, and the instructors are themselves military personnel rather than persons brought in from potential employers. It's a friendly gesture to keep the military instructors paid and busy, but the economic value of such activity is dubious.

Many experts believe that training programs should be conducted, not by the military, but by potential civilian employers. The Service Members Occupational and Training Act, passed by Congress in 1992, is an important step in this direction. Under the act veterans discharged after July 1990 are eligible for federally subsidized training by approved employers for amounts up to $10,000 per veteran. In the state of Tennessee, the Department of Employment Security has served more than 60,000 veterans since the inception of the law. Fifty percent were referred to job interviews and about 40 percent of those referred found suitable occupations.

Still more jobs would have been found had the economy been stronger.

Structural unemployment is the kind of unemployment that develops when the skills of potential workers are unsuited to the job openings that are available. An obvious example is when added job opportunities are created in the health care industries while the workers available to fill these jobs are people being released from the military and from defense industries. Attempting to reduce such mismatch by creating more job openings is often referred to as attempting to fit square pegs into round holes. Creating such job openings merely causes inflation unless workers obtain the required skills. By the same token, teaching usable skills is largely wasted when the job openings aren't there. That, in fact, is one of the greatest problems the economy faces today. Absorbing people out of the military and the defense industry into civilian employment is being hugely hampered by the sluggishness that has characterized the labor market since 1989.

The difficulty of obtaining credit is another deterrent to labor mobility. If you go to a bank for a loan to help finance relocation to another state, the bank is sure to turn you down because, since you are unemployed and intent on leaving, it regards you as a poor credit risk. Then, if you are fortunate enough to get to the new job site, it will be hard to get a loan to help you get settled in the new location because nobody knows you and you haven't had time to establish credit. A federal program of interest-subsidized relocation loans would be inexpensive and most beneficial. It would also be appropriate and important to target workers in declining industries in a manner that would extend their eligibility for unemployment compensation.

Reducing the pain associated with the movement of resources from declining industries into other productive activities should be a major public responsibility. Despite the fact that the effective relocation of military and defense workers is likely to be temporarily costly, the longer range gains in higher growth and productivity are certain to be far greater. It seems entirely appropriate to use a goodly fraction of defense savings for this purpose.

Tax Expenditures: Truth in Spending?[4]

Rather than provide direct subsidies for particular purposes, Congress hides an enormous amount of such subsidies by granting tax breaks. Instead of paying part of your medical bills directly, the government helps you pay them by allowing you to deduct a part of your out-of-pocket medical expenditures from your taxable income. Instead of encouraging home ownership by directly subsidizing your home purchase, the government does this indirectly by letting you deduct your mortgage interest and property taxes. The government attempts to help poor people and part of this is accomplished by earned income tax credits for low income workers and by letting people deduct their charitable contributions. You may also deduct your state income and local property taxes and, in this manner, the federal government adds to the subsidies received by state and local governments beyond its grants in aid. The elderly are assisted by taxing social security benefits at a lower rate than other income, while corporations benefit from preferential treatment of certain corporate outlays.

These tax breaks, or hidden subsidies, are known as *tax expenditures.* They represent a huge budget cost to the federal government. Since they reduce corporate and individual income tax receipts, they add to the deficit just as any other government expenditure. Estimates by OMB, shown in ***Table 8-2***, suggest that the expenditure equivalent of such hidden subsidies totalled $408.0 billion in FY 1993, an amount that would have increased federal outlays by 27 percent had they been made as expenditures rather than reflected in lower receipts. The biggest tax expenditure items were for housing, health, income security and subsidies to state and local governments.

Tax expenditures include exclusions of income such as certain transfer payments and fringe benefits, exemptions such as the personal and family exemption, deductions such as medical, charitable and homeowner deductions, credits such as the earned income tax credit, preferential rates such as the lower rates on capital gains and social security benefits, and tax deferrals such as IRAs.

4. The author owes a huge debt of gratitude to Mrs. Dorothy Rudolph for supplying much of the information and analysis contained in this section.

Table 8-2
Tax Expenditures Estimated as Outlay Equivalents
(Fiscal Years, Billions of Dollars)

Function	1988	1989	1990	1993
National Defense	2.2	2.2	2.3	2.1
International Affairs	6.7	7.0	7.5	2.9
General Science, Space, and Technology	2.6	2.8	3.0	3.3
Energy	0.8	0.9	1.0	2.0
Natural resources and Environment	3.1	3.2	3.3	1.6
Agriculture	0.5	0.7	0.5	3.1
Commerce and Housing Credit	143.2	152.9	160.7	177.1
Transportation	0.2	0.2	0.1	1.8
Community and Regional Development	1.4	1.8	2.2	2.4
Education, Training, Employment, and Social Services	20.7	20.6	21.6	21.8
Health	42.8	47.4	51.0	52.3
Income Security	81.6	82.9	89.3	73.6
Social Security	17.4	17.4	18.2	23.7
Veterans Benefits and Services	2.0	1.9	2.0	2.0
General Government	34.5	35.5	37.7	37.2
Net Interest	0.9	0.9	1.0	1.1
Totals	360.6	378.3	401.4	408.0

Source: Office of Management and Budget, *The Budget in Brief,* FY 1990, p. 90.

While many tax expenditures are familiar enough there are others that are not well known. For example, the IRS subsidizes business expenditures for research and development (R and D) by permitting R and D outlays to be treated as a current cost rather than as an investment expenditure. Above a threshold level, business firms are also permitted to deduct 20 percent of their R and D expenditures from their corporate tax liability.

While the federal government provides grants in aid to state and local governments, these grants by no means cover all federal assistance. The exemption of state and local taxes from federal taxation is one example, and the privilege of issuing tax free bonds is another.

The use of the individual income tax to promote social goals has been justified in a number of ways. It is said that the cause of equity is served when, for example, a person who accumulates large out of pocket medical expenses is able to reduce his tax liability. Similarly, because the tax systems of state and local governments are regressive, permitting state income taxes to be deducted from federal taxable income is said to serve the cause of equity. It is also argued that tax expenditures, such as tax breaks for home owners, promote such national goals as widespread home ownership. It is said that tax expenditures promote individual freedom as when charitable deductions permit individuals to select their own worthy causes rather than having this be done by the government. However, an honest appraisal of these arguments suggests that they are dubious half truths, and in the meantime the economy pays a very heavy price for the privilege of avoiding the term direct subsidy, which has a negative ring to it, by loading up the tax code with hidden subsidies.

Potentially the individual income tax of the federal government is far and away our best tax. There are numerous criteria for evaluating taxes. One criterion is that tax *incidence* should fall on the party against whom it is assessed. Payroll taxes charged to employers do not qualify in this respect because they are *shifted* in part to employees in the form of lower wages, and in part to consumers in the form of higher prices. Inasmuch as it is extremely difficult to obtain accurate measures of payroll tax shifting, it is not really possible to know where the incidence falls. To the economist this is another of the many liabilities of payroll taxes. To politicians, on the other hand, it is useful to fuzz up such issues as tax incidence. There isn't much doubt about who pays when income taxes are raised, but that is not true when payroll taxes are raised. That, perhaps, accounts for the popularity of payroll taxes with the Congress.

It is difficult to shift the income tax even though it has been argued that when marginal income tax rates are very high, this reduces the supply of labor effort and force up wages. This then raises prices and causes some shifting from wage earners to the general consumer.

A second criterion for a good tax is that its distorting effect on economic decisions is minimal. This criterion is called the *efficiency* criterion. For example, economic theory suggests that a flat tax rate applied to corporate income is efficient because it will not affect production and employment decisions.[5] Conversely, in the past there have been times when Congress has granted an investment tax credit (ITC) to stimulate investment, and President Clinton has asked Congress to enlarge the credit for small business. Such a credit permits businesses to deduct a fraction of the cost of new capital assets from its corporation income tax liability. But since, in the past, the credit applied to machinery and equipment, but not to new structures, it had the effect of causing business to put new machines into antiquated buildings. Similarly, payroll taxes raise payroll costs and provide an incentive for business to replace labor with capital in the production process.

Such distorting effects are thought to be largely absent in the case of the individual income tax. However, and as noted above, income taxes may distort the work-leisure decisions of individuals and therefore affect the supply of labor. For example, high marginal tax rates might deter the wife of a well paid worker from seeking employment because a large fraction of the extra income earned by the family would be taxed away.

The third criterion for a good tax is that it should be *stabilizing.* As explained in Chapter 2, all taxes have some automatic stabilizing influence because their yields rise and fall with the economic cycle. However, the taxes that have had the greatest automatic stabilizing

5. To grasp the point, have a look at the accompanying table which shows the profits of a hypothetical firm at different levels of output. When quantity is less than 11,000 increases in output raise revenue by more than they raise costs so that profits rise. However, increases above 11,000 units of output raise costs by more than revenue so that profits decline. Profits are therefore maximized at a production level of 11,000 units. The second column shows profits before tax. The third column show profits after tax assuming that there is a flat rate of 20 percent applied to corporate income. As can readily be seen, the same output level that maximizes pre-tax profits also maximizes after-tax profits. The flat rate tax therefore does not distort production decisions.

Quantity	**Profit**	
	Pre-Tax	**After-Tax**
10,000	$80,000	64,000
11,000	$100,000	80,000
12,000	$90,000	72,000

effects are the corporate profits tax and the individual income tax. Receipts from the corporate profits tax are highly responsive to the level of business activity because corporate profits are the most volatile component of the several sources of National Income--employee compensation, interest, rent, corporate profits, and income of unincorporated enterprises.

Personal income does not fluctuate as much as profits. However, receipts from the individual income tax fluctuate sharply because of progressive tax rates applied to different brackets. It's important to understand this so the explanation bears repetition. Suppose that a taxpayer pays an average rate of 20 percent, or $6,000, on the first $30,000 of taxable income, and that he pays 40 percent on any income over $30,000. If his taxable income is $40,000 he pays $4,000 in additional taxes on the additional income of $10,000. Since his total tax bill is $10,000, his *average* rate of tax is 25 percent (10,000/40,000). His disposable (after tax) income is then equal to $30,000.

If the economy enters a recession and this individual's taxable income declines by $10,000 to $30,000, this reduces his tax liability by $4,000, thereby causing $4,000 of the income loss to be absorbed by the government. His disposable income declines by $6,000 rather than the $10,000 loss in his pre tax income, and he and the economy therefore benefit from the fact that he is forced to reduce his consumption spending by much less than if he had to absorb the entire loss. Furthermore, his average rate of tax now declines from 25 percent to 20 percent. Consequently, it can be seen that the yield from the income tax falls both because there is less income to tax and because a lower average rate is applied to the lower income.

A fourth fundamental property of a good tax is that it should serve the cause of *equity*. Some would go farther and say that a good tax promotes a more equitable distribution of income. A flat lump sum tax that everyone has to pay regardless of his economic circumstances would certainly not qualify. Even though all taxpayers contribute equal amounts to the financing of government, such a tax would exact severe hardship on poor people and be barely noticed by the rich. A more equitable way to tax is to apply a flat tax rate to incomes. Such a tax is called a *proportional* income tax. Though far more equitable than a lump-sum tax, a proportional income tax is not thought to provide sufficient equity. The reason for this is that if you take one dollar of income away from both a high income person and a low income person, this will reduce the sense of well being of the high income person by far less than the sense of well being of the person with a low income. Therefore, to equalize the welfare loss to both persons, it is considered appropriate to apply a higher tax rate to the last dollar earned by the rich person than the rate applied to the last dollar of income of a poor persons. Such an argument implies that equity is best served by a *progressive* income tax under which successive blocks of income are taxed at increasing rates. The progressive rate structure causes the *average* tax rate to increase as the taxpayer's income increases, and therefore implies that higher income taxpayers pay a larger fraction of their income in taxes than lower income taxpayers.

Until 1985 there were as many as sixteen income brackets with higher *marginal* rates applied to the income falling within the successive brackets. At that time the number of brackets was cut to three and this had the effect of eliminating much of the progressivity of the income tax. However, the Revenue Reconciliation Act of 1993 added two more brackets and made the individual income tax substantially more progressive. For a single taxpayer the schedule that prevailed in 1992 was:

Taxable Income Bracket	(marginal) Rate
0-$21,450	15%
21,450-51,900	28%
Over 51,900	31%

The new schedule legislated in 1993 is:

Taxable Income Bracket	(marginal) Rate
0-$22,100	15%
22,100 to 53,500	28%
53,500 to 115,000	31%
115,000 to 250,000	36%
Over 250,000	39.6%

	Homeowner A	Homeowner B
Assessed Value of Home	$1,000,000	$100,000
Mortgage	800,000	80,000
Adjusted Gross Income	400,000	40,000
Deductions		
Interest (10%)	80,000	8,000
Property Tax (2%)	20,000	2,000
Total	100,000	10,000
Taxable Income	300,000	30,000
Taxes: 1992 Rates		
No deductions	119,655	8,412
Average Rate	30%	21%
With Housing Deductions	88,655	5,612
Average Rate	29.6%	18.7%
Tax Saving	31,000	2,800
As Percent of AGI	7.75%	7.0%

Comparison of the two schedules shows that the progressivity of the individual income tax has been increased. Individuals whose incomes exceed $250,000 now face a marginal tax rate of 39.6% whereas previously their marginal tax rate was 31%. It can be observed, as well, that the first three brackets have been slightly widened to prevent inflation from changing tax rates.

Although the new tax is far more progressive, this also has the effect of making tax expenditures increasingly regressive. This important and paradoxical circumstance is illustrated in the above table which illustrates the effect of the subsidy to homeowners. In 1993 the Federal government lost $13.1 billion in revenue by permitting homeowners to deduct property taxes, and $48.7 billion more was lost by permitting mortgage interest to be deducted.

In the hypothetical example shown in the table it is assumed that homeowner A has a mansion whose assessed and market value is $1,000,000 while homeowner B owns a modest home with a value of $100,000. It is also assumed that the values of their homes are proportional to their adjusted gross incomes (AGI) and that A earns $400,000 in AGI while B earns $40,000. Homeowner A carries a mortgage of $800,000 while B's is $80,000. If both pay mortgage interest at 8 percent and property taxes at 2 percent, their total deductions from AGI would come to $100,000 and $10,000, respectively. If there are no further deductions or additions to AGI, their respective taxable incomes are $300,000 and $30,000.

Inspection of these calculations shows that rich homeowner A enjoys a far greater tax saving than homeowner B. Not only is the dollar value of his saving absolutely far greater, it is also relatively greater as a percent of adjusted gross income. The higher a taxpayer's marginal rate, the greater the tax saving per dollar of itemized deduction.

Next compare how the equity situation is aggravated under the 1993 law.

	A	B
Taxes: 1994 Rates		
No Deductions	138,977	8,340
Average Rate	34.7%	20.9%
With Housing Deductions	99,377	5,540
Average Rate	33.1%	18.5%
Tax Saving	39,600	2,800
As Percent of AGI	9.9%	7.0%

Under the new tax rates homeowner A would pay $99,377 in taxes whereas B pays $5,540. Their average rates of tax are 33.1 and 18.5 percent, respectively. The good news is that A, with a higher income, pays a larger fraction of his income in taxes. The bad news is that A gets a far greater housing subsidy than B. A's taxable income is reduced by $100,000 and since his marginal tax rate is 39.6 percent, he saves $39,600 in taxes or 9.9 percent of his AGI. Under the old law his savings came to 7.75% of AGI, but under the new law the savings come to 9.9%. Homeowner B, on the other hand, deducts only $10,000 and since his marginal tax rate is 28 percent, he saves $2,800 or 7.0 percent of his AGI just as he did under the old law. Therefore the subsidy to A is not only far greater than it is to B, it is also proportionately greater, and the disproportion is increased sharply by the new law. Small wonder that tax expenditures are often characterized as upside-down equity.

The benefit to A is disproportionately greater than to B. However, both receive benefits that are not available to renters, the bulk of whom consist of low income families. Although the renter pays the landlord's property taxes and mortgage interest, there is no provision for recouping any of these costs via deductions from his income tax. Or, consider the fact that only the upper income 30 percent of tax payers find it advantageous to itemize deductions. It is, therefore, this upper income 30 percent that receives the bulk of the subsidies provided by the privilege of itemizing deductions.

With the obvious exception of the earned income tax credit, tax expenditures redistribute income in a regressive manner. It has, however, been argued that some tax expenditures do the opposite. Most state and local governments now have state income taxes. To the extent that these taxes are less progressive than federal income taxes, permitting them to be deducted from federal AGI lowers the average federal tax rate paid by low income persons to a greater extent than the average tax rates of high income persons. But this fact is more an argument for state and local tax reform than it is for the retention of tax expenditures. It is possible to argue, as well, that since illness is largely accidental, it is equitable for a taxpayer to spread his out of pocket medical costs to other taxpayers. But suppose he's just too cheap to buy health insurance? Should others have to subsidize him? Or, conversely, suppose he is a middle-aged self-employed person whose applications for health insurance are turned down by insurance companies. We'd sympathize with him. But wouldn't it be better to have comprehensive health insurance so that those who are denied coverage would not have to rely on tax deductions as a health care safety net?

Many would argue that tax expenditures, in whatever form, should be entirely eliminated. They would claim that it is bad policy to hide a large fraction of public expenditure from view, in part because this makes it more difficult to assess the true costs of the various expenditure functions of the federal government. Were these costs fully exposed to view, it would be far more difficult to justify the amounts spent for many of the functions. This is particularly true for housing, health, and income security. Is this truth in spending? Is this the way to control the budget?

Furthermore, the hiding of subsidies is done in a highly discriminatory manner. The same well-to-do person who is critical of direct federal housing subsidies for the poor, will be the first to defend the "legitimate" deductions he enjoys as a home owner. Is it fair or reasonable to publicize government benefits to poor people while hiding those that go to the rich?

Many tax expenditures adversely affect the distribution of income. If subsidies were exposed to view it would be far more difficult to subsidize the rich than is presently the case. Would it not be appropriate to suggest that the wealthy ought to be made responsible for paying for their own mansions and their own medical expenses?

Because the progressivity of the individual income tax is reduced, tax expenditures reduce the stabilizing property of the income tax. It can be argued that this can be offset by increasing the progressivity of the rate structure. But at the same time greater progressivity disproportionately increases the value of the tax deductions of wealthy people.

Tax expenditures promote a curious and inefficient method of administering government programs. If you were Commissioner of Internal Revenue, you probably would have to agree with former Commissioner Jerome Kurtz that:

> Each of the tax expenditure provisions is, in effect, a non-revenue related expenditure program written into the tax law. Each entails its own special set of issues, definitions and limitations...I find myself...administering programs of many other agencies.

A peculiar way to run a railroad, isn't it? Shouldn't federal housing policy be administered by the Department of Housing and Urban Affairs? Is the same not true for other categories such as social security, health, and science and technology?

All things considered, would it be fair to say that tax expenditures not only hide federal subsidies from view, they also hide the poverty of national policy from view? For lack of a rational health care system that insures all citizens, we ease the pain of those who are denied health insurance by permitting a portion of their medical spending to be deducted. For lack of a rational national housing policy we subsidize the housing of the rich. Instead of encouraging state government to reform their regressive tax systems, we permit state income taxes to be deducted. Because of these, and other, factors the distribution of income in the United States has become increasingly unequal and unfair. Beyond the customary hand wringing ritual over the "vanishing middle class," is anything being done about it?

Take another good look at Table 8-2. $408 billion in hidden subsidies, 43 percent of it for housing. Who gets the benefit? Mostly rich people and the construction industry. If you want to cut the budget, why not start there?

Part III

Deficits, Debt and the World Economy

9

International Crowdout: The Twin Deficits

The Twin Deficits

The influence of the federal budget extends well beyond the geographic United States. The accumulation of foreign debt is becoming a major problem and U.S. fiscal policies of the past fifteen years have profoundly affected the prosperity and growth prospects of other countries. To ease into this subject, have a look at ***Table 9-1*** which shows the relative shares of the major expenditure components of real GDP in 1979 and compares these with the shares for 1985. Consumption took 67.0 percent of the economic pie in 1985, up sharply by 2.5 percentage points over its 1979 share. Much of this reflects the effects of the income tax reductions sought by the Reagan administration. The share of government purchases also increased from 18.2 percent to 19.0 percent thanks largely to increases in defense spending. This had to mean that the share of investment fell sharply; or did it? Investment's share fell by only two tenths of one percentage point, not nearly enough to make room for the increased shares going to consumers and government. In fact if these three components are added together for 1985 the total is, not 100 percent, but rather 103.4 percent of GDP. Where did the rest come from? The answer, of course, is that it came from abroad in the form of a sharp increase in imports relative to exports, or net exports as this is called. Importing more than the nation exports is really the only way we can live beyond our means in the sense that it enables us to consume more output than we produce.

What accounts for this enormous deterioration in net exports, or trade deficit as it is sometimes loosely called? A part of it was simply the continuation of a trend that had been going on for many years. During the 1970s real GDP grew at an average annual rate of 2.8 percent. However, imports grew at a rate of 7.1 percent, outpacing the 6.6 percent growth of exports.

Table 9-1
Composition of Real GDP: Levels and Percentages
(Billions of 1987 dollars)

	1979		1985	
	Value	Percent	Value	Percent
Consumption	$2,448.9	64.5	2,865.8	67.0
Gross Investment	669.7	17.6	745.9	17.4
Government Purchases	689.3	18.2	813.4	19.0
Net Exports	-10.6	-0.3	-145.3	-3.4
GDP	3,796.8	100.0	4,279.8	100.0

This trend was all the more remarkable because, during the 1970s, imports became more expensive and exports should have become easier to sell because the international value of the dollar fell 14.2 percent relative to foreign currencies. Net exports in the national income and product accounts also include net income from overseas investment, and that had been in the process of dwindling as our net overseas indebtedness continued to rise. ***Table 9-2*** provides information on the components of net exports and also traces changes in the value of the dollar both nominal and real.

The nominal exchange rate is the dollar cost of foreign currency. When the exchange rate rises so that more dollars are needed to purchase a unit of foreign currency this has the effect of increasing the dollar cost of imports. At the same time foreigners can buy more dollars with a unit of their currency so that our exports become cheaper to them. The likely result is a decline in imports and a rise in exports. Therefore, a rise in the exchange rate makes the nation more competitive as exports rise and domestic production displaces imports.

Table 9-2
Exports, Imports and Exchange Rates
(Billions of Constant 1987 Dollars)

Year	Exports	Imports	Net Exports	Value of the Dollar Nominal*	Real*
1973	210.3	244.4	-34.1	99.1	98.9
1979	293.5	304.1	-10.6	88.1	83.2
1980	320.5	289.9	30.7	87.4	84.9
1981	326.1	304.1	22.0	103.4	100.9
1982	296.7	304.1	-7.4	116.6	111.8
1983	285.9	342.1	-56.1	125.3	117.3
1984	305.7	427.7	-122.0	138.2	128.8
1985	309.2	454.6	-145.3	143.0	132.4
1986	329.6	484.7	-155.1	112.2	103.6
1987	364.0	507.1	-143.1	96.9	90.9
1988	421.6	525.7	-104.0	92.7	88.2
1989	471.8	545.4	-73.7	98.6	94.4
1990	510.0	561.8	-51.8	89.1	86.0
1991	543.4	562.5	-19.1	89.8	86.5
1992	578.5	611.6	-33.6	86.6	83.2
1993	596.4	675.7	-79.3	93.2	89.9

* 1973 = 100

Sources: Department of Commerce and Board of Governors of the Federal Reserve System.

However, suppose that the exchange rate rises 5 percent and that at the same time domestic prices also rise 5 percent while foreign prices remain constant. The competitive gain caused by the rise in the exchange rate is then exactly neutralized by domestic inflation. Because of this a far better indicator of international competitiveness is the *real exchange rate,* which is the *nominal* exchange rate multiplied by the ratio of an index of foreign prices to an index of domestic prices. Specifically, let the nominal exchange rate be expressed as **e**, the foreign price level as **p***, and the domestic price level as **p**. The real exchange rate is then given by,

$$r = \frac{ep^*}{p}$$

By taking different inflation rates into account, the real exchange rate provides a measure of the number of units of domestic production needed to acquire a unit of foreign production. This ratio is often referred to as the terms of trade.

Be sure to notice (***Table 9-2***) that the U.S. exchange rate as reported there is inverted. Instead of the price of foreign currency in terms of dollars, the table expresses the value of the dollar as a weighted basket of major foreign currencies. Remember also that when we say the dollar appreciates that this is equivalent to saying that the price of foreign exchange falls.

The decline of the dollar was arrested in 1979 and the dollar then entered a lengthy period of appreciation that caused it to rise 59.3 percent by 1985. This had the effect of reducing the domestic currency cost of imports. Although imports were depressed during the recession, the combination of recovery and the rise in the dollar caused them to shoot up sharply in 1983. The appreciation of the dollar also had the effect of increasing the cost of American goods as seen by foreigners thereby causing exports to stagnate. Indeed, during this period imports (measured in constant prices) increased 49.5 percent while exports increased only 5.4 percent. You may, in fact, remember how foreign autos and other imports flooded into the U.S., and if you were lucky enough to have the opportunity to travel in Europe, how far the dollar went in paying for travel, food, and lodgings, and how you enjoyed picking up bargains in European stores.

What caused the appreciation of the dollar? In late 1979 the Federal Reserve began a restriction of monetary growth that reduced real M_1 by 4.3 percent between 1979 and 1982. In response to monetary tightening the yields on 60-day treasury bills shot up from 7.6 percent in 1978 to 13.8 percent in 1981 (an increase of 82 percent), yields on 10 year government bonds rose from 8.4 percent to 13.9 percent (up 65 percent), and yields on corporate Aaa bonds rose from 8.7 to 14.2 percent (up 63 percent). Seeing these sharp increases in U.S. interest rates, foreign investors became attracted to the higher-yielding U.S. financial assets. To acquire them they first had to sell domestic financial assets in exchange for foreign currency. They then took the currency to the foreign exchange market where currencies are traded and used it to purchase dollars. The dollars, finally, were used to purchase U.S. bonds and other assets. Because this generated a huge increase in the demand for dollars, this *capital inflow* caused the dollar to appreciate sharply. ***Figure 9-1*** shows the enormous jump in short term interest rates and ***Figure 9-2*** shows the value of the dollar relative to the German Deutschemark and the Japanese Yen. While the yen held its own against the dollar, this was not true for European currencies such as the Deutschemark.

Later, major tax reductions were enacted and defense expenditures were also increased. These budgetary policies converted a modest fiscal deficit of $16.1 billion in 1979 into a deficit of $196.9 billion in 1985, the bulk of which was structural. Between 1986 and 1990 the deficit continued at high levels ranging from a high of $206.9 billion in 1986 to a low of $134.3 billion in 1989. As the structural deficit widened, increased federal borrowing added further upward pressure to interest rates, and this helped to sustain the continued appreciation of the dollar. Therefore, and as can be seen from the data shown in ***Table 9-1***, the rise in interest rates caused by growth in the deficit and the debt during this period had only minor effects in crowding out investment, but a massive effect in producing international crowdout in the form of rising imports and stagnating exports. The budget deficit and the trade deficit therefore appear to be closely connected and that is why they are sometimes referred to as the twin deficits.

Some observers went so far as to say that U.S. policies were instrumental in creating a triple debt crisis. By driving up world interest rates, these policies directly aggravated the debt servicing problems of debtor countries, especially the Latin American countries. The stagnation of U.S. exports was partly attributable to the higher cost of the dollar. But exports were also greatly reduced by a decline in the ability of Latin countries to pay for American goods. Overall, the rise in interest rates and the rise in the dollar had a depressing effect on the U.S. economy that helped to offset the expansionary effects of tax cuts and increased defense outlays. Americans spent their tax cuts, but largely on foreign produced goods and services.

The appreciation of the dollar held down the domestic cost of

Figure 9-1
Short-Term Interest Rates[2]
(Period Averages In Percent per Annum)

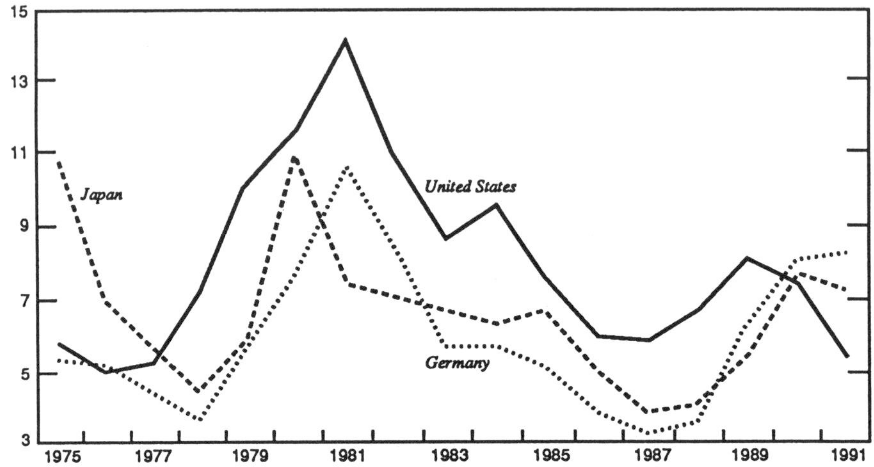

Figure 9-2
U.S. Dollar vs. Deutschemark & Japanese Yen
(Period Averages)

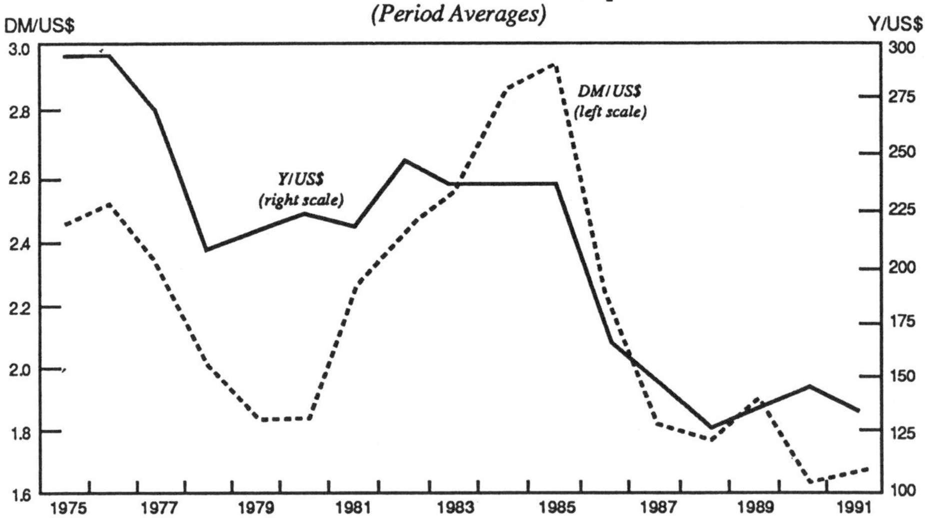

Source: International Monetary Fund, International Financial Statistics, Yearbook 1992

imports, and it thereby helped to lower the rate of inflation in the United States. The opposite happened to other countries that were being forced to pay more for dollar-denominated imports, including oil imported from OPEC. Seeing their currencies depreciating, their inflation rates rising, and their economies overstimulated by rising export demand, foreign countries began to imitate the restrictive monetary policies of the U.S. so as to stem the depreciation of their currencies. But since one country's appreciation is another's depreciation, all countries cannot appreciate their currencies simultaneously. Competition by countries to do so by the use of restrictive monetary policy had the inevitable consequence of causing excessive world monetary contraction, generalized interest-rate escalation, and recession. Not surprisingly, the world economy sank into its worst global depression since the Great Depression of the 1930s.

Three questions now present themselves: First, what are the consequences for the economy of a large and persistent deficit in U.S. international accounts? Second, how do the budget and trade deficits impact other countries? Third, is a reduction in the federal budget deficit likely to produce a significant reduction in the trade deficit?

Paying for Imports

How are imports paid for? It makes no difference whether foreign exporters accept dollars in exchange for their goods or whether they first make American importers buy their currencies in the foreign exchange market. Therefore, to keep it simple, assume that trade is conducted in dollars. Foreigners earn dollars by selling imports to the U.S., and they can then use these earnings to purchase exports. If the value of exports equals the value of imports, the same number of dollars flows in as flows out and the balance of payments is then said to be in equilibrium.

However, if the value of imports exceeds the value of exports there will be a net outflow of dollars. If foreigners sell the surplus dollars in the foreign exchange market, this depresses the value of the dollar relative to the value of foreign currency. Because this raises the dollar cost of imports while giving exports a competitive advantage, imports decline, exports increase, and the inflow and outflow of dollars tends to be equalized. In theory, a trade deficit tends to eliminate itself because of movements in exchange rates.

That is what the old international economics textbooks predicted would happen when exchange rates are market determined.

Instead of selling surplus dollars in exchange for their own currencies, foreign dollar holders have the option of using them to make investments in the United States. They may therefore purchase U.S. bonds both private and public, shares in U.S. companies, physical properties such as land and capital, and they may establish subsidiaries of their own industries in the United States. Such a reflow of dollars is called a *capital inflow* and it would then be said that the *current account deficit* (exports minus imports plus net overseas interest and dividend income) is matched by a surplus in the *capital account.*

When the capital inflow equalizes the outflow caused by a trade deficit, no surplus dollars accumulate in foreign hands and there are, therefore, no dollar sales such as would depress the foreign currency value of the dollar in foreign exchange markets. Changes in the exchange rate can therefore be seen to be determined both by trade in goods and services as well as purely financial transactions.

Over the years international financial markets have become increasingly accessible and integrated and the volume of international financial transactions has increased enormously. Indeed, on a normal trading day it is not at all unusual for as much as $200 to $300 billion in national currencies to be exchanged one for another. These amounts vastly exceed the amounts needed to finance trade in goods and services, and it has therefore become the swapping of financial assets that very often has the overwhelming influence over exchange rates. It is this dominant effect of capital flows that explains how it is possible for the dollar to rise even as the trade deficit widens.

The movement of financial capital, especially of the short-term variety, has proved to be extremely sensitive to changes in interest-rate differentials between domestic and foreign financial markets. Just let the Fed push up U.S. interest rates, as it did in late 1979, and watch the foreign capital flood in. Then, as now, these capital inflows finance the trade deficit. They also moderate the rise in interest rates as foreign investors create a demand for U.S. bonds.

Foreigners accumulate U.S. IOUs when they sell more goods and services to us than they purchase. If this goes on for a long period of time indebtedness to foreigners increases. This fact has important implications.

First, ownership of foreign assets provides interest and dividend income that permits the receiving country to finance part of its imports rather than having them entirely paid for with export earnings. Therefore a position as a net international creditor carries with it the potential for a higher standard of living since it enables the country to consume more than it produces. By the same token, a country whose net international creditor position deteriorates gradually loses this advantage, and this has been happening to the United States. Over the years the U.S. built up its creditor position by exporting more than she imported and receipts from foreign investment income grew to a maximum of $32.9 billion in 1981. However, because of the rapid growth of U.S. IOUs in foreign hands, such income dwindled to only $10.9 billion in 1987. If the United States continues to import more than she exports she will soon have to pay more in interest and dividends to other countries than she receives from them. This would imply that, in the future, overseas earnings will not be available to pay for imports, and this means a potential loss in the standard of living unless foreign investors continue to grant credit.

If foreign investors lose their taste for U.S. IOUs they can sell them in exchange for dollars and then use the dollars to purchase their own currencies. When that happens the foreign exchange value of the dollar falls as, indeed, it did between 1985 and 1992. Continued decline in the value of the dollar implies that each unit of exports earns less foreign currency and that each unit of imports therefore costs more dollars. More domestic production must therefore be sent abroad to pay for one physical unit of imports. This is called a deterioration in the *terms of trade* and it has an obvious adverse effect on the standard of living just as improvement in the terms of trade during the early 1980s added to the standard of living. In this sense the extravagances of that period were being paid for by attaching an international mortgage onto the future. Indeed, by 1992 the value of the dollar, and therefore the terms of trade, had fallen back to their 1979 levels and were 8.4 percent lower than they had been in 1973, when the international value of the dollar was first permitted to fluctuate in response to market forces.

False Alarm: Deficit Reduction to Avoid Depression

A few years ago, when the economy was moving towards full employment, many alarmists, including some highly regarded economists who ought to have known better, were loudly proclaiming that if the federal budget deficit were not quickly reduced, this would lead foreign investors to believe that nothing would ever be done about the trade deficit. Failure to take fiscal action would so alarm these investors that they would no longer be willing to finance our deficits and would, instead, cash in their U.S. government bonds and other U.S. IOUs. If that happened there would be a massive capital outflow that would drive U.S. interest rates up to unheard of levels thereby causing a severe depression. Because U.S. imports would decline when economic activity declines, other countries would lose export markets and the depression would spread to other countries. Because interest rates would escalate sharply, Latin American countries would be thrown into a new debt crisis. Awesome scenario isn't it?

Capital outflows imply that foreign investors are selling U.S. financial assets and this raises domestic interest rates just as capital inflows reduce them. However, there is no good reason why the Fed should permit interest rates to rise. The Fed can easily prevent such a rise by engaging in open-market purchases. With the Fed's unlimited ability to create credit, what is to prevent the Fed from buying U.S. bonds to offset foreign sales? This prevents economic contraction and, although it involves expansionary monetary policy, is unlikely to be inflationary because the Fed is merely replacing the foreign financing that has been withdrawn.

The argument that the budget deficit has to be gotten down to avoid a depression ignores the fact that such action requires deflationary fiscal policy that is far more likely to cause a depression than to prevent one. When interest rates fall in response to a reduction in the government budget deficit, this occurs because the restrictive fiscal policy slows the economy and therefore *reduces the demand* for money and credit. The idea of using restrictive fiscal policy to forestall recession is therefore pathetically fallacious. It makes sense if, and only if, the economy shows clear signs of overheating. In that event fiscal restraint would be appropriate and it would have an advantage over monetary restraint because it would tend to lower interest rates rather than raise them.

To get interest rates down without reducing economic activity, it is necessary to *increase the supply* of money and credit. That implies the need for expansionary monetary policy that drives up bond prices and lowers interest rates. Critics of the use of expansionary monetary policy to lower interest rates prove the point inadvertently by claiming that expansionary monetary policy is inflationary whereas budget tightening is not. That is surely true. Expansionary monetary policy could cause some inflation because it is an expansionary policy. Budget tightening will not cause inflation precisely because it is a restrictive policy.

One group of experts that sought to get the U.S. to pursue "responsible" fiscal policies was an international panel assembled by the Institute for International Economics in Washington D.C. in late 1987 that issued a paper entitled *Resolving the Global Economic Crisis.*[1] The specifics of their program were as follows: The United States budget would have to swing away from its budget deficit by $150 billion over the next four or five years. That meant deficit reduction of roughly $40 billion per year. Only in this way could the trade deficit be made to show similar improvement. Failing such policy, there would be a sharp rise in interest rates in the United States as the rest of the world loses patience and refuses to finance further American borrowing with the dire consequences already noted including wholesale default of Latin debt. What do your back-of-the envelope calculations tell you would happen to the U.S. and other economies if the advice of the experts had been followed?

Never believe nonsense no matter what the Wall Street Journal and other self-appointed experts say. The catastrophe hasn't happened; it probably won't happen, and if it does happen the Fed can prevent it from damaging the economy. One just has to hope the Fed has sense enough to do that, and that is by no means a foregone conclusion. The fact that both American and foreign economists were spouting such rubbish is probably due to the fact that they naively thought it might be a good way to frighten Congress into reducing the budget deficit.

1. Institute for International Economics, Special Report, No. 6, December, 1987.

Is the Trade Deficit Correctable?

The theory behind the twin deficits suggests that a rise in the budget deficit will be accompanied by a rise in the trade deficit. This relationship held up pretty well during the first part of the 1980s but hasn't looked so wonderful since that time. To sort things out, it is again essential to distinguish between the structural and the cyclical deficits.

When the cyclical deficit widens, as it did in response to the recent recession, reduction in purchasing power relative to purchasing-power potential causes imports to be lower than they would otherwise be. It would not be at all surprising, therefore, to find an increase in the cyclical budget deficit to be accompanied by a decline in the trade deficit. Clearly, the theory that the trade deficit rises when the budget deficit rises applies only to increases in the structural budget deficit.

The structural budget deficit rose in every consecutive year from 1988 through 1992 yet the trade deficit (as measured by net exports) declined until 1992, instead of increasing as the theory predicts. Both the trade deficits and the structural deficit increased in 1992, but the increase in the trade deficit appears to have been caused by a slowdown in export growth caused by severe recessions in Europe and Japan. Since the dollar had been falling and the trade deficit narrowing, could it be that the old textbook theory, that a trade deficit will be self correcting through currency depreciation, has once more become relevant? Or, could it be that the difficulty of reaching positive net exports has some structural elements that are not readily amenable to correction by changes in relative prices?

Many of the foreign inroads into U.S. markets that occurred during the 1980s have an air of permanence about them. Despite increases in price differentials between foreign and domestic cars, how many owners of Acuras and Preludes do you know who are in a mood to trade in their Japanese produced Honda products for an American make? Similarly, the revolution in consumer electronics brought about by Sony and other Japanese companies is likely to leave a permanent impression on the tastes of American consumers. The decline in the dollar may eventually make a significant difference in the pattern of purchases. But don't bet on a major reversal any time soon.

Good Neighbor Economics

As explained previously, the restrictive monetary policies of the early 1980s had the effect of increasing U.S. imports and slowing the growth of exports. Inasmuch as U.S. exports are somebody else's imports, while U.S. imports are other countries' exports, this meant that the restrictive monetary policy that started the U.S. on its way into recession must have had an inflationary effect on other countries. Similarly, the further worsening of our trade accounts as the consequence of President Reagan's fiscal policies added more expansionary thrust to foreign economies.

The older textbooks taught that, under a system of market-determined exchange rates, countries would exist in virtual macroeconomic isolation. This meant that inflationary or deflationary shocks arising in one country would not be transmitted to others. If, for example, the government increased its spending and this raised GDP, the resultant rise in income would increase the demand for imports. A trade deficit would therefore develop. Because foreign exporters would then accumulate surplus dollars, they would sell these dollars in exchange for their own currencies and the value of the dollar would then decline. Because this would reduce imports and increase exports, the trade deficit would be eliminated. The effect of the rise in government spending on other countries' economies would therefore be temporary and self correcting.

The experience of the last twenty years confirms that the world economy no longer works that way. Because exchange rates have fluctuated widely, countries' exports and imports have also fluctuate widely, and this has affected countries' GDP levels because higher exports increase GDP whereas higher imports decrease it. Much of the fluctuation in exchange rates arises from capital movements. Capital movements, in turn, frequently arise in response to widening interest rate differentials. These differentials are often the consequence of conflicting macroeconomic policies pursued by countries.

Considerations such as these suggest that the trick to effecting domestic policy changes without harming others lies in the prevention of sharp interest rate differentials between countries. Since expansionary fiscal policy tends to raise interest rates, while expansionary monetary policy does the opposite, the key to good neighbor macroeconomics lies in coordinating the two policies in a manner that neutralizes the interest rate effects of the individual policies. For example if taxes are cut to stimulate the economy, this measure needs to be accompanied by sufficient growth in the money supply to prevent the tax cut from raising interest rates. Such coordination would prevent the capital movements that cause exchange rates to fluctuate sharply and that, in turn, lead to the instability of exports and imports which, in turn, make for overall economic instability.

Good neighbor economics, as defined above, may have its drawbacks. Fiscal policy tends to lack flexibility, and when the deficit is large there may be little support for expansionary fiscal policy even when the economy is below potential output. Perhaps of greater importance is the fact that coordination of fiscal and monetary policy to prevent capital flows implies acceptance of the existing level of interest rates. When priority attaches to raising investment, a case can be made for lowering domestic interest rates even when this has unfavorable foreign repercussions.

A situation which illustrates the difficulty arose in 1992 when the Fed belatedly loosened its monetary stranglehold thereby lowering interest rates. The predictable outcome was a capital outflow that depreciated the dollar tending therefore to raise exports and reduce imports. While this was beneficial for employment in the U.S., it had the opposite effect in European countries. These countries found themselves caught in a squeeze between the low interest-rate policy of the U.S. and the high interest-rate policy of the German Bundesbank. The depreciation of the dollar increased already high unemployment levels and, at the same time, the affected countries could not take steps to expand their economies because they were obliged to harmonize their monetary policies with the conservative Bundesbank.

After the collapse of the Bretton-Woods system of fixed exchange rates in 1973, European countries formed the European Monetary System, EMS, which created an intra-European fixed exchange-rate system. In such a system a country running a deficit vis a vis other countries in the system must finance the deficit with currencies acceptable to creditor countries. Stock piles of such currencies, held by central banks, are called foreign exchange reserves. Exchange rates are fixed by the commitment of countries' central banks to buy and sell their own currencies at a fixed price in exchange for other currencies. Therefore, a country running a deficit will have to buy up its own currency in exchange for its foreign exchange reserves. This reduces the money supply and since reserves are limited they cannot finance perpetual deficits. Thus, deficit countries are forced to take steps to slow inflation and become more competitive. This, in turn, means imitating the monetary policies of the most conservative country in the system.

In late 1992 Great Britain found herself in a severe predicament because the appreciation of the pound relative to the dollar made her goods uncompetitive in U.S. markets and also made U.S. goods increasingly attractive to British consumers. The result was higher unemployment piled on top of an already high unemployment rate. To restore competitiveness it would have been appropriate for Britain to devalue the pound vis a vis the dollar. But since the entire basket of European currencies fluctuated in unison vis a vis the dollar, this was not possible without breaking away from the fixed exchange rates of the EMS. That, finally, is what Britain and others were forced to do. The effect has been to weaken the EMS as well as to threaten ratification of the Maastricht Treaty under which European countries intend to convert the EMS into complete monetary integration. As explained in the final chapter this treaty takes the radical step of abolishing national currencies in favor of a uniform currency and the creation of a European super central bank empowered to create money and manage monetary policy.

Although the Federal Reserve's lowering of interest rates in 1992 caused considerable discomfort abroad, the bulk of the anger was directed at the Bundesbank for persisting in its high interest-rate policy despite high unemployment and mounting evidence that the European economy was heading for a major recession. Under the circumstances it was clear that it was Germany' responsibility to lower interest rates rather than U.S. responsibility for raising them up again.

10

Deficits and Foreign Debt

The Latin Debt Crisis

The interest-rate escalation as well as the loss of export markets caused by the world recession of the early 1980s was heavily responsible for the third great surge in the growth of the foreign debt of non-oil producing developing countries. Two earlier waves--those of 1973-74 and 1979 – were associated with increases in the cost of oil imported from the OPEC countries and the consequent inflationary-recessions that afflicted the industrial countries. Following the quadrupling of oil prices in 1974, oil importing developing countries had to pay more for their oil, their export markets dwindled as the industrial economies slowed, and the cost of their non-oil imports increased because of higher inflation in industrial countries. The financial crisis that might have been expected to accompany the huge redirection of world income and wealth towards oil exporters was averted by a process of quickly recycling the surplus (petrodollars) earned by the oil exporters by lending them back to the countries that needed loans to pay for imports.[1]

But when the interest-rate escalation that began in 1980 and the subsequent recession in the industrial countries arrived, developing countries found their export markets dwindling just as their borrowing capacity reached exhaustion. The recession in the industrial countries lowered their export earnings, the appreciation of the dollar raised the cost of dollar-denominated imports (including

1. A large fraction of the increase in the so-called petro-dollars earned by the OPEC countries was deposited by them in banks in industrial countries. Having a huge inflow of resources, the banks found avid borrowers in the countries that needed to finance their higher priced oil imports.

OPEC oil), and the escalation of interest rates caused by the monetary and budget policies of the U.S. and other industrial countries added hugely to the cost of debt service. Since there was no surplus of petro dollars available for financing imports, the borrowers could no longer meet their obligations and the debt crisis, as it came to be perceived, struck with full force.

Table 10-1 provides data that help to study the debt problem. It shows that Latin American debt increased 580 percent during the ten year period 1973 to 1983. The ability of a country to finance its interest and amortization obligations depends on how much foreign exchange it has, and an indication of this is its export earnings. Therefore the ratio of debt to exports provides a useful measure of the debt burden. For the Latin countries this ratio rose 70.5 percent from 1973 to 1983, and its ratio of debt service costs to exports rose 60 percent.

The rise in world interest rates militated against rapid economic growth, and that was certainly an aggravating factor in the world debt crises because it meant that the export markets of developing countries could not grow rapidly enough and that their terms of trade would remain adverse as long as this were the case. Some therefore viewed the acceleration of economic growth (and inflation) in the industrial countries as an essential step in reducing the debt problems of developing countries. It was, however, widely claimed[2] that this could not be done until the United States put its budget in order because, until that happened, interest rates would remain high.

Others argued that, although the United States is an important actor in a very severe problem of global imbalance, it is by no means the only one. Getting the U.S. budget and trade deficits down would help but would only scratch the surface. Some went so far as to suggest that the appreciation of the dollar caused by U.S. monetary-fiscal policies provided other countries with export demand without which many of them would have been far less prosperous. While it is unfortunate that a relatively rich country such as the United States

---

2. For example, William R. Cline, *International Debt: Systemic Risk and Policy Response,* Institute for International Economics, Washington, D.C., 1984.

Table 10-1

External Debt of Non-Oil Developing Countries

Item	1973	1978	1980	1982	1983
Total Debt (billion $)	$130	343	485	650	686
Asian Countries	30	80	116	154	168
Latin American Countries	44	133	193	288	299
Ratio of Debt to Exports of Goods and Services (%)					
All non-oil Developing Countries	115	131	113	148	154
Asian Countries	93	76	68	81	83
Latin American Countries	176	218	188	283	300
Ratio of Debt Service to Exports of Goods and Services					
All non-oil Developing Countries	16	20	18	25	22
Asian Countries	7	10	8	11	10
Latin American Countries	30	42	36	55	48

Source: International Monetary Fund, *World Economic Outlook,* April 1984 and September 1984.

has been importing capital[3] from a relatively capital-poor world, it does not follow that a reduction in U.S. import demand would cause a redirection of export surpluses to the countries that are most in need of these goods and services. Indeed, taken by itself, a deflationary U.S. fiscal policy would be harmful for all concerned--the United States, as well as for other countries.

Deficit reduction, beginning in 1984, provided it had been combined with supportive monetary policy designed to avert recession, would have been appropriate for the U.S. acting in its own interest.

3. The phrase importing capital means that a country is consuming more than it is producing because its imports exceed its exports, and that it is paying for the difference with IOU's. The thought is that since the U.S. is a relatively rich country, it ought to be exporting capital, thereby providing resources to poor countries. The U.S. was a heavy importer of capital during much of the 19th century when imports of capital hgoods, especially from Great Britain, helped to underwrite the rapid industrialization of the economy.

But the question remained whether any of this would have eased the problems of the world's chronic debtors and creditors. A decline in the U.S. trade deficit means that others are exporting less relative to their imports. For the creditor countries this spells job losses and stagnation. For deficit-debtor countries, the loss of export markets in the U.S. widens their deficits and exacerbates their debt problems. Although lower interest rates would surely help, it is not at all clear whether, on balance, debtor countries would have been much better off as the result of deficit reduction by the U.S.

If the United States reduces its budget deficit, and if this reduces import demand, this releases resources for use elsewhere. That fact does not in any way guarantee that the resources will flow to where they are needed. To redirect Japanese production away from the U.S. and towards poor countries it would be constructive to encourage the Japanese and other surplus countries to provide far more financial assistance to the poor countries than they are currently providing. That would make far more sense than persisting in the annual ritual of browbeating the Japanese into making their markets more accessible. What Japanese person in his right mind would buy an American car when the American manufacturer can't be bothered to move the steering wheel to the right side of the vehicle?

In August 1982 the Mexican government announced that it did not have the foreign exchange needed to meet its current obligations to foreign creditors. Although Peru and Bolivia had earlier made similar announcements, it was the threat of Mexican default that produced major shock waves because a default by Mexico was seen as directly imperilling the viability of the banking systems of industrial countries. It therefore became the event that triggered the "third world debt crisis" into official consciousness and mobilized creditors, their governments, and the International Monetary Fund (IMF) into crisis management to prevent a major country from defaulting on its international obligations.

It was determined that the first priority would be to ease the immediate crisis by providing short term loans to the beleaguered Mexican government. The United States quickly pieced together $3 billion, European central banks provided another $1 billion, and the OECD[4] countries supplied $2 billion in export credits. All together some $6 billion in emergency relief was promptly arranged.

In exchange for this assistance the Mexican government was obliged to sign an agreement with the IMF committing her to take steps designed to reduce her foreign debt to more manageable proportions. To reduce borrowing it would be necessary to raise exports relative to imports. Import reduction necessitated reductions in national expenditures which, in turn, necessitated reductions in the country's fiscal deficit. Export expansion would normally have to await longer term measures designed to enhance productivity and competitiveness. But in the short run exports could be made more attractive in foreign markets by currency depreciation, and that would have the further beneficial effect of making imports more expensive.

The Mexican economy went into a horrendous tailspin almost from the moment the IMF's austerity program went into effect. Real GDP, which had risen at an average annual rate of growth of about 6 percent during the preceding twenty years, fell 5.3 percent in 1983. Combined with the continuation of a rate of population growth in excess of 3 percent, this meant a real per capita income contraction of close to 8 percent in one year. It was estimated that half the labor force either became unemployed or underemployed, while Mexico's official unemployment rate rose to 16 percent.

The increase in exports hoped for by the IMF required growth in Mexico's industrial capacity. However the growth of new productive facilities collapsed as investment declined 28 percent in response to the austerity program. The very problem the program was intended to solve got worse as Mexico's foreign debt continued to balloon and her ratio of debt to GDP increased from 49.4 percent in 1982 to 56.2 percent in 1985.

Mexico's imports dropped 42 percent in 1982, just as the IMF had intended. Unfortunately, this had to mean that someone else was losing export markets, and the economic contraction was therefore spreading beyond Mexico. It was hardly an accident that the merchandise exports of the United States dropped $22 billion between 1980 and 1983. Some of this decline was caused by the appreciation of the dollar, but much of it was attributable to the Latin debt crisis. About $14 billion of these U.S. export reductions were lost in Latin

4. OECD is an acronym that stands for Organization of Economic Cooperation and Development. Its membership includes nearly all major industrial countries including the United States.

America, Mexico alone accounting for close to one half of this total. This meant less production, less income, and the loss of numerous jobs in the United States. Thus, industry, agriculture, and labor, in both debtor and creditor countries, paid a heavy price for a decision, concurred in by the U.S. Treasury, the Federal Reserve, and the IMF, to engage in a futile effort to reduce Mexican borrowing for the dubious purpose of bailing out the commercial banks whose questionable lending had put them at risk by the possibility of a Mexican default.

The Role of the International Monetary Fund

The IMF has entered the discussion and a short digression on that institution and its mandate is therefore in order. The IMF, or Fund as it is called, was created in 1944 at an international monetary conference in Bretton Woods, New Hampshire. The International Bank for Reconstruction and Development, or World Bank for short, was created at the same time. The rules for the conduct of international monetary relations were also agreed to at the conference. The international monetary system that emerged was called the Bretton Woods system. One of the two primary responsibilities of the IMF was to police the system, and the other was to provide short-term credit to countries that were running deficits in their balance of payments. The need for such credit emerged from the circumstance that, under the rules, exchange rates were to be fixed by government action. This was to be done by having the U.S. treasury commit herself to purchase and sell dollars at a fixed (official) price in exchange for gold when asked to do so by foreign central banks. This fixed the gold price of the dollar in the market place because it was never necessary to purchase gold at a price above the official U.S. price, nor was it necessary to sell gold at a lower price. Other countries' central banks were required to purchase and sell dollars in exchange for their own currencies at a fixed official price. This fixed all currency prices relative to the dollar as well as to each other. No private party ever had to accept a lower, or pay a higher, price than the official price. Under the system gold and the dollar became the world's "reserve currencies" with which central banks dealt with each other.

A system of this sort is called a fixed exchange rate system. When countries export more to the U.S. than they import, or when U.S.

firms build overseas subsidiaries, other countries accumulate dollars that find their way into the hands of their central banks. These central bank accumulations are called foreign exchange reserves. But if a country imports more than she exports she loses her reserves and when reserves approach exhaustion the country is forced to take steps to stem the reserve loss. This usually means reducing import demand by slowing the economy and improving competitiveness by slowing inflation. In such situations the IMF helps by lending reserves to the deficit country so that the painful deflationary adjustments can be spread over a longer period of time. To make sure that the loans are repaid the IMF insists that the deficit country take steps to correct its deficits. Such IMF "conditionality" normally takes the form of insistence that the country reduce inflation by reducing its rate of growth of "domestic credit."

When the balance sheets of all a country's banks, including the central bank, are consolidated into a single balance sheet the result is called the monetary survey. The assets of the banking system are divided into domestic assets, otherwise known as domestic credit, and foreign exchange reserves. The sum of these two equals the nation's money supply which is recorded as a liability of the banking system. An open-market purchase by the central bank increases the banking system's holdings of government securities (domestic credit) and simultaneously increases the money supply. Similarly, as explained in Chapter 3, in developing countries government budget deficits normally must be financed by borrowing from the central bank so that the budget restraint is,

$$\Delta M = E - T$$

and there is therefore a direct link between the budget deficit, domestic credit, and the money supply. Thus reduction in the growth of domestic credit necessarily means reduction in the government's fiscal deficit.

After 1955 the U.S. began running steady deficits in its balance of payments. Although exports exceeded imports many dollars were also spent in making foreign investments. Because this caused a net outflow of dollars foreign central banks were obliged to buy the surplus dollars to maintain fixed exchange rates. At first the dollar outflow was welcome to increase international liquidity, but later it became excessive causing countries that were accumulating dollars to purchase U.S. gold. By 1967 the gold drain had been so huge that the U.S. was forced to ask other countries to stop buying what remained of the gold stock. Since gold could no longer be used to settle international accounts the Bretton Woods system became, in effect, a dollar standard.

Thereafter as the U.S. deficit widened, partly in response to the inflation caused by the Viet Nam war, foreign central banks accumulated ever larger amounts of dollars. But when foreign central banks purchased dollars they sold their own currency in exchange. This caused foreign money supplies to increase sharply and that, in turn, created severe inflationary pressures. In early 1973, with their money supplies out of control and inflation accelerating rapidly, the countries of the European Economic Community (EEC) found the situation so intolerable that they suspended their dollar purchases. The Bretton Woods system thus came to an abrupt end as exchange rates were cut loose to find their own levels as determined by the forces of demand and supply. Since 1973 the U.S. dollar has fluctuated more or less freely with respect to the Canadian dollar, the Japanese yen, and the currencies of the EEC. Flexible, or free floating, exchange rates are not, however, universal. The EEC very quickly created its own European Monetary System (EMS) under which the member countries created an intra-European fixed exchange rate system. The entire basket of European currencies was, however, permitted to fluctuate against the dollar and the yen.

Most developing countries felt it in their interest to retain fixed exchange rates and most of them linked their currencies to the currencies of their most important industrial-country trading partners. French speaking African countries pegged to the French franc. English speaking countries pegged to the British pound. And many Latin countries defined the values of their currencies in terms of dollars.

Although flexible exchange rates largely eliminated the need for IMF assistance to industrial countries, the retention of fixed exchange rates by developing countries continues the need for IMF assistance to such countries. Consequently, after 1973 the IMF increasingly became an institution concerned with the problems of developing countries, just as the World Bank had become following post World War II reconstruction.

The IMF solution for poor debtor countries has been finely tuned over many years of dealing with countries in need of balance of payments assistance. It was resurrected on a grand scale during the era of massive debt, without much apparent consideration given to its appropriateness, and applied to the problems of debt-ridden developing countries. The bitter deflationary medicine that the IMF prescribes had originally been intended to cope with the problems of a country that had permitted inflation and an overvalued currency to cause its balance of payments to deteriorate. It presumed, moreover, that the country was an isolated case, and that the world economy was functioning well so that deflationary pressures, imposed on one or two deficit countries, would not be excessively harmful to world employment. In that event, it was envisioned that the IMF could help the situation by providing short term financing to act as a buffer in return for efforts by the country to get its inflation under control and improve its international competitiveness.

By imposing its program on every debtor country that needed financial assistance, the IMF placed itself in the untenable position of behaving as if it wanted all countries to generate trade surpluses, without appearing to recognize that the end is unattainable and that the consequences of attempting to achieve it are disastrous. Applied indiscriminately, the logical outcome of IMF austerity programs is global deflation and depression. Debtors are denied essential imports, and creditors cannot sell their exports. Alfred Watkins aptly commented that:

> IMF policies were...designed to be implemented within the context of robust and sustained world wide economic expansion. As long as the world economy was growing rapidly, the austerity prescribed for one country would not have a noticeable impact on international economic growth rates.
>
> IMF austerity programs are not being implemented in one country at a time, but in over 30 countries simultaneously. They are not being applied within the context of a buoyant world economy, but on top of an international economy already plagued by slow growth and high unemployment. Debtor countries are not facing balance of payments imbalances caused by too much growth and too many imports. Rather, their

problems result from slow growth and too many required interest payments.[5]

Structural Indebtedness

The experience of Argentina, Mexico, and a host of other countries makes clear that the problems many debtor countries face cannot be classified as temporary emergencies that can be palliated by buffer loans and a short spate of deflationary belt tightening. Many of today's debtor countries suffer from what has been described as "structural indebtedness," which means that such countries cannot grow and prosper without more or less continuous foreign borrowing. The key facts responsible for this condition are rapid population growth combined with inadequate domestic capital goods production capacity. In such a situation, a country's ability to grow and employ its work force depends directly on its ability to pay for imported machinery, equipment, and other capital goods. Denied such capital-goods imports, the country will not have the tools needed to provide the new entrants into its work force with jobs. Without the precious imports, economic growth comes to a halt, and unemployment increases as labor force entrants find themselves without equipment with which to work.[6] The need for capital goods is so acute that even after the collapse of 1982, roughly 92 percent of Mexico's import expenditures continued to be made on capital goods and intermediate inputs vital to the productive process.

A similar problem arises when the IMF insists that a debtor country reduce its fiscal deficit. Since the IMF is reluctant to tell a country which expenditure categories to cut, politically sensitive governments have tended to take the path of least resistance and have cut the capital budgets that finance public investment projects. Such cuts offend the fewest vested interests and create the smallest amount of immediate political fallout. Consequently, when the IMF moves in, this usually means that public expenditures for transpor-

---

5. Watkins, Alfred J., *Till Debt Do Us Part*, Roosevelt Center for American Policy Studies, 1986.

6. This is one of the key points documented in a splendid study by Thomas O. Enders and Richard P. Mattione, Latin America: *The Crises of Debt and Growth*, The Brookings Institution, *Studies in International Economics,* 1984.

tation facilities, public power projects, schools, and hospitals get slashed. However, curtailing public investment is very much like cutting capital goods imports. Without public transportation, communications, and power facilities, factories cannot operate profitably, and without profitable factories the growing labor force cannot be employed.

The decline in investment, and the resulting inadequacy of the capital stock in Latin America, is one of the most damaging consequence of the IMF austerity programs. To take an extreme example, real private net fixed investment in Argentina was negative during the 1983-88 period. The country's stock of productive facilities not only failed to grow, it had not even been maintained as it deteriorated. Thus the capital stock in 1988 was not even adequate to employ the labor force that it had been capable of employing five years earlier. Several years of IMF style austerity programs made shambles of the economies of much of Latin America. By 1988 the drop in Mexican per-capita income had ballooned to between 15 and 20 percent. Similar disastrous declines in per-capita income afflicted much of the remainder of the hemisphere. Bolivia, the worst case, suffered a collapse in per capita income of close to 40 percent. Per capita income dropped more than 20 percent in Argentina, Venezuela, Peru and Ecuador. Jeffrey Sachs commented on the catastrophe as follows:

> the real economies of these countries has fallen back to the levels of the early 1970s--15 to 20 years of lost economic development...Economic development has been lost to an entire generation, with few signs of sustained economic recovery in prospect.[7]

Chronic Creditors: More Structural Problems

Although there is occasional recognition that the Latin countries have deep-rooted structural problems, there is virtually no recognition that many creditor countries also have such problems. For every debtor there must be a creditor. Many of today's creditor countries have a strong interest in maintaining that status. Does that make

7. Sachs, Jeffrey, "The Debt Crisis at a Turning Point," Interview in *Challenge*, May/June, 1988.

sense--extending unlimited credit thereby giving away goods and services? It doesn't seem to and yet there are several countries -- Germany and Japan being conspicuous examples -- that appear to have had to do exactly that in order to keep their highly productive labor forces employed. The structural problems of these countries are every bit as serious as the problems of the debtor countries but they go largely unnoticed because, in today's curious world, creditor status is equated with virtue and evidence of sound government economic management, whereas debtor status suggests profligacy and the government's inability to control inflation. The problem, however, is that the urge to maintain large and widening export surpluses greatly compounds the difficulties of others in balancing their international accounts. Foreign debt reduction requires debtor countries to expand exports relative to imports. But all countries cannot do this simultaneously. And if the habitual creditors are busy boosting their own trade surpluses, how can the debtors hope to adjust?

Just as rapid population growth helps to account for the import dependence of Latin countries, so also is slow population growth a major factor in explaining the export dependence of Germany and Japan. Japan, a country of some one-hundred million people, has little population growth and an acute shortage of land. Although its domestic market is large, that market does not keep pace with productive capacity. Japanese post World War II economic development was built up largely in industries that produce durable goods. Such industries tend to show rapid growth of labor productivity, and, as a result, each Japanese durable goods factory must increase production five or six percent a year merely to keep its existing work force employed. At the same time, the absence of population growth means that the domestic market for such goods quickly becomes saturated. When, for example, Japanese workers began to enjoy the fruits of post-war recovery during the 1950s, their need for inexpensive transportation caused them to purchase motor bikes that were produced by Honda and a few other firms. Within a period of three years, nearly all of the Japanese workers had been supplied with motor bikes. Subsequent demand would then either have to be replacement demand or it would have to come from abroad. Honda, obviously, had no choice but to market its motor bikes overseas and to expand into other lines of activity if it expected to survive and prosper.

Honda's case was typical. Indeed, any Japanese durable-goods industry hopeful of survival and growth had to look to foreign markets in order to do so. Also, as the invasion of foreign markets took hold, Japanese firms discovered the important fact that increased output allowed exporting firms to enjoy scale economies[8] that reduced unit production costs, thereby greatly improving their ability to compete effectively in the domestic market. Japanese firms quickly learned that exporting was a key to survival in the home market.

Personal saving as a percentage of disposable income is far higher in Japan than in the United States. An acute shortage of land is one of the factors that helps to explain this fact. With narrow roads, small plots of land, and small, closely-juxtaposed and thinly-constructed houses, Japanese families cannot make use of the large automobiles, ear-shattering hi-fi equipment, and major appliances that are routinely purchased by families in other well-to-do countries. Ambitious to become home owners, while faced with the tremendous cost of land, Japanese workers save large fractions of their incomes for this purpose. Add to this a traditional lack of enthusiasm for imports, and it can readily be seen why the Japanese must generate trade surpluses if they expect to maintain high employment. The domestic economy simply does not provide adequate demand to purchase the output of the highly productive and efficient Japanese industrial establishment. This was especially so during the 1980s when the terms of trade were such that the prices of primary imported goods were cheap relative to the value of Japanese exports.

A somewhat similar situation exists in Germany. Stationary population combined with rapid advances in labor productivity also characterizes the Germany economy. Germans also suffers from a pathological fear of inflation that has caused their government and central bank to pursue conservative policies that have had the effect of persistently improving international competitiveness and therefore supporting continuous export expansion. Add to this the celebrated German virtues of "sparsamkeit" (frugality) and

8. The term economies of scale refers to the fact that, up to a point, the unit cost of production in most manufacturing industries declines as the level of production increases. A small firm cannot, for example, take advantage of the assembly line methods used by large firms.

"tüchtigkeit" (industriousness), as well as the notion that the government should live within its means to prevent inflation, and you have another country that has gotten itself into structural dependence for its prosperity on large, and widening, trade surpluses.

If there is a group of debtor countries that must import more than it exports in order to employ its work force, and a group of creditor countries that must do the opposite, this suggests the presence of a natural symbiosis between debtors and creditors. Both parties are addicted. But, by mutual enabling -- that is sustaining a relationship of resource transfer from creditor to debtor -- they can operate their economies at high employment levels. Unfortunately, as in the case of many addictions that are gratified by reciprocal enabling, there are powerful forces tending to undermine the arrangement. The seeds of breakdown arise from the circumstance that a process of continual lending by creditors to debtors carries with it steady increases in foreign debt. That in turn implies increases in interest payments which, if the borrowing continues unabated, eventually grow so large that new borrowing is necessitated merely to pay the interest on existing debt. As this goes on, the chronic debtors find it increasingly difficult to finance badly needed imports, and the creditors find it harder to sell their exports even though the size of their loans is growing steadily. Continuation of this symbiotic relationship implies ever growing red ink and threatens ultimate economic breakdown for the parties that have come to depend on it.

The chronically export-dependent countries would long ago have had to come to grips with their horrendous structural problems had the United States not shown such an enormous appetite for their autos, electronic equipment, and tourist attractions. An impeccable conservative, the late Malcom S. Forbes Jr., concurred. He noted that,

> If it had not been for the American market, Europe's economy would be even more stagnant than it is, the Third World would be in even worse financial shape, and even Japan would have had considerably lower growth rates.[9]

---

9. Forbes, Malcom, "Extending the Reagan Revolution," *Cato Policy Report*, May/June, 1988.

If what has been said is at all near the mark, it suggests that the United States, although its monetary and fiscal policies played an important role in the debt crisis, is not at the center of the fundamental problem. The U.S. does, to be sure, need to get its budget under better control, but this does very little to scratch the surface of the basic structural problems that are plaguing the world economy. The solution, if there is one, lies in finding an appropriate recycling mechanism that enables the creditor countries to continue to finance the import dependence of debtor countries for as long as it takes to alleviate the structural problems that afflict both sets of countries.

The suggestion here is that economies such as West Germany and Japan must run large and perhaps widening trade surpluses in order to maintain high employment. The hypothesis implies rejection of the idea that domestic demand can be expanded to substitute for international demand. One reason for such rejection is that much of the investment that goes on in export-dependent countries is geared to the construction of productive facilities and capital goods for the export industries. Therefore, when export demand declines, so also does investment demand. It is difficult to conceive how monetary and/or tax policies can change this situation. Since investment and exports march in step, it is not reasonable to expect to be able to raise investment by amounts capable of compensating for declining exports.

On many occasions during the last twenty years American officials have attempted to prod the Japanese and European governments into implementing internal demand-expansion measures. During the slow recovery that followed the recession of 1975, the Carter Administration urged the Europeans to expand more rapidly but largely to no avail. Since inflation accompanied unemployment at that time, reluctance to expand demand was understandable. But, recovery from the depression of 1982 was again accompanied by slow growth in Europe, and this time the problem of inflation seemed far less severe. Nevertheless, reluctance to move aggressively against slow growth and unemployment persisted. It is important to ask why there is such continuing resistance to domestic demand expansion? Europe and Japan are again suffering severe recessions. Yet the German Bundesbank has been reluctant to reduce interest rates. What, besides the traditional fear of inflation, could account for this?

As frequently claimed by representatives of European countries it is their belief that internal demand expansion is not likely to be capable of replacing the demand that would be lost by a reduction in their trade surpluses. A common European explanation for this puzzling hypothesis is that wages rise automatically when prices rise. So-called money wages are indexed in whole or in part to the cost of living.

Such lock-step movement of wages and prices prevents relative prices from adjusting so as to provide the changes in cost-price relationships that are needed to motivate firms to expand production and employment. Economic theory teaches that such incentives arise from an increase in selling price relative to the unit cost of production. Any businessman will tell you the same thing. A rough, though inverted, indicator of this ratio is the so-called real wage rate, which is calculated by dividing an index of hourly money wages by an index of prices. A decline in real wages provides employers with an incentive to increase production and employment. A rise in real wage rates does the opposite. But if money wages rise proportionately whenever domestic prices rise, real wages cannot be lowered and production and employment will then not increase in response to a rise in total spending in the economy. Rather, the added spending is wasted in inflation, as wages and prices rise in step, while output and employment remain the same.

Rising export demand is the one source of aggregate expenditure increase that may not run afoul of the downward real-wage problem. Suppose that Audi, BMW, and Mercedes-Benz conduct successful advertizing campaigns that substantially raise German overseas car sales. This increase in export demand raises Germany's current-account surplus and therefore tends to appreciate the deutschemark. The appreciation reduces the domestic currency cost of German imports. And since imported goods enter into the cost of living as measured by the consumer price index, German workers observe this as a decline in the cost of living and therefore as a rise in their real compensation. This, in turn, makes it possible for the increased export demand to pull up domestic prices without this raising the cost of living above its initial level, and this averts wage escalation. Because of the rise in domestic prices, unaccompanied by wage increases, employers perceive an improved domestic cost-price relationship. Production and employment then increase.

On the other hand, a rise in internal spending induced by government policy tends to depreciate the currency because, among other things, it raises the demand for imports. This raises the home-currency price of imports and therefore increases the consumer price index. Automatic wage indexing then raises money wages. The real wage therefore cannot be lowered, and the added spending merely adds to inflation as wages and prices escalate even when there is heavy unemployment.

These considerations help to explain the odd reluctance of Germany to expand its economy despite the presence of extensive unemployment. They offer a reasonable explanation for the seeming paradox that export demand is viewed as "good" demand that raises production and employment; whereas internally generated demand is viewed as "bad" demand that causes inflation.

What about other European countries? Under the rules of the European Monetary System (EMS), the exchange rates of European countries are pegged to each other. Suppose that France considers her unemployment rate to be too high and that she therefore takes action to expand her economy by the use of monetary policy. The Bank of France therefore drives down interest rates by purchasing government securities. Since this makes the financial assets in a high interest rate country such as Germany more attractive, a capital flow from France to Germany develops. French investors convert their francs into deutchemarks at the Bank of France and France therefore lose her reserves of deutchemarks. Since the stockpile of reserves is limited in size, the outflow cannot be permitted to continue. France must therefore abandon the attempt to lower interest rates. Indeed, in a fixed exchange rate system, the policies of all countries participating in the system tend to be largely dictated by the policies of its most conservative member.

Good Neighbor Economics: Upside Down Version

Perceived export dependence is likely to make for economic policies that enhance, rather than reduce, export dependence. The government of an export-dependent economy will support its export industries with tax credits, export subsidies and the like. Such policies are the diametric opposite of conventional concepts of international economic cooperation. Cooperation implies that if a country is running an export surplus, its government should pursue policies that reduce exports and raise imports thereby fostering international adjustment. Policies that support these goals are tariff reduction and expansionary monetary-fiscal policies that raise import demand and permit domestic prices to rise so that the economy's competitive advantage declines. But a country that attempts to maximize exports and minimize imports will do the opposite. It will discourage imports by raising tariffs and pursue restrictive policies that hold down inflation in order to improve the country's competitive position in international trade.

Such behavior greatly complicates the policy problems of other countries because it is not possible to escape the conclusion that deflationary policies must reduce spending and cause unemployment somewhere. Although monetary-fiscal austerity is universally admired, this admiration has obscured the fact that these conservative policies have acted systematically to undervalue the currencies of the creditor countries, thereby providing substantial and continuing cost advantages to their exporters. This has led to high employment and prosperity for these countries. But since they have been stealing demand from elsewhere, their employment gains have come at the expense of employment in other countries. Since continuation of these policies means that other countries will tend to continue to import more than they export, it also contributes to the growth of global debt.

In conclusion, it has been important to note that the fiscal deficit can have powerful effects on other countries. It has been equally important to note that not all the world's economic problems can be laid at the feet of U.S. budgetary and other policies.

Real wage indexing is an important matter because of the frequency with which it has been suggested as rational policy for the United States. Senator Edward Kennedy has long advocated such a policy and President Clinton spoke favorably about it early in his term. However, both European experience and economic analysis teach that it would be a mistake for the United States to index its wage rates to the cost of living. Although there are cost of living escalators in some labor contracts, and although the minimum wage is raised periodically to offset the effects of inflation, there still is sufficient flexibility in the economy to allow for real wage adjustment.[10] However, if wages are adjusted automatically every time the cost of living rises, this will build in a structural barrier that, similar to European experience, makes it increasingly difficult to raise employment.

---

10. Increases in wages, including minimum wages, raise the labor cost of employers thereby causing firms to reduce output and employment. If the decline in production equals 10, then that much income is lost. However, inasmuch as consumption is likely to fall by only 8, there develops excess commodity demand of 2. The excess demand then leads to a rise in the level of prices. Therefore part of the gain in real wages is lost to rising prices. If the increase in unemployment caused by the wage increases causes the government to engage in expansionary policies to eliminate the unemployment, the net effect will be to raise prices in exactly the same proportion as the original wage increase. Real wages and employment will therefore return to their original levels. The increase in money wages does nothing to raise the real wage that workers receive. Most observers believe that the effects of minimum wage increases tend to be neutralized in this manner.

It is important to be concerned about the living standards of low paid workers. But the raising of the mimimum wage is hardly an effective way to deal with the problem. Government financed wage subsidies or tax credits would be far more effective and far less detrimental to the economy. This would raise the standard of living of low-wage workers, and since it could also lower labor cost as seen by employers it would raise production, employment, and also slow inflation. Raising minimum wages does the opposite.

11

Economic Integration

Trade Integration: the EEC and NAFTA

The countries of Europe have been creating a free trade area that rivals the United States as one of the world's largest. It is somewhat ironic that the model of the United States seems to have been used by the Europeans as evidence of the prosperity, growth, and efficiency that could be achieved in a large free trade area. The European example then became instrumental in the planning and adoption of the North American Free Trade Agreement, NAFTA, by Canada, Mexico, and the United States.

Imagine that the United States were divided into 50 separate sovereign states each of which maintained tariffs against the goods of other states. Out of state goods would then become more expensive so that in-state producers would gain competitive advantages. If the tariffs were high enough, it might then even pay to grow hothouse oranges in northern states even though this would be far more costly than growing them in Florida and California. Steel producers would be faced with higher cost iron ore imported from Minnesota and it might therefore pay to establish steel mills in that state even though shipping costs for finished steel from Minnesota to other states might become astronomical. If you live in Tennessee a few miles from the Kentucky border you might nevertheless have to obtain a passport and a work permit if you got a job in Kentucky. You would have to stop and show that passport each time you crossed the state line. And its possible that you might have to pay taxes in both states. If the barriers are onerous enough you might decide to take a job in Tennessee for which you are overqualified and under paid, while someone with less competence than yourself gets the job in Kentucky. Its not hard to see how such legal barriers would severely misallocate resources and retard economic growth.

Its not surprising that all past American Nobel Laureates in economics, of whatever philosophical persuasion, were in support of NAFTA. Indeed the superiority of free trade over restrictive practices by countries against each other, is one of the few issues over which virtual unanimity exists among American and European economists. When Adam Smith published his *Wealth of Nations* in 1776 he laid the intellectual foundation for free trade by pointing out that "the division of labor is limited only by the extent of the market." During the early 19th century the English economist, David Ricardo, sharpened the argument for free trade by stating his *law of comparative advantage.* To illustrate, suppose that you are the owner of a small business and that you hire a number of employees to perform various duties including person X charged with paper work, typing, bookkeeping, and the like. You discover that occasionally the books are not quite correctly kept and that the paper work moves more slowly than had you attended to it yourself. Do you discharge person X and do the work yourself, or do you lower the standard of efficiency that you apply to yourself? You reason that although you yourself are better at routine office work than person X, you cannot take on those duties because your time is far more valuable in managing other aspects of your business including its policies. Since your business would really suffer if you took time away from these duties you reason that person X, despite occasional errors and inefficiencies, is, in fact, a valuable employee. You couldn't replace person X at the same wage and hope for improvement. And you certainly wouldn't want the government to come along and impose a heavy tax on you for employing person X. But that is what tariffs and other obstructions to the free movement of goods and services do.

If the world's highly capable persons were left to do all the world's work they would have to spread themselves thin and there would be no economic role left for the less capable. The law of comparative advantage explains that real income will be maximized if everyone does that at which he is best, or, if you will, turns those things that are not worth his time over to someone else. Such things as tariffs, quotas, export subsidies and the like roll back comparative advantage and this deprives the world economy of its full potential real income.

The original name for a regional free trade arrangement was customs union. Such a union was formed shortly after World War II between Belgium, the Netherlands, and Luxembourg; hence the acronym Benelux. Multi-national free trade areas can be established for specific commodities. In the Schuman Plan the European countries created the European Steel and Coal Community which removed tariffs and other obstructions thereby providing advantages to the most efficient producers of steel and coal. The movement towards freer intra European trade has continued steadily so that the European Economic Community, EEC, has become one of the world's largest free trade areas; rivaling that of the United States.

The North American Free Trade Agreement (NAFTA) recently approved by the Congress is another giant step in the direction of trade liberalization. The agreement virtually eliminates all barriers to trade between Canada, Mexico, and the United States thereby creating an enormous free trade area of the kind that has already been created in Europe. NAFTA promises to provide substantial gains in U.S. exports and therefore jobs. Increased exports stimulate the economy raising both the rate of economic growth and the level of employment. NAFTA may even have beneficial effects on the Federal deficit. Because of greater prosperity the cyclical deficit will be lower.

There are two reasons for being optimistic about job creation. Mexico's population is growing far more rapidly than population in the U.S., and Mexico's tariffs against U.S. goods averaged 10 percent as opposed to the 3 percent average tariff that the U.S. imposed. For both of these reasons the job gains through export expansion are likely to be far greater than the jobs lost to import competition. Principal opposition to NAFTA came from nervous labor leaders and loose cannons, such as Ross Perot, who argued that NAFTA would cost American jobs. Some jobs will surely be lost to import competition. However, the overall effect on U.S. jobs is likely to be positive.

Prior to NAFTA some Mexican tariffs against U.S. manufactured goods were as high as 30 percent. With the removal of these tariffs American firms will find it profitable to export to Mexico rather than to establish factories in Mexico for the purpose of servicing the

Mexican market. Jobs will therefore be created in the U.S. rather than in Mexico as had previously been the case.

Regional free trade should not be confused with world free trade. Indeed, it is entirely possible for the establishment of a NAFTA type agreement to reduce economic efficiency. Consider a simple case designed to illustrate the point. Let there be three countries A, B, and C. A and B produce automobiles. C does not and imposes a 25% tariff on car imports. A is the more efficient producer and can deliver a car for $10,000 to C. B, the less efficient producer, can deliver a comparable car for $12,000. Counting the tariff A's car costs $12,500 in C's market, whereas B's car counting the tariff costs $15,000. A, the efficient producer, gets the business in C's market. Now suppose that B and C form a customs union. The 25% tariff is eliminated on B's cars but not on A's. Since A's cars continue to cost $12,500 whereas the price on B's cars is reduced to $12,000, B, the inefficient producer, gets the business in C's market.

It is clear from the example that the formation of a free trade area does not necessarily improve efficiency. NAFTA, for example, gives the U.S. an advantage in Mexico, and it gives Mexican producers an advantage in the U.S. But at the same time more efficient producers in other countries may be frozen out of the NAFTA market by the continuation of tariffs against their goods.

Therefore, if NAFTA and other free trade areas are to enhance overall economic efficiency, it is essential that as they eliminate trade barriers between themselves, they also greatly reduce trade barriers to the outside world. This is why it is now so important to follow up NAFTA with successful GATT negotiations designed to reduce tariff barriers between all countries.

GATT stands for General Agreements on Tariffs and Trade which date from the early post World War II years. Under GATT tremendous progress has been made in reducing world trade barriers.

The procedure at GATT meetings is for a schedule to be set up for bi-lateral negotiations between "principal suppliers." For, example, suppose the U.S. is the principal supplier of automobiles to Canada while Canada sells more lumber to the U.S. than to anyone else. The negotiators then negotiate "reciprocal" tariff reductions--Canada reduces auto tariffs to the U.S. while the U.S. reciprocates by reducing lumber tariffs. The next step, and this is crucial, is that these tariff cuts are automatically extended to all other countries enjoying "Most Favored Nations" status. Since other countries are simultaneously engaged in principal supplier negotiations, the U.S. and Canada will automatically enjoy the benefits of negotiations between other countries.

The negotiations don't necessarily end there. After the U.S. gets through with its Canadian negotiations, its representatives move to another room where they again engage in principal supplier negotiations with another country with which the U.S. is a major trading partner.

Tariff schedules can be incredibly detailed and complex and it is not always clear where a commodity should be classified. The U.S. may, for example, have different rates applicable to all the different cheeses produced in France. But through the principal supplier negotiating process and through the extension of the results on a Most Favored Nations basis, remarkable progress can be made in a fairly short period of time.

Monetary Integration

Economic integration implies the free movement of goods, labor, and capital, and it may also profitably include monetary integration. That is what the Europeans are striving for in the Maastricht Treaty, projected to be put in place in 1999. If the treaty is ratified this will mean, first, the abolition of national currencies in favor of a uniform European currency. It also means the creation of a single central "superbank" which would be the only bank empowered to create money and to manage monetary policy. Europe would, therefore, become like the United States where the Federal Reserve manages the entire nation's money supply. Individual countries would remain free to manage their own fiscal policies, but borrowing would be at competitive rates and could no longer be from countries' central banks.

In order fully to understand the implications of monetary integration and the extent to which it is desirable, it is important to consider the benefits and drawbacks of fixed and flexible exchange rate regimes. The case for fixed exchange rates is based, primarily, on considerations of efficiency. Imagine what it would be like if each of the 50 United States had its own currency issued by its own central bank and if these currencies fluctuated on a daily basis against each other. Doing business in other states would then be vastly more complicated and expensive. Not only would you have to keep track of prices, you also would have to be able to forecast exchange rates. To hedge against exchange rate loss a forward exchange market would develop as an entirely large new industry that uses resources that would be completely unnecessary if currency prices were fixed. It's not hard to see how economic development in the United States would be severely retarded by such a system. Fixed exchange rates, or a uniform national currency, would be far more efficient.

There is, however, another important side to this coin. Suppose a sizeable region of the country such as the Northwestern United States suffers a recession because of a decline in the demand for lumber. Having no central bank of its own it is unable to reduce interest rates to stimulate regional economic activity. Nor can the Federal Reserve be persuaded to do this because the consequence of such action would be inflation in the rest of the country. The Northwest is, therefore, powerless to change monetary conditions.

Next suppose that the Northwest has its own currency and its own central bank but that it maintains a fixed exchange rate against the U.S. dollar. If the Northwest central bank increases the money supply to lower interest rates this will induce an immediate capital outflow. Citizens of the Northwest will cash in Northwest currency at the central bank in exchange for U.S. dollars which they need to buy higher yielding U.S financial assets. Since the supply of such U.S. dollar reserves in the central bank of the Northwest is limited, the outflow cannot be permitted to continue, and the central bank quickly learns that she must abandon the low interest-rate policy and harmonize her monetary policy with that of the Federal Reserve. It is important to recognize that even though the Northwest has its own central bank and its own currency, she is powerless to affect monetary conditions as long as fixed exchange rates are maintained.

Finally, assume that the Northwest permits her currency to fluctuate freely against the U.S. dollar. The capital outflow induced by the low interest-rate policy then causes currency depreciation. This makes lumber cheaper in the U.S. and raises Northwest lumber exports. At the same time U.S. goods will become more expensive in the Northwest and this reduces imports. The effect is a rise in spending in the Northwest and the elimination of the recession. It can therefore be seen that the advantage of flexible exchange rates is that they are beneficial to the maintenance of high employment. Under flexible exchange rates each central bank is free to pursue its own monetary policy. Under fixed exchange rates this is not the case.

The discussion suggests that the case for fixed exchange rates is primarily based on efficiency considerations. The bad news is that the state, region, or country cannot pursue an independent monetary policy. Flexible exchange rates imply the opposite. The question that should now be asked is whether there exists the possibility of a happy medium. Such a happy medium is called an *optimum currency area.* In each such area exchange rates are fixed relative to the other countries in the area. The entire basket of currencies is then permitted to fluctuate in response to market forces with respect to other optimum currency areas. Europe and the United States are good examples of existing optimum currency areas. Intra-European trade is much more important to European countries than trade with the United States. And interstate trade is far more important to the U.S. than trade with Europe. Moderate variations in the price of the dollar vis a vis the European currency basket are not likely to cause major disruptions to either area. Efficiency losses caused by fluctuating exchange rates are apt to be small. And, most important, each area is free to pursue its own independent monetary policy.

The story is completely different inside Europe. Flexible exchange rates are anathema to heavily trade-dependent countries. The smaller the country and the greater the percent of GDP involved in trade, the greater the aversion. In countries such as Belgium, Denmark, and the Netherlands at least 50 percent of GDP is exported to European neighbors, while an equivalent volume is imported. If the Dutch Guilder were to appreciate 20 percent against other European currencies there would be a sharp drop in exports, a huge increase in imports, and a severe recession. Conversely, if the Guilder depreciates 20 percent this increases the cost of imports by 20 percent. Since imports represent 50 percent of the weight in the CPI, there would be an immediate inflation in consumer prices of 10 percent.

It is clear that if a country has a neighbor with which it does a lot of business, both countries will be better off to fix their exchange rates. And its not difficult to see why the European countries quickly adopted their own fixed exchange rate system after the collapse of Bretton Woods in 1973.

Why is it deemed more advantages to adopt monetary union in preference to retention of the fixed exchange rates of the EMS? On the surface they look very much like the same thing. What are the differences? The adoption of a uniform currency would enable travelers inside Europe to avoid the nuisance of having to exchange currencies each time their travels take them to a different country. Goods and services would be invoiced in a single currency thus contributing a great deal to the efficiency of trade and finance. A uniform currency system is clearly more efficient than a multi-currency fixed exchange rate system.

As explained earlier, participants in a fixed exchange rate system have little or no control over monetary conditions in their countries. They are, rather, forced to harmonize their monetary policies with those of the largest and most conservative member. In the EMS monetary policy for the entire group of countries is, in effect, made by the German Bundesbank.

Under monetary integration existing central banks would lose the power to create money. This power would be transferred to a superbank. This bank would have a board of governors on which all member countries would participate and have voting rights. Monetary policy decisions would therefore become European decisions rather than the decisions of the Bundesbank.

So much for Europe; what about the Western Hemisphere? Clearly not all is well. Rampant inflation is destroying the economies of Latin America. The entire hemisphere is a mendicant to the remainder of the world. The Latin countries are hopelessly in debt and this is true for the United States as well. Compared to Africa Latin America is well off. The same is true for the United States relative to Europe. The rich are receiving continuing credit from the poor. Does this make sense?

Recall the conversation of Chapter 3 between the Governor of the central bank of a major Latin American country and an old pal from graduate school days. The conversation took place at a pleasant bar and grill just a few steps from the IMF in Washington,

D.C. The Governor's message had been bleak in the extreme: no way to slow inflation; no way to obtain the capital goods imports needed to put the labor force to work; no apparent way to reverse the continuing deterioration in per capita income.

However, after the second drink the Governor's mood brightened considerably and he volunteered: "I do have a radical solution. I'll tell you what it is if you promise not to laugh."

"I promise."

"The obvious way to stop inflation in Latin America is to abolish all the central banks and all the currencies except the U.S. dollar. In other words, persuade the U.S. to form a monetary union that would include all the hemispheric nations. Without borrowing from the central bank we couldn't have inflation, and that would be the most important step we could take to right our economies. Price stability would permit rational production and investment planning, and without the option of borrowing from the central bank our fiscal deficits would have to be radically reduced. And incidentally, that goes for the U.S. deficit as well."

"How would you get a project such as this off the ground?"

"Canada, Mexico, and the U.S. have taken an important step towards economic integration. Let them also move towards monetary integration by having them create a single currency, call it the dollar, and have it issued by a single central bank. To get U.S. participation that bank would probably have to be the existing Federal Reserve. However, representatives from Canada and Mexico would have seats on the Board and voting power in the Open-Market Committee. The next step would be to invite the other hemispheric countries to join. Those that are reluctant would quickly realize that they have little choice. Requirements for entry into the union would be abolition of their currencies and their central banks."

"What happens to your job as Governor of your central bank?"

"As I told you before I'm just a flunky for my finance minister having to provide him with as much credit as he dictates. Frankly, I'd much rather represent my country on the Board of the Superbank where I can be involved in genuine, rather than sham, monetary policy decisions."

"What happens if there's a slow down in your economy not shared by the rest of the Hemisphere?"

"We'd still have fiscal policy at our disposal. If we had to spend more on unemployment compensation we'd have to borrow. But this would have to be at competitive rates, and borrowing from the central bank would no longer be possible. Of course if there is a general recession throughout the hemisphere it would be the responsibility of the superbank to buy debt paper from the various governments in order to increase the hemispheric money supply and lower interest rates."

"Sounds like a winner to me. How do you propose to sell the idea?"

"Don't forget that the Europeans are setting an excellent example with the monetary union they're forming. So its not as if the idea of monetary union had been pulled from a hat."

Index

-- E --

-- F --

-- G --

-- H --

-- I --

-- J --

-- L --

-- M --

-- N --